Glory Days

Tales of a North Shore Dangerboy

TOM TERRILL

ISBN 978-1-0980-2164-1 (paperback)
ISBN 978-1-0980-2166-5 (hardcover)
ISBN 978-1-0980-2165-8 (digital)

Christian Faith Publishing, Inc.
832 Park Avenue
Meadville, PA 16335
www.christianfaithpublishing.com

Printed in the United States of America

Dedicated to
Lincoln Steffens and Mrs. Neely
and
The farm where they met

Acknowledgments

Long Day
Written by Rob Thomas
Copyright (c) 1996 EMI April Music Inc., EMI Blackwood Music Inc. and U Rule Music
All Rights Administered by Sony/ATV Music Publishing LLC, 424 Church Street, Suite 1200,
    Nashville, TN 37219 International Copyright Secured All Rights Reserved
Reprinted by Permission of Hal Leonard LLC

Baba O'Riley
Words and Music by Peter Townshend
Copyright (c) 1971 Fabulous Music Ltd.
Copyright Renewed
All Rights Administered in the USA and Canada by Spirit Four Music, Suolubaf Music and ABKCO
    Music Inc.
International Copyright Secured All Rights Reserved
Reprinted by Pennission of Hal Leonard LLC

Lake Shore Drive
Words and Music by Eugene Von Heitlinger
Copyright (c) 1971 Sony/ATV Music Publishing LLC and EVH Publishing
Copyright Renewed
All Rights on behalf of Sony/ATV Music Publishing LLC Administered by Sony/ATV Music
    Publishing LLC, 424 Church Street, Suite 1200, Nashville, TN 37219
International Copyright Secured All Rights Reserved
Reprinted by Permission of Hal Leonard LLC

Here I Am To Worship (Light OF The World)
Song ID: 27636
Song Title: Here I Am To Worship (Light Of The World)
Writer(s): Tim Hughes
Label Copy:

Contents

Preface

When Bruce Springsteen released his 1984 album *Born in the USA*, I heard the song "Glory Days" for the first time. Along with millions of his fans, I immediately loved the song, as it struck a deep chord within me. A happy feeling about my past.

The song moved me to reminisce of my own "Glory Days" stories, and over the years, I've had quite a few. Maybe more than my share. At least it seems that way. I treasure my Glory Days, and it got me to thinking.

Tom Terrill in his Kenilworth All-Stars sixth grade uniform

As a child, I loved the storytellers in my life. Capturing the excitement of a moment long past but bringing it alive in the present resonated with me. My father-in-law frequently said, "Never let the facts get in the way of a good story." That made me laugh.

But my memory is too clear and the stories so unique (according to my mother) that I have no need to change the facts.

We all have our Glory Days. Yours are unique to you and likely special to a lot of people in your life. Same with mine.

I hope you will enjoy reading my Glory Days and trust that it will bring you back in time to recall some of your own.

Bozo's Circus

In Chicago, during the sixties and seventies, the most popular TV show with kids was *Bozo's Circus*. The hour-long show started at noon and broadcast Monday through Friday. Mr. Ned was the ringmaster, and the star of the show was Bozo the Clown.

Kids tuned in on WGN-TV while they ate their lunch, laughing at the antics of Bozo who usually had the last laugh at the expense of his other circus clown friends.

The show aired live and had the "cast of thousands," which amounted to a crowd of two hundred children and parents lucky enough to get tickets. The waiting list was many years long, and it was rare that anyone knew anybody who ever got to go to the show.

My father was a master of making the impossible happen and procured tickets for our family. I'm not sure what it cost him to acquire these coveted passes, but it must have been substantial. With the same excitement of opening presents on Christmas morning, our family drove down to watch the show live in the seats my father obtained.

Photo courtesy of WGN-TV and Larry Harmon Pictures Corporation

Every show had two important games. The Grand Prize Game was the biggest of all, where one boy and one girl were selected at random with the TV's "magic arrows." Each child would attempt to toss a Ping-Pong ball in a series of six consecutive buckets. The second game varied each day from one set of skills or tasks to another and comprised of kids competing against one another.

We pulled into the parking lot of the WGN Studios on Chicago's North Side. Unable to show restraint, my siblings and I ran from the car to the entrance while Mom strolled in at a reasonable pace. (Dad was hard at work and could not come.) Once inside, we experienced the phenomenon of "hurry up and wait" as we got in a long line with other families. It seemed as if this was taking forever, and boredom set in.

After some fifteen minutes, a young woman, maybe twenty-one, came over to the roped line and asked me a question. "Young man," she began with a smile, "would you like to play a game?" I was confused by the question.

"No," I replied. I couldn't imagine what she was thinking. Couldn't she see I was in line to see *Bozo's Circus*? Why would I want to go with this stranger to play some games, like *Monopoly*, with her? I didn't know her and just wanted her to leave me alone.

My mom understood what she was asking and was puzzled by my response. "Tommy," my mom said, "why don't you go play a game?" Michelle, Kathy, and Jeff all too kept telling me to go and how lucky I was and how much fun it would be.

I did like games, but still, I came to see the show. And why did my family want to get rid of me? I was lost in a state of confusion. Reluctantly, I went with her but only because of the pressure from my family.

"Will we be done in time to see Bozo?" I asked as I walked down the hallway with this intern.

She now looked at me, perplexed herself. "Yes," she replied, "you will see Bozo."

Relieved now, I continued into a room where I saw five other boys my age standing and waiting. A man who seemed to be in charge explained that the six of us would sit together while we watched the show. Then we'd be brought to the center ring to compete in a game with Mr. Ned officiating.

Only at this point did I finally understand; however, I was not all that happy about it. I wanted to sit with my sisters and brother and, of course, my mom. I didn't know these guys, and I was pretty shy around strangers. As young boys, we eyed one another and looked away upon making eye contact. It was quite awkward, but there was no turning back.

I watched the show begin from my new seat, and to my great surprise, there were far fewer people in the audience than it seemed like when I would watch on TV.

"Why aren't we in the normal place?" I whispered to the boy next to me. The whole studio seemed so small that I figured we were in an alternate room. It is incredible how something on television can look so much more impressive than it is in real life, a lesson I wish I would remember more often as an adult.

"Boys, follow me," a man said as he guided us out onto the center ring. Mr. Ned came over and asked each boy his name and hometown. "Tom Terrill from Kenilworth, Illinois," I said with about as much pizzazz as Eeyore from *Winnie-the-Pooh*.

"OK, boys," Mr. Ned began, "you each have a supply of rope pieces eighteen inches long. You will tie your best knot to this hitching post and then tie successive pieces of rope to one another. After one minute, whoever has the longest rope wins! But be very careful, boys, because before we measure, I'll give a tug on each one… And if it breaks, then you will be eliminated. So tie your knots well."

I took heed to his warning. Mr. Ned was a big man, and I had a feeling he was pretty strong too.

"OK, boys, when I say 'go,' you will start, and when I blow my whistle, you will stop," Mr. Ned explained. "Ready…set…go!"

Each boy quickly began their task, and I too was off to the races. I measured my pace while replaying Mr. Ned's words of caution in my mind. Doing my very best to tie each knot extremely tight, I secured the ropes to one another. Methodically, I proceeded and never looked to see how far along my competition was in their growing length of rope.

Suddenly, the silence was broken by Mr. Ned blowing his ringmaster's whistle, and we all came to a stop. Four boys were well ahead of me with just one boy who was at my equal length. Mr. Ned came over to me first. "Well, young man, you did a fine job. But remember I have to tug at your rope to see if it breaks or not." He took the end of my rope in his big hand while Bozo secured the hitching post, and Mr. Ned gave a solid jerk to my effort. It held fast. "Good job, young man. Now let's see about the next contestant." Mr. Ned went to the boy tied with me and gave a yank on his rope. This boy's line held too. So each of us was securely tied for last place and not eliminated.

Mr. Ned continued going from the shortest to the longest, and so at the third boy, he gave a tug, and the rope broke. His knots were not well tied. The boy looked ashamed, and we all felt a bit embarrassed for him. Then came the tug on the fourth boy's rope, and it too broke easily. Then came the fifth boy, and his line broke also.

Wow, I thought to myself. Three boys in a row all had their ropes break. "Boys and girls, moms and dads, now we'll test the final rope to determine who our winner is today," Mr. Ned exclaimed, building as much excitement and tension as he could in the studio. Taking the longest rope of all in his hand and giving a solid yank as he did all the others, Mr. Ned's effort broke the longest one as well.

I went from last to first and was so excited. Of course, I was tied, but it was still first place, and Mr. Ned congratulated the two of us for tying such strong knots. "Well, Bozo," Mr. Ned queried, "what do our winning contestants receive?"

Avalanche created by Frank Sinden

Bozo came out with two boxes and handed one to each of us. "Mr. Ned," Bozo said with his jovial voice, "each of our two winners gets the exciting marble game Avalanche."

I took my game in hand and, with a big smile, held it up to the camera. Now proud as a peacock, I looked around to see everyone watching me. Escorted back to the seats, I now was able to sit with my family. My siblings looked at the game and congratulated me as did my mom.

The show ended, and the family drove back home. It could not have been a more successful day for me, and I just loved my first-place prize. For weeks, I'd invite friends over to play my game and tell the story of my proficient knot-tying skills. As the show was live, I never saw myself on TV, but my friend, Andy Furst, told me he saw me on TV and was cheering for me the whole time.

Junior High

At Joseph Sears School, we didn't really have a junior high. It was a pre-K-to-eighth-grade school, and there was nothing different by entering the seventh grade than any other year. Six hundred fifty kids or so comprised the ten grades, and for the most part, there was very little change from one year to the next of those kids in your class. Our school was a very close community. Partially the result of little movement out of Kenilworth and to some extent because of the baby boom. Most students had numerous siblings, so almost everyone knew various students throughout the other grades as well as their own. This environment allowed for a sense of family that permeated the school.

Like most people, my seventh- and eighth-grade years were both transitional and formational and, for me, very memorable. A few events stand out as being unusual to me and my maturation.

Waterbed

In seventh grade, I bought a king-size waterbed for thirty dollars at Khaki's in Evanston. I did not have a frame or anything to secure it but instead just purchased the bladder, which I put in my room on the third floor of our house. Our house was not air-conditioned, except for a window unit in my parents' bedroom, and the heat that rose to the third floor made it unbearably hot during the summer months.

I had the entire third floor to myself, which was an enormous space, including a bathroom with a claw foot tub. When I got home with the waterbed, I went upstairs and laid it out on the floor on top of a big hook rug. Then I went outside and wrapped up the very long garden hose, carrying it upstairs, where I proceeded to insert the one end into the waterbed and dropped the other end out of window, lowering it slowly to the ground. Quickly running downstairs and outside, I hooked up the hose to the spigot and turned on the water. I hustled back upstairs to find the waterbed slowly filling up with fresh cold water. Surprised by how long it took, I anxiously waited for the bed to be completely full.

All in good order, I turned off the water and removed the hose and put everything away. Finally, my waterbed was ready to try out, and with great excitement, I climbed on and got swished and rolled as I settled into a comfortable spot. Immediately, I noticed how cool the bed felt, which was a great benefit to the hot and humid air in my third-floor bedroom. Sleeping on it was a difficult transition with all the rocking, and often, I'd wander back downstairs to the second bed in my brother's room and sleep there.

After a few days, the water temperature equalized with the air temperature, and the cooling benefits were gone. Being smarter than the average Joe, I emptied the waterbed and refilled it with cold water. This process was repeated some half a dozen times and became part of my routine. I got to the point where I knew how long it took to fill the waterbed and would wander downstairs to see what was on TV.

One afternoon, I was home alone and watching my beloved Cubs playing an afternoon baseball game. A heat wave had hit the Chicago area, and it seemed like an excellent time to get some fresh cold water in my waterbed. I went through my routine setting up the refill and then returned to the family room to continue watching the Cubs. I became fixated on the game and forgot about the water. While lying down on the couch watching the game, a drop of water landed on my face. Looking up at the ceiling, I saw a small spot where water was pooling on the ceiling, and I thought how odd. Suddenly, it dawned on me where this was coming from, and I bolted upright running up the stairs three at a time.

Reaching the second floor, I discovered that an inch of water pooled in the landing area and the ceiling above was raining down. Without delay, I continued up to the third floor to come across what seemed unimaginable. The hose had popped out and was blasting water at full throttle onto the floor. The waterbed was pouring additional water out of the unsealed opening onto the floor. There were two to three inches of water sitting on the floor, all leaking its way down through the house.

Very quickly, I opened the window that was holding the spraying hose and let it free fall down to the ground. I shut the valve on the waterbed to stop any additional leak and then threw open the front window and started in vain to bail water from the floor out the window.

My good friend and next-door-neighbor, George Haydock, was walking by. "George!" I shouted. "I need your help! Please get up here and help me bail water!" George looked at me with a kind of puzzled look on his face and explained he was late getting home and couldn't help. Had he fully understood what was going on, he would have rushed in to help.

I was nervous that the very floor I was standing on might collapse with the additional weight. I pulled the waterbed off the large hook rug and started to roll the waterlogged rug into a long cylinder. With a herculean effort, I pulled the rug to and out the window, letting if free fall to the driveway below. Fortunately, it held much of the water, soaked up like a sponge within the fibers.

Traveling three flights of stairs to the basement, I grabbed as many buckets as I could carry and brought them to the second floor. Strategically placing them to catch the water pouring down from the ceiling while on the first floor, I covered any spot where water was leaking with a myriad of towels replacing them as they got semifull.

At this point, I could only sit back and let the water work its way through the ceiling and floors of both levels of the house. To my amazement, the house did not collapse, and it all cleaned up reasonably quick. My initial panic and worst fears subsided as the conditions improved. When my mom came home with Kathy and Jeff, it seemed more funny than scary. I showed them through the house, like a museum docent, ignoring the fact that my carelessness caused this.

Neither ceiling had any damage, and only the hardwood floors on the third floor suffered. Over the next few weeks, the wood began to expand and buckle upward so that every two boards created a peak an inch or so higher than the actual floor itself.

To my good fortune, my parents were not upset. I think they had other things to worry about, but also, they allowed their children to make their own mistakes. They knew we would learn about life by falling down and getting up on our own. Helicopter parenting had not yet been invented.

Likely, the fact that the house was a rental had something to do with it too.

I have never slept in a waterbed since then and have a feeling that it was a one-hit wonder in my life.

BB Gun

My father had given my brother Jeff and me two guns to use in the backyard. A CO2 pellet gun and a BB gun. Dad bought a steel trap target that would catch the projectile and secure it in a ricochet-proof compartment. Carefully explaining that we could only shoot at the target and had to be sure the target was in the backyard with no one behind it. Following these rules carefully, we typically positioned toy army men in the trap to shoot at and pick off one at a time.

When we traveled to the family lake house in Wisconsin, the rules were completely different. We could shoot out into the lake from the pier as long as no one was swimming and at will in the open field and woods. How much fun it was to walk around with a gun shooting at whatever we wanted. I was never reckless and became quite comfortable with the gun.

One summer day in 1972, Jeff and I were sitting on the front porch of our home in Kenilworth. Jeff had the BB gun and was telling me what a good shot he had become. "See that squirrel on the elm tree?" Jeff asked, not expecting an answer. "I bet I could hit it from here," he said with an air of confidence.

Never mind that the strict rules required we only shoot at the trap in the backyard. Without any comment from me, Jeff took aim and shot. He missed the squirrel and squarely hit the tree. A few more shots were fired off when we noticed Mr. Springer walking from his yard and across the street to our house. Mr. Springer looked a little like Mr. Wilson in the old *Dennis the Menace* TV show.

"Dennis the Menace" courtesy CPT Holdings, Inc.

He looked very angry, and Jeff and I wondered what was up. Walking up to our house and ascending the ten steps to the front porch, he exclaimed, "You shot a hole in my window!" Grabbing the gun from Jeff's hands, he demanded, "Are your parents' home?"

"No, Mr. Springer, they are not. I'm sorry I shot your window. I was aiming for a squirrel," Jeff calmly said. His young age gave him a still-true sense of innocence in the sense that he didn't intend to shoot the window.

Jeff did, however, have to pay for the window, which was just. However, neither Jeff nor I got in trouble with our parents, although that ended our redneck days shooting from the front porch.

Ice-skating and Skitching

In Kenilworth, the winter ice-skating rink was set up each year at Townly Field. Ice-skating was a big deal, and in fact, we had two weeks of gym class after Christmas where everyone was required to skate. Without exception, every student at Joseph Sears learned how to skate, and most loved it. There is something to the blend of grace and power combined into gliding across the ice in a rhythmic dance of athletics that drew me in and captured my heart.

My mom, Grace Terrill, and me on the Kenilworth ice rink in 1994

During the winter nights, kids from all over town would come to ice-skate after their family dinner and meet up with friends. For boys like me, this was a chance to steal the hat of a cute girl like Alison Kerr or Susie Buckingham and actually have them chase you. That alone was enough to bring me to the rink, but we also had games of pom-pom. A catch-one, catch-all game that left the very best of skaters weaving in and out of a mob, trying in vain to get a hand on the elusive master of the rink.

Playing pom-pom was where my skills improved dramatically by watching older kids with their cuts, quick stops, and tricks that I could later try on my own to imitate.

Hockey too was a central part of the skating. A separate hockey rink with the full boards was at the south end of this enormous rink. Here is where I honed in my hockey skills, again learning from those who were far better than me.

The rink stayed open until 9:00 PM every weeknight, and it was the routine to stay out until then. The ice rink became a hangout for much of our school. Skating under the lights while the loudspeakers would play songs by the likes of James Taylor, Carole King, the Beatles, as the evening passed. It was understood that everyone would come to skate unless you were sick or out of town. Most of my life hanging out had been with boys, but this setting broke down the barrier of boys and girls every single night of the week. I loved it!

When the rink would close, the girls and younger kids would go home, but the boys still had another activity to keep the adrenaline pumping. Skitching was the means to this rush, and if there was snow on the road, we were skitching.

With hockey sticks in hand and our laced ice skates around our neck, we'd grab onto the bumper of one of the cars picking up the younger kids. At a minimum, we'd skitch toward home, but it was such a thrill that we'd often continue this exploit around town. Any car that came to a stop sign was our target, where we would sneak behind and grab on the bumper as the unsuspecting driver proceeded down the village street.

Whenever we had a fresh snowstorm, we'd skip the skating because the rink was full of too much snow. Our alternative was to skitch instead. One evening, a group of guys were at a favorite intersection of Melrose and Warwick where we'd take a ride in any of the four directions a car was going. Brian Avery, Brett Johnson, Bill Fillion, and I were having a fantastic night when the four of us secured a long ride all the way to Sheridan Road—laughing all the way there until the car pulled up to the stop sign. Brian and I let go, but Brett and Bill hung on.

"Hey, what are you guys doing?" I called out incredulously. This seemed crazy as Sheridan Road was heavily traveled, so not only was another car likely to be right behind you increasing the danger but the amount of traffic naturally melted the snow quickly so only a remnant of wet slush remained.

Brian and I watched as the car turned south, pulling our two friends onto one of the forbidden roads of the skitching world. Some fifteen minutes later, Bill and Brett returned to our intersection with a wild story of smoking boots from the friction while they hung on for a block and half down Sheridan Road. It seemed unbelievable until Bill showed us the heel on his steel shanked boots which were worn down about an inch from normal. This was the stuff junior high legends were made of, and Bill and Brett had two eyewitnesses to their achievement.

Breaking in the School

Most of the nighttime activity centered geographically around our school grounds. It seemed like a common place to congregate and meet up with other peers. A neighborhood-based event for kids in seventh and eighth grade called the "Drop In" took place at the community center next to the ice rink that continued long after the temperature rose and the ice melted.

This evening event initially had no name. The adults in charge were looking for something clever and created a suggestion box. I noticed how we kept coming, then leaving, and coming back. I suggested it be called "Drop In, Drop Out." The next week, it was officially named the "Drop In," and I knew my idea was the source of the name. I told my friends, but no one believed me. I guess it's hard to gain fame for something so trivial.

Given enough time, junior high boys will gravitate toward trouble. Girls too, if the boys are there and trying to impress the girls.

In the eighth grade, my friends and I now found we were the big fish in our small pond of Joseph Sears School. One fall weekend, as usual, a large portion of our eighth-grade class found ourselves hanging around the school at night. There were large metal grates around one side of the building where warm air was expelled from the heating system for the school. We liked to sit on these grates to keep warm but also to have a place to talk in mixed company. One of the girls saw the school's janitor through a window and knocked on the door, asking if she could come in to use the bathroom. Being a nice man, he accommodated her request, but when she left, she made sure the door lock did not click behind her. After finishing his work, he left for home, and a large group of kids pulled open the door and entered our school on Friday night.

Initially, we were walking around, feeling a bit daring to cross this distinct line of right and wrong. Exploring the confined box of our "life of rules" had grown tired. Willingly, this gang of students, full of groupthink, left the box behind, traversing into unknown territory. We split up into different groups, some going left and others right and still mostly trying to act cool and impress girls or get noticed by the boys. I don't think any other reason can explain our willingness to enter the school.

No one was in charge, and we had no plan. The evening unfolded unpredictably like a shifting whirlwind. Somewhere nearby, I heard some glass breaking and laughter following. I thought to myself, *What was that?* as I couldn't conceive of intentionally breaking a window. However, that is precisely what happened. One of my classmates had some heavy leather gloves and punched hard into a sturdy window and broke it. This was now another lined crossed and one that I was feeling a bit uneasy about stepping over. But not enough to leave. Shortly after that, another window broke and more laughter. This second window brought everyone together tracking the sound down to the math classroom. Joe Thompson was standing in front of the broken window, with a look of shock on his face.

"I can't believe I did that," Joe said. Vandalism was not a part of his life experience. After some initial conversation from various people in the group, Brett Stone, with his leather gloves protecting his hand, punched in another window.

These initial actions unleashed the restrained propriety of a few other boys who started to break one window after another. The more that broke, the more kids crossed the line into willing vandals. Light fixtures in the walls were now kicked in, desks overturned, and the blackboards became the target of words that shouldn't be written in chalk.

"Joe," I asked, "did it hurt your hand to punch that window?"

"A bit," he replied. "I don't think I'm going to do that again. I need to protect my arm for when the Cubs sign me to that big contract."

I think the most fun part of the night was watching Phil Upton and Jack Smith blast the fire extinguishers at one another. Modern-day gladiators with the tools of 1971. Patty Miller came down the stairs from the second floor and told us that Brian Avery had just picked the lock on the school safe. The funny thing was that Brian wasn't even there that night, but it added to his reputation of being a lot smarter than the rest of us.

Throughout the entire evening, I watched but never broke anything. It didn't have any appeal to me, and I didn't think this would impress any of the girls. At least not the ones I wanted to impress. At some point, the thrill wore off, and everyone left. Our school in shambles but without any trouble from the police, it seemed as if we partook in some senseless, reckless, and shameful behavior that would never have a price to pay.

On Monday, I went to school and honestly forgot about it until I saw some of the plywood where a window used to be. Walking through the hallway that morning, I caught the eye of some of those who were inside with me over the weekend. No one said anything, but the expression on everyone's face was one that said, "I'm not going to squeal, and you better not either."

Coach K was the school assistant principal. He was our gym teacher for grades 1 to 5, after which he took a job in the administration. Every kid in school respected Coach K; he was a big man who was a friend but also a stern disciplinarian. He was not to be messed with by anyone.

Walter Calhoun was our student council president, and he was called to Coach K's office first. Under normal circumstances, Walter would have been in the thick of it, but he had been grounded by his parents for minor offenses and was at home all weekend. Walter was not a firsthand witness, but he knew pretty much what went on. Doing his best not to name names, he took the approach to tell Coach K the names of those who were not guilty of the vandalism.

Needing to find out who the guilty students were, Coach K called into his office a girl from our class who was tough but also willing to be honest. Sitting in science class, she came down from the office and walked up to Joe Thompson. "You're wanted in Coach K's office," she said. Off went Joe, who looked back, making a face of impending doom to the rest of the class. After about ten minutes, Joe came back and walked up to Jack Smith. "Your turn, Jack." Phil Upton, Rick Goff, and John Kerns all took trips to Coach K's office; and eventually, I too was called.

When it was my turn to face the music, Coach K said, "Tom Terrill. I am surprised to see you in my office."

"I'm surprised too," I said, not really knowing how to respond. He didn't crack a smile as he picked up a piece of paper and said, "Tom, I have you down for four windows, two light fixtures, and a fire extinguisher."

"What?" I asked, quite confused.

"Your friends have reported that this is how much you broke. What do you have to say for yourself?"

"I didn't break anything," I protested, claiming complete innocence.

"Are you trying to tell me you didn't break into the school?" He fired back. Well, I was not sure what to say. I never thought that I actually broke into the school but instead entered in through an unlocked door. However, I was confident he didn't care about such a technicality.

"No, I came into the school, but I didn't break anything," I admitted, not sure how deep the trouble was.

"Well, then who did break these if not you?" Coach asked. It was the million-dollar question and the one that I dreaded more than anything. I knew a lot and could easily attribute probably half of the damage to four to six people. But should I tell? I was perplexed and didn't have time to think it out. I was in a jam and had no idea how to resolve it.

"I can't say" was my reply.

"I understand. However, this doesn't end here. Go back and get Brett Stone." As the day played out, more and more people were called into Coach K's office. Some people summoned were wholly innocent and were not even there, and others were as guilty as guilty could be.

At the end of the day, my homeroom teacher informed me that I could not go home but would need to go to a specific classroom. I walked into the classroom to see most everyone who was there that night. After a few minutes, everyone else arrived. We were all caught, and it only took one day. Mastermind criminals in the making we were not.

The room was silent, except for some nervous breathing from others like me who were not used to this sort of trouble. To my fascination, some of my classmates looked almost bored here in this room of detention.

"OK, boys and girls," Coach K began, "here on the chalkboard, we have an inventory of everything broken over the weekend, and we are going to meet here every day after school for an hour until each broken item is accounted for." It was a long list, and so far, no one had confessed to anything. As we sat, I looked around the room, looking at those whom I knew had broken various things that fateful night. After thirty minutes, not a word was spoken by a single student. We all sat silently. Coach K was not in any hurry and was willing to wait us out. The first day produced nothing.

At 4:00 PM, we were excused to go home and told we had all better be back at 3:00 PM the next day. So we started the process over again the next day, and there we sat. Having nothing to confess, I began to resent my punishment, waiting for those who were guilty to confess. However, I was not interested in pressuring anyone either. I was ready to sit as long as it took, without breaking the confidence of my friends.

About forty-five minutes into day 2, Joe Thompson raised his hand.

"Mr. Thompson, do you have something to say?" Coach K sternly inquired.

"Put me down for one window," Joe said with a casualness in his voice that struck me. The middle child of a big family, Joe was one of my closest friends through grade school. All the Thompson kids were tough, and Joe broke the ice. A few minutes later, Brett Stone piped in, "Two windows and a light fixture for me."

Now we were getting somewhere. However, I was aware that Brett had done more damage than that. Phil Upton, moments later, included himself in winnowing down the list. The day continued with the list almost complete, but not fully filled in. "OK, kids, we didn't quite finish today, so I will see everyone back here tomorrow," Coach K concluded as he released us from our confinement.

The next day, the gaps closed entirely, and we were done sitting in this room, accounting for the damage. No formal school enforced punishment occurred other than recovering the cost of the damaged property. Each student's punishment was what they'd receive at home, and mine was limited to a lecture about making good choices.

I was relieved to put this chapter behind me, and I think most of my friends felt the same. I wish I could say we learned our lesson, but I don't think we did. We were just too young to absorb the meaning of our actions. It would take time to learn how wrong this was. More time than I care to admit. To my amazement, the class, a year behind us, repeated our mistake when they were in the eighth grade, breaking into the school and vandalizing it as we had. Everyone was caught just like we were. I guess sometimes you can't learn by others but have to suffer through it yourself.

Falling in the Ice

As the cold water enveloped my body, I gasped for breath…

In February of 1971, I was a seventh grader. My friend, Brian Avery, and I decided to go bowling; and my younger brother, Jeff, came along with us. We walked to Bleser's bowling alley in neighboring Wilmette and had fun knocking down some pins, and in the winter, it was an enjoyable diversion.

The day was sunny, and in the afternoon, the temperatures rose into the fifties, melting much of the remaining snow. We left the bowling alley and aimlessly wandered north on Ridge Road, eventually arriving at Indian Hill County Club. As it was February, the golf course was closed, and we decided to walk out onto the grounds.

Two twelve-year-olds and an eight-year-old younger brother rarely have much of a plan, and we certainly were without one. It was a Saturday, and we were walking and talking, letting the whim of the moment dictate our path.

The golf course was 50 percent snow covered, and the rest exposed soggy grass. Eventually, we arrived at a frozen pond. Curious about the ice, we stepped out at the edges to see if the ice would hold us. Even pounding our feet a bit to be sure it was solid, we learned that it was rock-solid and safe to cross.

Our journey started, leaving a path of footprints in the thin snow layer on top of the ice. We had crossed over three-quarters of the way when suddenly my left foot broke through. There I was with one foot fully submerged and now in a crouched position with my hands on the ice.

I gave a frustrated groan as my leg was soaked and cold. Brian and Jeff laughed, not knowing any better.

I shifted my weight to my right leg and pushed, uplifting my wet left leg out of the narrow hole. Suddenly, my right leg broke through as well, expanding the hole in the ice. Now both hands were at my side, bracing me from falling farther. The laughter stopped as my heart began to race. This was a serious problem, and we were ill-equipped to handle what was coming.

I was wearing a heavy down jacket, corduroy pants, and a hat and gloves. Not exactly swimwear.

As I tried to lift my legs up out with all my weight on my hands, a large crack broke open, and I plunged into the frigid pond wholly submerged. My clothes soaked up the water and felt like I had an anchor wrapped around me. In a panic, I hurriedly swam for the surface. Luckily, I came up at the hole and gasped for breath. The cold had compressed my lungs, and fear now had my full attention. Like an elephant on my chest, it was nearly impossible to inhale in the freezing water, leaving me with a limited ability to speak at all. In vain, I tried to call out for help, but what could Brian or Jeff do? They stood on the ice, terrified that they too would soon be joining me.

I placed both hands on the ice and started to push up, attempting to climb out. Once about halfway out of the water, the ice would again collapse, and under I went. Popping back up and struggling for air, I tried this over and over again. The open water was expanding, and Brian and Jeff kept backing up farther toward the middle of the pond.

Suddenly, Jeff too had the ice break on him, depositing him into the open water. My mind was racing, and nothing seemed like the slow motion that supposedly happens in a crisis. I'm not sure what was going through Jeff's mind, but he wisely kept his eyes focused on the shore moving through the water, breaking the ice as he went toward land. I was able to only get a single word out to Brian at this point: "Help." I knew I couldn't survive this much longer and was unable to do this on my own.

Suddenly, I saw a gift there on the ice. An eight-foot long dead tree branch was lying to Brian's left. I never noticed the branch until that moment when Brian, catching a glimpse of it out of the corner of his eye, picked it up and extended it out toward me. I grabbed hold while Brian pulled me up out of the water onto the ice. This time the ice held, as I laid on my back breathing heavily. Glancing over to see Jeff stumble out of the water onto the grass as he collapsed on the ground, lying on his back to recover. *OK*, I think to myself, *at least Jeff won't die here.*

Brian and I, however, were still on the ice of this pond. We stood up, trying to figure out what to do. We looked back to see the footprints from where we came, but to retrace these meant going farther from land. We debated among ourselves that the ice held us on the way out, so it should hold us back again. Straight ahead was now open water with chunks of floating ice. To our immediate right, we could traverse parallel to the open water and have the shortest walk to land. But would the ice hold us?

We decided the shortest way was the best, and if the ice broke, Brian and I committed to moving toward land like my younger and wiser brother Jeff had done. With trepidation, we began this harrowing journey. Nervously laughing and trying to encourage one another, we made our way the twenty-five paces or so and safely arrived on the shore. Land never felt so good. We walked around to Jeff, who was now sitting up but with a dazed look upon his face. The temperature was warm for February, but fifty-degree air in soaking wet clothes created more than a chill. We were a mile plus away from home and needed to dry off before showing up there. Brian recalled that Steve Miller lived nearby, just three blocks away.

Steve was a classmate, but not a close friend. I'd never been to his home nor met his family. The three of us showed up and rang the doorbell, where Mrs. Miller opened the door. I can't imagine what was going on in her mind. She had no idea who we were and why two of us were wringing wet. She kindly invited us in, and our clothes were rung out and thrown in the dryer. Steve invited us to play some cards while we waited for our clothes to dry. It all seemed so relaxed after nearly dying. Once dry, Mrs. Miller gave us a ride home, and Brian was dropped off at his house on Cumnor Road first and then another four houses down to Jeff's and my home.

I was afraid to tell my parents the story. I kept trying to figure out some way the day's event and trauma wouldn't sound so bad. I had nothing but the truth to tell, and that is what we did. I anticipated being punished for such reckless behavior, especially with my younger brother. To my surprise, my parents just hugged us both. Long and hard, happy that they were able to do so.

As a parent myself, I now understand why that was all they could do.

I look back on that day with a few questions. How did that dead branch get on the ice? Other kids? God? Coincidence? If that branch wasn't there and I succumbed to the cold, what would have happened to Jeff and Brian at that point? In the summer of 2010, I went back to that spot one summer day, walking out to the pond. It was just as I remembered it. I took the time to thank God for sparing me that day and for my wife and kids and all that I had experienced since then.

When I die and go to heaven, I hope to be able to ask God to show me that day replayed and learn what was happening that I didn't see at the time.

Aspen

Chateau Dumont. The red door on the 3rd floor was our unit.

In 1968 my parents purchased a 50% interest in a newly built condominium in Aspen, Colorado. Chateau Dumont #21 was now owned by a combination of my family and the family of one of my best friends, Brian Avery.

I was 10 years old and my skiing had been limited to a few times at the local hills in Wisconsin. This acquisition would change the trajectory of the lives of everyone in my family. Not only did we become a skiing family, but each of my sisters and I lived in Aspen for a part of our lives and my brother went to college in Colorado as a result of the time spend here.

Skiing was synonymous with my family. Growing up my friendships that were the deepest were with those with whom I spent time on the ski slopes. Those friendships have lasted for many decades.

Half a century has passed since then. My siblings and I all continue to ski as often as we can. My two sisters live in the mountains, and my brother and I often travel back to ski in the Rockies.

I kid my two brothers-in-law who love to ski that they owe my parents a huge debt in raising two daughters who can ski better than most men.

Tom Terrill with Aspen city limit sign hanging on my bedroom wall in college

The Early Days

Thanksgiving of 1968, our family loaded into the family station wagon and drove west to Colorado. We stopped for three days to ski Vail before heading to our final destination of Aspen. The mountains were new to my siblings and me, and we quickly fell in love.

Our new vacation condominium was just one block from the Little Nell chairlift on Ajax. We could walk to the slope and ski back right to our front door. Aspen Highlands was where the kids took lessons while Mom and Dad skied on their own. Initially, the trips were family only, and we really bonded together as siblings. The extended time of a typical ski day allows for such relationships to flourish. Riding chairlifts, taking turns picking the run to ski, and lunch together. This was so much more time with one another than if we were at home, on the beach, or anywhere else. We also loved the physical challenge of skiing and improving together.

In the eighth grade, my family went out to Aspen the week of Christmas for nine days. The Avery family would go the week of New Year's on an eight-day trip. Brian and I were best of friends since the age of three when we met in preschool. Neither of us remembers the earliest days and relies on our parents telling us stories of our very early friendship.

As the family trips were developing, Brian and I had a lightning strike of combined genius. We'd each invite the other to go on the family ski trip. This would mean seventeen days of skiing out of twenty consecutive days. It also meant missing some school before and after the normal two-week Christmas break.

Brian Avery and Tom Terrill riding the lift at Little Nell

Our parents agreed, and the trips were set. All our friends from school were very envious, and we welcomed the attention it brought our way. Our family drove the 1,168 miles from our house in Illinois to Chateau Dumont in Aspen in the family station wagon. My mom, dad, and five kids along with my dog, Fritzy, were squeezed inside, with our suitcases in the soft luggage carrier on the roof of the car. The cars were bigger back then than now, and most people were smaller, but still, it was crowded.

We stopped in Boulder to visit my mom's college, the University of Colorado. A boring part to the kids but fun for my mom to revisit where her college career started.

Brian and I skied every day together, and our abilities took off. The competition and comradery, combined with being a perfect recipe for fast improvement. We loved to race down the slope and see who could get to the bottom first. Brian was a faster skier than me, but we learned to handicap our races by giving me a single chairlift lead. Then we'd always end approximately at the same time.

It was more fun to talk and think together about dangers ahead; it was safer to meet them shoulder to shoulder. I enjoyed our many many days of free play. *

As thirteen-year-old boys, we were interested in athletics and girls. We knew how to handle the athletics, but our shyness and ignorance kept us from any sophisticated plans to meet girls our age. One day at Aspen Highlands during lunch, we did notice three girls close to our age, and we deliberately sat at a table near them. They all looked cute to us, but one, in particular, stood out. She had long blond hair and was undoubtedly the leader of this group.

The girls were clearly aware of our presence but acted like they did not know we were there. Still, their conversation was not meant for one another but Brian and me. It was painfully obvious to us, but as thirteen-year-old boys, we were naive to what we should do about this attention. So we silently went about our business of watching them while pretending not to be watching them.

While the blond leader was cute and clearly of interest to both Brian and me, she also was loud and boisterous. We privately gave her the nickname of Loudmouth Yellow Jacket, proving the cleverness of thirteen-year-old boys is relatively limited.

For several days, we'd see this group skiing around the mountain. We followed them, and they followed us, but we never intersected to meet formally. On the third day of this adolescent dance on skis, Brian and I saw the girls just one hundred yards in front of us stopped on the hill. Instinctively, we took off down the slope skiing hard and fast, showing off as it had never been done before. I was in the lead and Brian right behind me.

After passing them by some fifty yards, I decided to stop hard, punctuating my impressive skills. Brian, however, was looking back to see if they were still watching. He did not see me stop and crashed into me at full speed. We tumbled down the run, leaving hats, goggles, and ski poles behind. We were sprawled out on the run; the girls skied by us. "Nice job, boys," Loudmouth Yellow Jacket called out. Our egos were bruised more than our bodies. We never saw them again.

---

* Quote from "The Autobiography of Lincoln Steffens" Page 47 Chapter 6 'A painter and a page'

While skiing dominated the daytime activities, our evenings were filled with a different type of winter sport: skitching. Skitching is done on a snow-covered road. When a car comes to a stop sign, one sneaks behind the vehicle, dropping down to a crouched position while grabbing onto the bumper of the car. I've never seen the driver notice this as they pull forward continuing their journey. Happily sliding on our shoes (loafers were great for this activity), we'd hang on for blocks on end.

Brian and I would head out after dinner to the streets of Aspen for several hours. If a line of cars came along, the last one was always selected to avoid having another car right behind you. Sometimes other random people would see us and would run to catch the car and join us. The snow-covered side streets naturally kept the car's speed down to some ten to fifteen miles per hour. Once it would get faster than that, we'd just let go and slide to a gradual stop.

Tom Terrill, Brian Avery, and Michelle Terrill at Aspen Highlands

In those days, Aspen did not throw much rock or dirt for traction on the road, and we were able to glide on a very smooth surface. Typically, we went home once our feet were too wet and cold from all the snow and ice that accumulated over time.

My parents knew what we were doing and had no objection. In fact, my mom was known well by my friends at home as the only mom to take her kids skitching. She figured that if she were behind the wheel, she'd know that her kids were safe. A fresh snowstorm at home meant my mom would be driving her yellow Chevy station wagon around the streets of Kenilworth with her kids hanging on the back bumper.

My father did a great job of teaching his kids the value of hard work. From the eighth grade on, his kids had to pay or work for their lift tickets. Aspen Highlands had a great program that offered anyone who signed up to clean the midmountain restaurant at the end of the day a free lift ticket the next day. Brian and I would show up at 3:00 PM, thirty minutes before the lifts closed for the day, at the Merry Go Round restaurant. Gwen and George ran the restaurant back then, and Gwen hired us on the afternoon crew. Vacuuming the carpet, wiping tables, and cleaning the restrooms for sixty minutes and a free ticket was waiting for you the next morning at the ticket office. We didn't mind the work and learned to appreciate the value of our effort for our pleasure skiing. The ski patrol made their final run at 4:00 PM to check for anyone still on the slopes, and they left right before we did. Brian and I knew this meant that the entire mountain was free and clear of other skiers. We could then ski as fast as we could and fly over blind jumps without worrying about anyone below. We took advantage of this and let our skis air out all the way to the bottom.

One day at the bottom of the mountain, the Aspen Highlands Ski School had a makeshift softball game on skis. As we came flying down the hill after our cleanup work, Brian didn't see what was going on. He hit the last steep section of the slope with the reckless abandon Brian was known for, and by the time he realized there was a game going on at the bottom, it was too late to stop. He came in hard from what was center field. Streaking through the infield, Brian went into a hard hockey stop, sliding all the way to home plate. Dropping into a full slide, he crossed home plate, forcing the catcher to leap out of Brian's trajectory. The softball players all stopped and stood silently. Clearly disrupting the game, Brian stood up without saying a word either. Trailing the commotion, I glided by at a slow speed out of the way. To my surprise, the instructors never said a thing, but they did stare at Brian, wondering who this kid was.

The best part of the restaurant work was that our lift tickets had a vital word stamped on it: **"Employee,"** providing us with a 50 percent discount on food. As growing boys, this did not mean it cost any less for lunch but instead twice as much chocolate milk, brownies, and cheeseburgers.

Brian and I did one thing that led to improving our ability more than anything else: skiing on one ski. We didn't realize it at the time, but this turbocharged our skills. We assumed it was against the rules to ski on one ski, so we sneakily did all this. Removing one ski while riding on the lift and holding it in our hands, so when we got off the chairlift, we'd ski down the ramp on one ski. At first, this was difficult, but we got the hang of it quickly enough. Eventually, we tested the limits by leaving our ski at the top of the lift and skiing down the entire run on one ski. Figuring if we got in trouble, we'd have to ride up to get our ski. To our surprise, no one cared. Our sneaking around was met with indifference by the mountain authorities.

When we got home to Chicago, there was a big event with the local kids' ski club. The Snowflake Club took kids from ages seven to fourteen to the local small ski hills in Illinois and southern Wisconsin. The trip to the Playboy Club was the biggest of all as members could bring friends. This hill was a true bunny slope with nothing steep at all. It was too easy. After a little while, Brian and I got bored and decided to ski on one ski. Chuck Caldwell and Tom Porter were our classmates and friends on the evening trip, and they joined us on one ski. Brian and I had mastered this skill while Chuck and Tom Porter did an admirable job for their first time on one ski. Soon, we were the talk of the ski hill. People would stop and point to the four guys skiing down on one ski. The four of us played it cool, acting like this was no big deal. Secretly, we loved the attention, especially from the girls. If only Loudmouth Yellow Jacket could see us then.

During my freshman year of high school, I had my most painful skiing fall ever. Skiing at Aspen Highlands, I was coming fast down Exhibition Run when my marker bindings released prematurely, causing me to lose my balance and fall backward landing on my back. The free ski flipped over with the tip digging into the snow. The ski stopped hard as my rear end caught up to the ski, meeting the flat edge of the ski's tail. This force snapped my Rossignol Strato 102 in two with my tailbone taking the brunt of the force. Underneath the chairlift, people were calling down asking if I was OK.

All I could do was nod my head yes, as I was too embarrassed to tell anyone how much my butt hurt. You can't really grab your butt either to soothe it. At least not without looking creepy. I gathered my gear and put my remaining good ski on my right leg. Picking up the broken ski still held together by the P-Tex base and metal edges, I skied down on one ski to the bottom of the hill. It took about six months for my tailbone to heal fully. When I returned to school, I found it very painful to sit in a desk chair, but what choice did I have. Each class was literally a pain in the butt.

A year later, my family traveled to Aspen again for Christmas. Per usual, Brian was there with my family for a fun-filled time. My sister Michelle had graduated high school and had moved to Aspen, where she was teaching skiing at Aspen Highlands, and the rest of the family was excited to visit her. My parents had a great evening event planned with a party at our condominium. Many of Michelle's new friends were invited, including Bill Hovanic. Bill was your classic ski bum. Living in an apartment above Crossroads Drugstore, he was one of many of Aspen's classic characters. My mom and dad carefully crafted a treasure hunt competition. They had planted six clues at various places throughout the town of Aspen. Dividing the group into two teams, they sent everyone out into the Aspen night trying to solve each clue as they covered block after block in the town.

Bill Hovanic in the red vest with Andy Heath on Steeplechase at Aspen Highlands

Brian and I were on different teams, with Brian ending up on the same side with Bill and five others. My folks had the teams go in reverse order so that we'd not be in the same place at the same time.

Everyone had so much fun that evening, etching a pleasant memory into each one of our lives. When the night got late, the party concluded with everyone wearing a big smile on their face. Brian and I went to our room to go to sleep, but the fun of the evening had us still full of energy. Instead of sleep, we each lay in our beds and talked for a while.

"That guy Bill is kind of weird," Brian started.

"Oh, really? He is a lot older, but I don't think of him as weird," I responded.

34

"Well, you should have seen him when we decided to skitch. We knew we had to get across town fast, and I suggested we skitch. While we were hanging on to the back of a pickup truck, he couldn't stop laughing. Moreover, he just kept saying, 'I can't believe I'm doing this.' He made it out to be such a big deal."

"Brian! You know he only has one leg, right?" Bill was a helicopter pilot in Vietnam. While flying a mission, he took fire that ripped through his leg at the knee. He lost his leg, but in the years that passed, he had a wooden prosthetic.

"He only has one leg?" Brian queried while laughing and thinking I was needling him.

"Yes, he does," I said. "He has a wooden leg from his knee down. I know he does because I've seen him take off his wooden leg."

"You're kidding!" Brian said in a stunned voice. "No wonder he was so slow. I just thought he was in horrible shape."

Brian and I cracked up with laughter. I had forgotten to tell Brian and, with long pants on, Bill's wooden leg is not apparent. Eventually, we fell asleep after a memorable day in Aspen.

The Transportation

Getting to Aspen was frequently an exciting travel adventure. Typically, Nana, my mom's mom, was traveling with us. She became a widow the year we bought the condo, and so leaving her at home was just not what our family would ever do.

The first trip out, we flew to Denver and rented a car there to drive to Aspen. Our family station wagon was packed with eight people, our dog, and stacks of luggage tied to the roof of the car for the drive to Chicago's O'Hare airport. The thirty-minute drive to the airport had an ominous start. The bags on the roof were not well tied down, and at seventy miles per hour, several suitcases flew off the top of the car into oncoming traffic.

Jeff and I were in the third row, which faced the back of the car, so we had a front-row view of my dad's suitcase being run over and flying open. His clothes exploded out of the suitcase as we pulled off the road onto the shoulder. My dad and Edward Morgan, my grandmother's houseman, ran back, trying to gather the clothes and debris without getting run over. A few shirts were ripped to shreds, and tire marks on some underwear created an interesting fashion opportunity for my dad. It was an exciting ten minutes and gave us all something to laugh about once the crisis was over.

The next year, my dad decided to save some money and drive the twelve hundred miles. Once again, our station wagon was full of people, pillows, and animals. Most of the luggage, now correctly tied down, sat securely on the roof. My dad was behind the wheel with Jeff and my mom sharing the bench seat in front. My sister Kathy was right behind my dad and kept putting her feet into the back of the driver's seat. This drove my dad crazy anytime, but the dog barking and an environment of chaos from the overcrowded car triggered a moment of insanity and genius at the same time.

Suddenly, the car swerved across three lanes and onto the exit for the airport. "Tom, what are you doing?" my mom demanded of my father.

"I can't do this. We're going to fly!" My dad drove straight to the departures level at O'Hare and pulled up to the United Airlines entrance. The kids piled out of the car while my mom found a sky-cap. My dad ran to the airport ticket counter and bought seven tickets to Denver on the next plane, which was leaving in forty-five minutes. We hustled through the terminal to our gate, and without the security of current times, we were able to arrive quickly and board immediately.

Upon our arrival in Denver, we deplaned and were walking to baggage claim when my dad stopped to make a quick phone call to my uncle. "Lee, I need you to do me a favor. I'm in Denver as I pulled an audible, and we flew to Colorado. I left the family car at O'Hare. It is at the curb at departures with the keys in the ignition. Would you go pick it up for me?"

My uncle didn't flinch and thought nothing unusual about this situation. He drove with my aunt and found the car exactly how and where we left it four hours earlier. No ticket, no tow truck, no screaming policeman. Just a Chevy station wagon with the keys in the ignition.

In the years to come, we'd drive, take the train, and fly. The driving trips were typically routine and monotonous; however, there were moments of terror on the highway. Fog so thick your only hope was to find a semitractor truck to follow a set of red lights or ice so slick that the highway was littered with cars and trucks in the ditch. Somehow, we never joined them off the road, to which my father credited to the posi-traction option he added to the family station wagon.

On one such occasion, we were in a blinding snowstorm in rural Nebraska. The sun had set long ago, and we were just hoping to find an exit and a motel to spend the night. A Holiday Inn sign was spotted, and we got off, thrilled to be out of this storm. As we pulled into the parking lot, we were following another car that lost control and slid into the ditch just fifty yards from the motel entrance. My dad, with our posi-traction vehicle, went right around them and pulled up to inquire about a room.

I walked in the lobby with my dad, to which we were greeted by the motel manager. "Are you looking for a room for the night?" the manager asked.

"Yes. In fact, we'd like two rooms adjoining please," my dad said.

"Sorry, but we have just one room in the entire facility left, and it's yours if you want it." We took the room, and with some rollaway beds crammed in, we made due. We did wonder what happened to the people in the car that went into the ditch. Score another victory for the posi-traction.

The most fun we ever had as a family on the trip to Aspen were the two times we took the train. The

California Zephyr began her journey in Chicago on the way to San Francisco. The classic train travel with Pullman sleeping cars, dining cars, and the Vista-Dome car. We boarded our train and went to our four side-by-side sleeping berths. Jeff and I shared one room, with Kathy and Michelle next to us. Nana had her own berth and then my parents.

We often took the train to Chicago or the three hours to Appleton, Wisconsin, but never before had we spent the night on a train sleeping in a real bed. Impressed by the way the beds tucked into the wall, allowing us to sit in comfortable chairs with our own view out the window as the Midwest countryside eased on by.

Tom, Jeff, Michelle, and Kathy Terrill with our dog Fritzy

Jeff and I were bouncing with excitement and quickly left our room to find Michelle and Kathy. They were carefully organizing their room with the nesting instincts of female birds, which made no sense to us boys. "Hey, let's go explore the Vista-Dome cars!" I proclaimed with an effervescent sense of urgency. Patient I was not, but my sisters willingly complied, and off we scurried through one car and the next, taking turns pushing the button to open the door.

Everything seemed new in our moving playground. When one door opened, we burst into the dining car. Although no one was dining yet as we just pulled out of the station, we slowed our pace down and walked through as if we were in a museum. "This is the table I want to eat dinner at," Michelle said. "Me too," added Kathy, to which Jeff and I selected another one just because they were all open. Our imaginations were running at an accelerated pace, which we embraced with the playful approach to life that all children possess.

The Vista-Dome car. The four kids with Nana.

We continued into the next car, which had steps leading up to the seats in the Vista-Dome car. Up we went, and all grabbed a row of our own. Here we would stay until my parents arrived some twenty minutes later. The entire trip was one of back and forth from one end to another of the train. I don't think I stayed in one place for more than thirty minutes except when sleeping. The next morning, we awoke to the eastern plains of Colorado, and after a delightful breakfast of french toast, bacon, and hot chocolate, we started the climb into the mountains. Seeing the mountains from the Vista-Dome Car was idyllic and something I'm grateful to have experienced as a child.

We arrived in Glenwood Springs, Colorado, which was our stop. We rented a car and drove the fifty minutes to Aspen. On Highway 82, one passes the majestic Mount Sopris outside Carbondale. My parents liked to encourage us kids to take note and learn the many sights along the way.

Mount Sopris Photo courtesy of Brian Wright

"Does anyone know what mountain that is?" my dad asked. I was a prankster and whispered in Kathy's ear, "Mount Everest."

Kathy eagerly shouted out, "Mount Everest!" to which my dad told her no, but that was a good guess. I then turned to my other side and whispered in Jeff's ear, "Mount Sinai."

Jeff, taking the bait, said, "Mount Sinai."

"Who is telling you two to say that?" my dad, now angry, demanded to know. My humorous deception had crossed the line with my dad, and the laughter ended quickly. The awkwardness in the car lasted some twenty minutes, but as with similar events, we all laughed about it in the years to come.

1975-76

I held my breath as Ski School Director Lefty Brinkman read the names of those selected to teach skiing at Aspen Highlands. More than anything, I needed to hear... "Tom Terrill" in that group.

In 1971, the announcement came that the Winter Olympics for 1976 would be held in Denver. I figured that in the winter of 1976, I'd be a senior in high school, but that would be a problem. If I was going to win a gold medal for my country that year, I'd need to be finished with high school.

I asked my sister who was a freshman if it was possible to finish high school in three years. Michelle researched this idea and found out that it was in fact possible. One needed to double up on classes and have a term of summer school after sophomore year. Well, that settled it for me, and I publicly declared my plan to graduate early. I kept the gold medal thing to myself.

My sister, two years ahead of me, thought it was such a good idea she too would graduate in three years to pursue a career in acting. No Winter Olympics in her future.

Very soon, I admitted to myself that while I was a good skier, I was not a racer. I loved to ski but didn't love to race. I modified my plan and reaffirmed that I would finish school early and added that I would move to Aspen to become a ski instructor. I'm not sure anyone took me seriously, but I was fully committed. As plans change, Michelle too had an epiphany of her own. She didn't want to be an actress, but instead, she would be a ski instructor at Aspen Highlands.

Wait. What? I said to myself. *Michelle is stealing my idea, and I have no way to do this first.* Initially, I was upset but fairly quickly gave up my own ego of fulfilling my own idea first and would let her clear the trail two years ahead of me. Truthfully, I was very supportive of Michelle, and my path was made much easier because of the many friends and connections she made.

Michelle was seventeen and living on her own in Aspen. She was handpicked to be music icon Cher's private ski instructor. I remember in high school looking at a *People* magazine with a picture of Cher and her daughter Chastity skiing. Michelle was in the picture too, but only her leg. *People* magazine didn't care about Michelle. It was Cher and Chastity they wanted to cover.

I did finish high school early as planned, graduating at sixteen. That fall, I moved to Aspen in my rear-wheel drive 1969 Chevy Impala along with my good friends, John Thompson and Tim McGuane. The first week, we stayed in my folks' condo as I went through "The Clinic" at Aspen Highlands where about half of those attending would be hired. Thrilled to pass the weeklong test and join the ranks of the Aspen Highland Ski School, I had accomplished what I planned to do four years earlier.

Like my sister before me, I was seventeen and living in Aspen on my own. My parents had assisted in finding a house for me to live in, and I rented a room from the Britvar family. Their son, Paul, was in high school and became a friend. I lived there for several months up in the McClain Flats section across from the airport.

While I never saw them, my neighbors were actress Jill St. John and singer John Denver. Not many homes were in this area, but both of them took the same road home that I did. Cemetery Lane across the Roaring Fork River then climbing uphill on McClain Flats Road was no easy drive, especially when a fresh layer of snow covered the road. My car had balding tires, and when it did snow, I could not climb the hill to my home. Being in Aspen, it snowed a lot, which meant I often did not make it home.

I kept a sleeping bag in the back seat of my car just in case. If my parents' condo was not occupied with renters, I could stay there, but more often, I ended up in one of two parking garages. Typically, my parents' condo garage, which had twelve spots inside. If there was an open spot on a snowy night, I'd pull in to park, climb in the back seat, and settle into my orange fiber-filled sleeping bag for the night. It wasn't a great way to sleep, but it beat being outside. I also knew the code for the Aspen Square parking garage as my friend Mark Jiganti's family had a condo in this building. It was a bigger garage and warmer too.

The approach to the Britvar's home where I moved in November 1975

The idea of the sleeping bag came shortly after I moved in to the Britvar's home. John Thompson was still in town with me, and we got stuck trying to climb the road. After dozens of failed attempts, we gave up and decided to head back to town. On the climb back up from the river crossing, the car slid off the road into the ditch, requiring the car to be towed out. John and I walked to the main road and hitchhiked into town.

We walked into the Jerome Hotel at 11:00 PM. Attempting to enter the bar, our fake IDs were not the quality required to get past the bouncer. So instead we hung out in the lobby on the ancient couches from the silver mining days decades ago. The snow continued to fall, and John and I realized we were spending the night here, or at least until we got kicked out. Shortly after midnight, the Jerome Hotel had a major power failure. With the lights out, it became easier for the two of us to fall asleep and not be noticed by the employees who were concerned with getting the power back. We woke early in the morning to find the sun out and the roads beginning to clear from the ten plus inches of fresh snow. This experience taught me to have a well-stocked emergency kit in my car with the orange sleeping bag as the first item.

John would be leaving Aspen soon and going back to Chicago. A few days before he left, we were in the City Market getting some groceries when John noticed a single ski glove on the ground. It was old and clearly discarded. On a whim, John picked up the glove and placed it on my car antenna which was on the passenger side in front of the windshield. The 1969 Chevy Impala had an antenna that would go up and down with the push of the volume knob, but mine never retracted all the way down. As we drove with the glove on the antenna, the wind from the car's speed blew back three of the fingers in a curved fashion, leaving only the middle finger boldly making a statement to the people we passed. John put his window down and would call out to people, "Hey! Get the message?" We laughed and laughed at this comical circumstance. When John left for home, his humor went with him, and I was on my own now until Christmas.

Aspen Highlands had embraced the GLM technique of teaching skiing. Graduated Length Method was created by Clif Taylor, one of a handful of 10th mountain division men who fought in World War II and came back after the war to make a career in skiing. People who never skied before would start on very short three-foot skis, staying on these for two to three days, before progressing to four- and then five-foot skis by day 5. It was a remarkable thing to see people who had never skied before quickly have the skills to go to the top of Aspen Highlands at Loges Peak.*

My view at breakfast each morning from the Britvars' home

As a new instructor and also just a kid, I had to prove myself to the supervisors. Smitty, John, Bonnie, and Squatty were the four supervisors at Aspen Highlands. Each day I made sure I was the first one to the morning meeting and then first out to the slope, waiting to get called down for a new class. Day after day, I was ignored as classes were handed out to other instructors who showed up well after me despite the rule that an instructor would get a teaching assignment in the order of their arrival that morning. A new class would last a

---

* In the seventies, the top of Aspen Highlands was called Loges Peak as the trail maps of that time clearly show. Today the S has been dropped, and it is called simply Loge Peak. To me, it will always be Loges.

good four to six days before the vacationers went back home, so eventually I'd get one. One day, all the classes were set, leaving some ten instructors without work that day. Nine of them gave up and went skiing, but I was determined. I had been standing for over an hour and watched some thirty instructors that arrived after me get an assignment. I was mad at being ignored and was not going away. I just stood there waiting.

Three women in their thirties showed up late, struggling to walk in their ski boots and carry their skis. They wanted a lesson, and only one instructor was available still. Smitty called me down, and I introduced myself to my group of three. But before I could even meet everyone, more latecomers showed up. They came in bunches of four and five. Smitty had no one left but me, and so they were all fed my way. Before I knew it, I had a class of twenty-six new students. This was crazy, as a typical class had six to ten students.

None of these people had ever been on skis before. Exhilarated by the demand of the moment, I had two lines of thirteen facing each other and fifteen yards apart on a small hill. I was in the middle, and I'd call out people one at a time to glide down a gentle slope. Amazingly, I immediately remembered every name of these twenty-six people. Surprising myself, I was doing a fantastic job in an impossible situation when a voice called out from behind me.

"Hi, young man. Mind if I join you?" I turned around to see who it was. "My name is Clif Taylor, and I'm in town to see how things are going at Aspen Highlands."

I was stunned. The inventor of Graduated Length Method and a legend in ski instruction was asking if he could observe me.

"Smitty said you might need some help with this big group," he said with an infectious smile.

"Sure, Mr. Taylor," I reverted to the respectful formality of addressing someone as I would in Chicago.

"Please call me Clif, and I'll call you Tom. Deal?" Clif said.

I responded positively with delight. For about thirty minutes, he watched me, occasionally giving me some suggestions and tips. At that point, he came over and patted me on the back and said, "You don't need any help here. You're doing a great job."

Tom Terrill, 1975-76, Aspen Highland Ski School

This affirmation was exactly what I needed. Moments later, out of the corner of my eye, I could see Clif talking to my boss Smitty and pointing back at me. I knew he was telling Smitty what a good job I was doing. Confident that things would be different now and I'd get the respect that I deserved. And it did get a little better, but what I didn't realize at the time was that many of my fellow instructors were doing this for their livelihood. I was just here for a season and then would head off to college. It was the right decision to give classes to people with families they were supporting before me.

Peter Johnson was a local kid a year older than me who also taught at Highlands. Peter and I would go skiing together when we didn't get a class and rip up the mountain.

One day, Peter shared an idea for something unique. "Let's ski on our three footers and cut into some really tight trees on a steep slope," Peter suggested. It sounded a little risky to me, but I was game to give it a try. We rode up the Exhibition lift and headed for the tight trees next to the expert run "Moment of Truth." With no poles and short skis, we stood on a service road staring down an extreme pitch filled with trees. These trees were so close together that it would be unthinkable to ski with normal equipment.

"How is this going to work?" I asked Peter, still unsure how we could get down without crashing into many trees. Peter looked at me and shrugged his shoulders. He too had no idea, but then he cast a certain smile that conveyed a "damn the torpedoes" attitude and dropped in. Peter sunk deep into the untracked snow, sitting low as if in a rocking chair with his gloved hands out in front of him. He'd tap a tree to initiate a turn and then another and another. All this at about four miles per hour. The slow speed allowed him to sneak down a path that only existed in a world of serpentine imagination.

I followed Peter's lead and hopped into my own path. A new form of skiing for both of us and to the best of my knowledge for anyone. The three-foot skis were the maximum length for this effort. I loved the slow-motion sensation of working my way down the slope. The depth of snow arrested our speed, allowing us to travel at a strolling pace down a forty-degree slope. I felt like a pioneer in new territory. We were skiing in an area that was "out of bounds," and if caught, we'd be in a lot of trouble from the authorities. But we were in an area that no one would ever suspect anyone would ski. We left the heavily wooded pitch some one hundred fifty yards down joining an open run.

At the bottom, we came to a stop and looked at each other as if we were ten-year-old boys doing something naughty. The combination of the novelty and rule breaking accounted for 50 percent of the fun. We continued to the chairlift and repeated this another two times. It remains a great memory but one I never repeated. It was a one-hit wonder on skis.

*****

Christmas vacation arrived with my family coming to Aspen. I was excited to see not only my family but also my many friends who would be there with their families. Chuck Caldwell, Peggy and Mary Shields, the Jiganti siblings, Teri, Mark, Jeanine, John, and Paul would all be there. Jamie Carmel would be traveling with her cousins, and my good friend Jim Cameron would arrive too.

I decided to stay in my family's condo while they were visiting. While I was excited to see everyone, I also knew I'd eat much better if my mom's home cooking was an option. After dinner one evening, I left my family and went to the Jigantis' condo two blocks away. While I loved being in Aspen, I also was very homesick for my friends back in high school, and this chance to see many of them here was a treat. After an hour or so of catching up, Paul Jiganti and his cousin came in announcing that a whole condo complex just two blocks away was on fire.

We all ran out to see, only to discover it was my parents' complex on fire. I found my family all safely outside watching the fire consume a fair amount of the back of the building. The fire started in unit 14, and our unit, number 21, looked OK as long as they could get the fire out in 14. A young teen had taken lighter fluid and sprayed it on an open fire in the fireplace to try to give it a boost. The flame ran back on the stream and to his hand, and he responded by tossing the container in a panic onto the sofa. The whole living room quickly went up in flames.

The firemen successfully put out the fire, and we were able to spend the night if we wanted to. The smoke damage was overwhelming however, and so I decided to go back to sleep at my rental. It took a few days for everyone's clothes to lose the strong odor or smoke which permeated every bit of fabric in our condominium.

Shortly after Christmas, my family left Aspen and went back home to the Chicago suburbs. During the Christmas break, I began to date Peggy Shields who was here for just two weeks with her family. The average life span of a dating relationship at these ages was roughly four weeks, but the fact that we saw each other every day and her entire stay was only two weeks, the odds for a durable relationship were stacked against us. Peggy also was sixteen going on twenty-eight, and her interest in me was certainly influenced by the coolness factor of me being a ski instructor. Once she discovered I was really only as cool as any other seventeen-year-old kid, my days of holding her attention were numbered.

Jim Cameron arrived in town and was staying with me at the Britvars' home. On December 31, 1975, I had a class to teach, but I really wanted to be skiing with Peggy.

"Jim," I started that morning, "will you do me a favor? I want you to ski with my new girlfriend, Peggy, while I'm working."

"What does she look like?" Jim asked, kidding around. He had never met Peggy back home but agreed to take her to Ajax.

I went off to work and arranged for Jim and Peggy to connect at the Little Nell lift. At 4:00 PM, I picked them up in town so I could see Peggy and drive Jim back to my place. I was delighted to see how well they hit it off and naively thought this was a good thing.

That night, we'd meet at the Silver King apartments where my good friend Doug Carlson lived. Doug and his roommates were having a New Year's Eve party, and my friends from home would all be in attendance. Chris Kessler and Doug Carlson both taught with me at Aspen Highlands, and I was excited to be coming to this bash. The shindig had good food, plenty of beer and wine, and a large crowd on excited revelers. Chuck Caldwell and Mary Shields started a new romance in the festive environment. Both of them were going back to Illinois, so this relationship might in fact have a chance but for the fact that Chuck's current girlfriend, Jamie Carmel, might not approve. Jamie was in Aspen but didn't make it to the party due to family commitments in Snowmass.

"Ten minutes 'til midnight!" Doug called out. "Make sure you know who you'll be kissing to bring in the New Year," he encouraged all his guests.

I looked around for Peggy, but she was nowhere to be seen. Wandering outside on the balcony, I saw plenty of people, but my girlfriend was not one of them. Down the stairs and into the parking lot, I searched trying to imagine where she might be. As I passed by my own car, I heard voices from inside and noticed the back seat was occupied. Grabbing the door handle, I whipped the back door open to discover Peggy and Jim inside, making out.

"Well, that's just great!" I loudly said as I slammed the door shut. I got back to the party to hear the last six seconds of the countdown to midnight. All I could see was everyone kissing someone else, except for me. It was like a surreal movie scene where everyone was happy and joyful, except for me in the middle of room. Stunned by the reality, I found Chuck and asked if he could have Jim spend the night with his family in Snowmass as I was going home.

The next day, I did not have a class and was free skiing at Highlands. While doing laps on the Olympic chair, Jim showed up, and we rode the chair together. Wordlessly getting on the chair, I was not sure what to do or say. Forty-five seconds into the ride, I broke the silence.

"Give me one good reason why I shouldn't throw you out of this chair," I self-righteously said to Jim.

"You should," Jim said. "Honestly, I can't believe what happened yesterday. But I have to tell you, Tom, while you didn't know it yet, you and Peggy were done." Jim went on to tell me Peggy had made it clear that day skiing with Jim she was looking for someone new.

I knew Jim was right and accepted this truth, which freed me from my anger toward him. Jim, Chuck, and the Shields family all left the next day, leaving just me with Jamie Carmel. Jamie still knew nothing about Chuck's new romance with Mary, but Chuck told me he intended to break up with Jamie in a week when they were both home.

Jamie came over to ski with me that day, and we had a great time. She was always a good friend, but we had never dated. I was fairly certain Jamie was experiencing some feelings toward me, and she was as cute and nice as they come. I rationalized that the only thing that was keeping me and Jamie apart was that she didn't know Chuck had moved on. In the most selfish move of my immature dating life, I told Jamie about Chuck and Mary. I knew Chuck would have to forgive me, and I wasn't likely to be kissing Jamie unless she was mad at Chuck.

I recall telling her, and later that day, our sparks attempted to catch fire. But a few kisses seemed more awkward than natural, and the fire never developed. Jamie went home, and I incurred Chuck's wrath from afar. We all moved on from that crazy two weeks, remaining friends with stories we can laugh at today. Now getting back to normal life in Aspen, my focus would correctly realign with skiing.

Tom Terrill outside the Silver King apartment

Aspen Highlands was going to host a major professional freestyle skiing event on the run Thunder bowl. At our morning instructors' meeting, it was announced that some volunteer help was needed. Everyone not teaching was asked to ski the run to build up the moguls, which I gladly did, but the second part was what intrigued me. The jumps needed to be built, and only those who helped would be allowed to go off the jumps in the week leading up to the competition.

I quickly volunteered to help build the jumps. I loved to get air, but to go off the jumps designed for the pros was electrifying. Four of us signed up and joined the jump designers with shovels in hand. It was very hard work, and I learned quite a bit of the science behind the jumps themselves. Once complete, we got to go off any of the three jumps as much as we wanted. One jump was for front flips and another for backflips. Then there was the floater for upright aerials.

I could flip on the diving board or the trampoline, but I never wanted to try this on skis. I was too intimidated. The floater was right up my alley, allowing me to fly some ten to fifteen feet above the snow to a perfect landing. It felt effortless to soar over the jump and enjoy the time suspended in the air.

Here I met Eddie Lincoln. Eddie was an instructor technically, but I don't think he ever taught at Aspen Highlands. I understood him to be skiing for himself with some sponsorship from the Highlands. Eddie had invented a new jump called "the Lincoln Loop," where he would rotate counterclockwise as if his body were the hands on a clock.

I was doing my standard tricks of a spread eagle, daffy, and tip drop. I could do a 360 but never tried it on a jump this big. Eddie recommended I do a twister and double twister to build toward the 360 off the floater. While his encouragement was helpful, I never did try the 360. Watching him jump was great fun, a unique opportunity for me.

Jane Northrup second on right in and Shenia Bhote far right in my class, March 1976

About a year later while back at home in Chicago, I went with friends to see the new James Bond movie, *The Spy Who Loved Me*. The opening scene has an amazing chase scene on skis in the Alps. While the close-ups are all Roger Moore, it was Eddie Lincoln who was the stunt skier in those scenes. I was not surprised, knowing how great a skier he was.

Doug Carlson had come from Boulder to teach skiing the same year. A year or two older than me, Doug soon became one of my good friends. In my life, I've met just a few people who seemed to be everyone's best friend, and Doug had that charisma and infectious joy of life that drew me to him. He lived in Silver King at the base of Red Mountain along with Chris Kessler, Bill "Chef" Reno, and a third guy I never met.

One night while hanging out with Doug and his roommates Doug read a letter he got from the absent roommate. The letter explained that he would not be coming back to Aspen, and would not be paying his portion of the expensive phone bill he owed either. In closing, he mentioned he'd come back in about a week for his car.

Doug decided that if he wasn't going to get paid the money he was owed, he'd get it in the value of a broken car window or two. Following Doug's lead, the roommates and guests that evening, like myself, went out to the parking lot with a baseball bat. Taking turns taking a whack at the rear window, which was surprisingly resilient, we eventually cracked it. I watched one guy take a towel and wrapped it around his fist, which he then smashed into the windshield, breaking it in a single blow.

We weren't vandals. At least we rationalized that we weren't as Doug made clear he would pay for all the damage out of the money he was owed. We went back to the apartment, which now had an empty bed to be rented. Doug could sell ice cubes to an Eskimo, and he needed a new roommate. It didn't take long before I was moving out of the Britvar's home and into the open twin bed in Doug's room. This life was so much better for me as I had friends that I could see all the time.

Shortly after moving in, I decided to take a quick trip back to Chicago in February to see family and friends. On the return trip, I brought Greg Stuhr, John Thompson, and Chuck Caldwell with me. My Chevy was a workhorse of a car but never meant for mountain driving. We left Illinois and drove straight out to Aspen. Tired and weary when he hit the climb up Vail pass, we tried our best to rally the additional three hours to Aspen.

My last day. Little Nell, April 1976.

I was behind the wheel and Chuck in the front passenger seat as I passed a semitruck slowly making the climb. The snow-covered roads had become wet with the traffic, and the truck laid a layer of dirt-filled frozen water on my windshield. Quickly turning on the wipers only made it worse with an impenetrable smear. At sixty miles per hour, this immediate loss of sight is a frightful thing but only made worse when I hit the spray to discover it was frozen. No wiper fluid came out. Chuck immediately put his window down while John grabbed a pillow and took off the cotton pillowcase, handing it to Chuck.

Chuck was sitting on the door while Greg held his feet down to prevent Chuck from falling out of the car. With great speed and vigor, Chuck cleared a small circle for me too continue to drive. Once I could see again, I safely pulled over on the shoulder. We threw snow on the windshield and cleared the mud off. But this was only temporary as each vehicle we passed or that passed us by would cover it again.

For twenty miles, we did this over and over and eventually got pretty good at giving me a peephole to traverse over Highway 6. I'm not sure what would have happened if I was alone in the car and didn't have this team assembled to address the problem.

We arrived in Aspen eventually and had five days of great skiing together. Peter Johnson guided us through a section off Olympic that was not open but provided some untracked powder after ducking under a ski area boundary rope. My friends flew back to Chicago to finish the school year, and I continued my time teaching skiing in Aspen.

Back home, my New Trier East High School was starting spring break, and two classmates of mine came out to ski and take lessons. By sheer coincidence, Jane Northrup and Shenia Bhote were assigned to me. Neither of them knew I had graduated a year early and were quite surprised to find their peer from back home as their Aspen ski instructor. I'm not sure if it was a disappointment to not have an instructor with an Austrian accent and instead just have it be a guy you knew from back home. Nevertheless, we had a wonderful time.

I finished my season in Aspen in April, leaving my new friends behind. It was a magnificent experience with memories I treasure.

John Thompson returned to Aspen once again to drive back home the final time. My car was filled with all my belongings, including a hundred-or-so empty beer cans that were a collection of Colorado beers. In Nebraska with John behind the wheel, a State Trooper pulled us over for speeding.

My Chevy Impala with the ski pole at the side of the car

As the officer looked in the back seat, his eyes caught a glimpse of a full Hefty garbage back stuffed with empty beer cans. "Did you guys just drink all those?" he asked. What could he have been thinking? I had enough sense to tell the truth and say no, but I still wonder if he felt as stupid asking that question as he sounded to us. If we just drank one hundred beers, I don't think we could be talking, let alone awake.

As he pulled away, we went to start the car. It wouldn't start. Rural Nebraska and the sun setting put us in a bad place. We walked a mile or so to an exit and found a mechanic to tow the car to his garage. My bull wheel had one-half of the teeth stripped from a bad starter motor. The car could start as long as the bull wheel stopped in the right place, but that was a fifty-fifty chance. So I needed to use a ski pole and climb under my car to force the bull wheel to turn enough so the starter motor could catch it.

I arrived home penniless with a car I sold for one hundred fifty dollars about a month later. My life would now shift to a new job until college in the fall.

Addendum: In 1984, I was newly married and living in Glencoe, Illinois, when I heard the news of an avalanche in Highlands Bowl at Aspen Highlands. I learned that Chris Kessler, who became a ski patrolman, was killed along with two of his co-workers. I called a few friends still in Aspen with whom we hung out with Chris back in the midseventies. It was such sad news to learn of his death.

I lost touch with Doug Carlson but learned that he was the cofounder of Fiji Water, serving as the CEO. Even though the company was sold in 2005, I regularly buy Fiji Water as it reminds me of my friend Doug and all the others who spent that remarkable ski season with me.

College Years

Independence Pass

My freshman year in college was spent in Carbondale, Illinois, at Southern Illinois University. Transitioning back to school after fifteen months without classes was a challenge emotionally. In my heart, I was still yearning to ski and greatly missed Aspen.

My family planned a ten-day trip to Aspen over Christmas. Excited about the prospects of getting back to the mountains, I called Aspen Highlands Ski School to see if they needed any extra instructors over the Christmas rush. To my delight, they were in need, and I was offered to teach as many days as I wanted during this ten-day trip, but a significant problem was developing: Drought!

Snowmaking was not yet prevalent in the 1976-77 ski season, and Mother Nature was offering a significant drought year in the Colorado Rockies. The snow accumulation that season was the worst drought in ski season history. For lack of snow, skiers at Aspen Highlands could not ski to the bottom of the mountain and instead were loaded into trucks and snowcats to drive the dirt roads the last one-quarter of the ski hill.

People canceled trips left and right, and now there was a shortage of people wanting instruction. Still, I did get a five-day class upon my arrival, which surprised me. I thought the supervisors would need to give any class to those that were there for the entire season. I loved to teach people to ski. The pleasure I enjoyed guiding someone's first time gliding downhill on skis remains one of the most fulfilling sense of accomplishment I've experienced. The delight in their face was unforgettable, and to be a part of the process was immensely rewarding.

The last five days, I would ski with my friends from home that made a similar pilgrimage each year with their families. This year, we found a way to make lemonade from the lemons of the drought. During the winter, Highway 82 usually is a dead end upon arrival in Aspen. The narrow road up Independence Pass was closed every winter, except this one. A lack of snow allowed the road to remain open over Christmas. Five of us decided to drive a car up to the top of the pass and then hike up from there into a terrain that we had never skied. No chairlifts, no ski patrol, and no lift ticket to buy. One earned every turn you made by the hike uphill at twelve thousand plus feet.

Mark Jiganti, Jim Cameron, Brian Avery, Peggy Shields, and I embarked on this new venture with excitement. We took my parents' Oldsmobile station wagon from the Aspen city limits up to the summit one morning and put on our ski boots. Another four or so people were already there upon our arrival, skiing down toward the parking area. We climbed up the north facing hill, taking about thirty minutes to get to the top. The conditions were very rough with snow compressed from sun and wind and time into a washboardlike surface. Our skis chattered on each turn, and the effort was considerable compared to skiing groomed inbounds runs. No one would ever call the actual skiing as fun but the fact that we were in the middle of nowhere in otherwise forbidden territory and foreboding conditions.

In a mere five minutes, we were back at the parking area full of smiles and congratulations on the first trip down. Immediately, we took off our skis and started back up. This time at the top, we surveyed the back side and fantasized about skiing it, which would be ten times the length of our run back to the car, but it seemed a bit foolhardy. We were already in an unregulated area, and the dangers of wandering into the unknown territory were clear. As we skied back toward the car, the level of enjoyment dropped considerably the second time down. The novelty was wearing off quickly, and the reality of the conditions was giving us second thoughts about how many times we'd do this. The hike was challenging due to the altitude and lack of acclimation from being at sea level a week earlier.

On the way up, we all kept talking about how we needed to ski the back side. That would be different, and we convinced ourselves the conditions would be better than the front side. The problem would be that we'd all be stuck at the bottom of the pass with very little vehicle traffic to hitch a ride back up. Once at the top, we all looked down longingly at the back side. We could hear the siren's song luring us to come hither when I had an epiphany.

"The four of you can ski down the back side, and I'll go get the car from here and meet you," I said.

We all looked far downhill to see a hairpin turn in the road well down the mountain. It appeared to be a clear straight shot down to the turn, which would be a secure pickup spot. Mark, Jim, Brian, and Peggy all agreed and headed down. Their shouts of joy echoed into my ears as I watched them start the trek down.

I took my time skiing alone on the front side, knowing my trip was much shorter than that of my friends. Scanning the majestic mountain peaks as I descended my third and final run, I felt a peace flowing through my spirit. When I ski and study the surrounding peaks in the distance, the presence of God is self-evident for me. Something about being in the altitude just feels closer to heaven.

I got to the car alone and imagined my friends having the time of their lives as I took off my ski boots and put on my shoes for the drive. The car was cold as I drove to the appointed pickup spot, which was 100 percent in the shade. Leaving the car running to keep the heat on, I got out of the car and walked a bit to see if I can see anyone yet. Not a soul in sight, which is a bit of a shock. My friends are all accomplished skiers, and they should be here soon. I walked back to the car to stay warm.

Thirty minutes after my arrival and I didn't see anyone yet. My imagination started to travel down a "what-if" road, hoping no one had gotten hurt.

"Jigs, Crams, Boaves!" I shouted the nicknames of the guys. "Can you hear me? Peggy, are you there?"

Nothing but silence. I went back to the car, thinking maybe I came to the wrong hairpin turn. I drove farther down the mountain, hoping they were below me. I drove some five miles and now could tell for certain I was at the correct spot, to which I immediately returned. In vain, I hoped they would be standing on the road when I got back to the appointed pickup spot. But no one was there.

I parked the car and began to walk up a snow-covered mound about thirty yards up to get a better view. The walk was difficult as the snow was not packed, and even in this drought year, each step, I sank past my knees. As I reached the top of this mound, my view dramatically improved. I could see how the topography was a lot of ups and downs and not a steady downhill run. I still didn't see anyone, and I shouted again, to which I received no reply.

The sun would set in about an hour, and I didn't know what to do. Should I spend the night waiting? Should I leave to go get help? But who could help? And what would they do differently than me? I kept hoping that my friends were all OK, but it didn't seem possible with the length of time that had now passed since they took off from the summit.

"Mark!" I screamed again.

"Tom, I'm here!" Mark responded exasperatedly as he walked out from some trees some forty yards away.

I was gratefully relieved to see Mark. "Is everyone OK?" I asked.

With an out-of-breath cadence, Mark said, "Yes, but…that…was a…bitch."

Shortly after that, I saw Peggy, Jim, and Brian emerge from the same place from where Mark came. Everyone was exhausted. Mark had now reached me and explained that the mountain was much different than it looked from the top. They had to climb numerous times from low points that you could not see until you were there in the midst of it.

As we got to the car, darkness had now fully set in. They arrived with no time to spare. We were young, inexperienced, and ill-equipped for such an effort and were fortunate to get out without any harm. I drove back to Aspen where we all agreed to ski in bounds at Ajax the next day.

Basalt and Other Assorted Bunkhouses

In 1977, I was able to arrange a three-plus-week stay in Aspen during the semester break. I left home right after Christmas, driving with Jim Cameron in his car. Jim was on his way back to Utah and would stay with me for a week of skiing. John Thompson would join us, but he would fly into Aspen.

My sister Michelle and her husband, Andy, were living in a house near Basalt some twenty miles outside of Aspen and invited us to stay. We followed the directions Michelle had given me and pulled into their snow-covered driveway. They were renting a curiously designed house or cabin, and we were thrilled to see them.

Michelle came bounding outside with her usual enthusiasm to greet us. "I am so excited to see you, Tom," she said, giving me a hug. "And, Jim, it is great to see you too! I'm hoping we will get to ski with you during your stay."

We grabbed our ski gear and suitcases and carried them inside. This rustic accommodation would do, and being the freeloaders that we were, nary a word of complaint crossed our lips.

"I'm sorry about how cold it is inside," Michelle said as she turned on the electric oven in the kitchen. "This is the source of heat for the kitchen and your room," she added. Uncertain if she was kidding or not, Jim and I silently glanced at each other. "Down these steps is Andy's and my bedroom. It has a woodburning stove, but it only heats our room. It will get pretty cold where you two are sleeping, so you'll want to wear long underwear to bed."

Michelle pointed to a futon on the floor that looked like a double bed. "Michelle," I started, "remember we are picking John up at the airport today. We need a place for three to sleep, and this looks like it is for two to share."

"Well, this is all we have," Michelle explained with a smile. "I think it will work," she added. My sister had an amazingly positive attitude and would turn any complaint upside down and into a positive point of view. Michelle had a couple of sleeping bags along with some pillows and blankets for us. "Oh, and here is the bathroom," Michelle said, directing us through a door. "Sorry, it's just a tub, but the hot water will feel good and help warm you up."

At this point, I thought a hot bath might feel good compared to the fifty-five degrees inside. But instead, we spent the time talking and catching up. Later, we went to the airport to pick up John Thompson and bring him back to our lodgings.

Getting ready to go to sleep, we unzipped the two sleeping bags to use as blankets and piled on the other blankets as well. The three of us squeezed into this too-small futon laying side by side and closer to one another than was comfortable both physically and emotionally.

Michelle and Andy were toasty warm with their woodburning stove while John, Jim, and I were freezing and bumping into one another. But these are the lengths one will go to when you want to ski. Chasing the white powder was an addiction, and we were willing to put up with a lot to get our fix.

We made it through the night but didn't like the thought of doing this over and over again for another six nights. After breakfast, where the open oven door lay as a reminder that this house was not heated, we drove into Aspen to do some skiing. We had a great first day on the mountain. The familiarity of Aspen and our core friendship set the stage for a rich time. However, in the back of my mind lingered the thought of a cold night sleep in twelve hours. To my way of thinking, we were going to have to just grin and bear it. John was ruminating on this temperature dilemma, and his out-of-the-box thinking went beyond my own limitations.

"Guys, I know what we can do!" John suddenly exclaimed. "We take the two sleeping bags and zip them together. Then the three of us climb in the combined larger sleeping bag where we will better share body heat."

"Are you nuts?" Jim retorted. "I'm not getting in a sleeping bag with you two."

I had to admit I agreed with Jim. We already were a bit too close while sleeping, and this would only accentuate the undesirable part of our predicament. Still, John persisted making his case that these sleeping bags were already a bit oversized, and there would be enough room. And we'd sleep better if we weren't so cold.

Chuck Caldwell in our bunk room at the Dormez Vous in Aspen

So when we got back to Michelle and Andy's, we went to work on fashioning the zippers together. There was not much to do other than laugh at the problem and the solution. We gave it a try, and John was right. We felt like the Three Stooges in bed together, but it worked.

Jim decided to leave early and head back to Utah, leaving John and me to finish the stay in Basalt.

Good fortune smiled upon us as John's Miami of Ohio friend, John Webster, was coming to Aspen with his folks. They were staying in a luxury condo in downtown Aspen and invited us to stay with them for three nights. Grateful for my sister's accommodation, we nevertheless jumped at the chance to have a room with two real beds and honest-to-goodness heat.

Chuck Caldwell in the office condo of Chateau Dumont where we stayed for four nights

Three days came and went all too quickly with John departing Aspen and Chuck Caldwell arriving. My merry-go-round of friends and places to lay my head continued. Chuck and I started in a bunkhouse dormitory lodge called the Dormez Vous. Fifteen dollars a night for a cot in a bunk bed in a room with four beds. You'd share the room with strangers and get a continental breakfast in the morning. Here we stayed for four nights.

This was close by to Ajax with an easy walk to the lift 1A base or to a bus stop to take us to Aspen Highlands.

My ski trip continued with Chuck as we moved on to the office unit of Chateau Dumont. The property managers for the condo unit had a basement two-bedroom condo for their office. Remarkably, they agreed to let us stay in their office for free as long as we were not there during regular business hours. This worked out perfectly as we would leave for the ski slopes at 8:30 AM and then not return until after 5:00 PM. We slept on a couch and had access to a kitchen and two full bathrooms. The bedrooms were crowded with desks and file cabinets, but we didn't care. It was a perfect arrangement, and we were able to stay for four nights for free.

My time in Aspen was coming to a close, but I still had more skiing. I took a bus to Vail to meet Greg Stuhr. Greg's family had moved to Evergreen, Colorado, the year earlier, and he would drive to Vail to meet me. Greg and I would ski for a day at Vail and then go back to his parents' place in Evergreen. We'd ski one final day at Winter Park before I hopped on a plane back to Chicago.

Tom Terrill on "Look, Ma" at Vail. Chair #3 and chair #4 in the background and Mid Vail to the left.

Lincoln Steffens

Christmas break of 1978, I again returned to Aspen to teach some but mostly to free ski and ski for free. The teaching job not only provided some income, but on days I didn't teach, I could ski on my own without having to purchase a lift ticket. That allowed me to extend my stay each year of college between semesters as I could really stretch a dollar.

One day, I had been skiing alone at Aspen Highlands when I came down to the midway loading spot on the Exhibition lift. I saw my sister's friend Bill Hovanic in the lift line ahead of me.

"Hey, Bill. Are you single?" I called to see if he was riding the lift alone.

"Tom! Yes, I am," Bill said, glad to see a friend. "Come on up and join me."

Bill skied every day and often alone, and he was glad to have the company. As we rode the chair, we caught up on what was going on in each other's lives. I told Bill I was in my junior year in college and studying history and political science and planned to get involved in politics in Washington DC.

"Have you read Lincoln Steffens?" Bill asked.

"Who?" I quizzically responded.

Bill pulled out of his backpack the oldest-looking and the thickest book I had ever seen. "This is *The Autobiography of Lincoln Steffens*, and it should be required reading for anyone who ever wants to get involved in politics." With great passion, he went on and on about how this book had turned on a light of understanding regarding government and politics with which he had never had before. Bill's enthusiasm was so compelling to me that I promised I would check the book out of my university library and read it.

When I returned to college, I kept my promise and checked out the book. It took me weeks to read it due to its length and other reading I had to do for my coursework. Bill was right. The book should be required reading to anyone studying history and political science. I thoroughly enjoyed the book and have recommended it to many people since. It is long out of print, but old copies can be found at used-book stores. I have given this book away to more people than any other and promised that anyone who reads about the Neely Farm and Lincoln's time there will have a smile on their face and peace in their soul while reading this delightful chapter.

Above the Clouds

I was skiing alone at Aspen Highlands one day in a heavy snowstorm. Most people didn't bother to ski that day, and the few that did spent most of their time huddled by the fire in the mountain restaurant. I was riding the Cloud Nine lift doing laps on Floridora when I rode up single with Andy Hanson. Andy was an acquaintance of mine but a good friend of my sister and brother-in-law.

He said he was going to ride up one more chairlift to the top of Aspen Highlands.

"Seriously?" I asked in an incredulous tone. "It is snowing so hard here, and you want to go farther up into the storm?

"I have a feeling about this," he said. "Come with me and see if my hunch is right."

I had no idea what his hunch was, and he would not tell me. Curious to see what he was thinking and enjoying the company, I decided to join him and ride the next chairlift to the peak some eleven thousand plus feet above sea level.

As we got on the Loges Peak lift, the snow was falling so fast and hard that we could barely see two chairs ahead. But after a minute or two, the snow stopped, and the clouds thinned.

"Yes! This is what I was hoping for," Andy said as the blue sky suddenly appeared. In the same way we had all experienced an airplane ascending through a cloud and breaking into the open, we experienced a brilliant blue sky and bright sunshine half the way up the chair.

"This is amazing," I said, a bit awestruck by the contrast from where we just were. I dusted the snow off my coat and hat and enjoyed the warmth of the sun on my cheeks. Andy shared with me how he had experienced this before, but only once. We got off the lift and looked down at the low-lying clouds below us. I felt as if I was privy to something so majestic and glorious, and indeed I was. We started our descent with laughter and shouts of joy as the only two people skiing in the sun that day. As we arrived at the cloud layer, we reentered the snowy conditions. Visibility shrank back to almost nil, and we found our way back to the lift to do it again.

Pulling my face down into my jacket for protection from the storm as I sat on the chair, we rode back up to experience the same thing all over again. I could hardly believe my good fortune. Upon completing our second unique run, we tried a third time. This time, however, we never got above the clouds. The storm had gained elevation, and we were in the heavy snowfall the entire way up.

As we skied down at some point, we got separated, with Andy going one way and me another. Once at the bottom of the mountain, I called it a day and prepared to drive home. I never skied with Andy Hanson before or after this. Neither of us could ever improve on the experience we had together, and leaving it as a one-hit wonder seemed appropriate.

Utah—at Long Last

Until March of 1980, all my skiing had been in Colorado, and most of it in Aspen with a few days in Vail sprinkled in here and there. Jim Cameron had been singing the praises of the Utah snow for three years now since he arrived at the University of Utah and persuaded my friends and me to come out to stay with him.

John Thompson with his Old Style and Jeanine Jiganti at the football stadium in Boulder

Airfare from Chicago to Salt Lake City was quite expensive; however, a flight from Denver to Salt Lake City was only twenty-nine dollars each way. John Thompson and I decided to drive from Chicago to Denver and then fly from there. Sharing the gas between the two of us and another girl I found from the "ride board" at Madison made the trip to Utah affordable.

We stopped to visit Jeanine Jiganti in Boulder. She was a junior at the University of Colorado, and we had a fun time visiting with her before our flight from Denver's Stapleton airport. Upon our arrival in Salt Lake, we picked up Win Craven who was joining us on this trip. Win was a couple of years ahead of us and in need of a good ski break from the pressure of medical school.

Jim Cameron came to the airport to pick up John and me and, an hour later, Win. Chuck Caldwell would fly in later from Los Angeles and join us at Jim's apartment.

We'd start with Alta on our first day. Driving up Little Cottonwood Canyon, John Thompson surprised us all.

"Hey, guys, I brought some lemons for anyone like me who wants to get the blond hair of their youth back," John said. After we all laughed thinking he was pulling our leg, he continued, "I mean it! I had blond hair until high school, and I want it back. Only Crams still has natural blond hair, and look at all the girls he gets. It has to be the hair."

Jim Cameron never lost his blond hair, and John had a point. I was blond until about age sixteen, and this sounded like a good idea to me. John cut a lemon in half and just squeezed it right onto the top of this head. He then massaged it in as if it was hair tonic from Floyd, the barber on *The Andy Griffith Show.*

"Give me the other half, John," I said. I imitated John and soon had sticky rock-hard hair. John even had a few seeds stuck in his head, which he thought gave it just the right look for the idiots we were. Win, Chuck, and Jim just laughed at us.

Chuck Caldwell and Tom Terrill atop Snowbird. March 1980.

We rode up the chairlift, ready to ski High Rustler, a famous run at Alta. It was a fantastic day of skiing. Excellent spring conditions with plenty of sun and short lift lines. Even the lift tickets were much cheaper than the posh Aspen prices that I was used to.

The next day, we stopped off at the slightly closer ski hill Snowbird. I had never skied a resort with a tram before, and this would be a fun first. Whisked quickly to the top, this new experience was a hit.

Chuck and I posed for a picture with my hair still as dark as it was the day before when I added the lemon to my hair in the failed experiment.

We were on Jim's home turf, and he was our guide. Ready to both impress and challenge, Jim led us across a ridgeline to a run called Upper Cirque.

Standing at the top was a cornice with a drop straight down for about ten feet, and then it continued in a hair-raising steep pitch like I had never seen before. We stood there talking for a few minutes when Jim exclaimed, "Did we come here to talk or to ski?" and he immediately jumped into the run. I watched Jim masterfully ski this run as only Crams can do. He had a confidence about him that was admired and unmatched by all of us.

Win Craven, John Thompson, Jim Cameron, Tom Terrill, and Chuck Caldwell

"Well, I can't do that, but I sure can try," Chuck said as he followed Jim's lead. Understandably a bit shaky on the beginning, but after his third turn, Chuck had his ski legs back, and he continued down making giant slalom turns on the wide-open run. Win cursed under his breath and then shouted out like the Sundance Kid did when he and Butch Cassidy jumped from the cliff into the river below. He too was now cruising smoothly down the mountain.

I stood alone as John had wisely ridden the tram back down. I was nervous, thinking to myself that this was the steepest entry I had ever seen before. Finally, I too hopped in and began my accelerating descent. Like Chuck, my legs gave a couple of quivers on the first two turns, but then I clicked into the familiar grove that I knew all too well. The mountain was my dance partner, and I now comfortably took the lead swinging down with adrenaline coursing through my veins. I caught up to the others gathered at a resting spot, but I had too much energy to stop. I flew by with a shout of "woohoo" and continued down, not sure of where I was going but sure that going I was, as the others quickly followed suit.

Slowing down enough to let Jim easily catch and pass me and resume his tour guide work, we connected to a chairlift where John was able to meet us, having missed this incredible opening run. We skied hard that day and loved every moment. At the end of the day, we gathered at the base of the tram to relax and debrief the events of the day. But in some ways, we didn't debrief but instead disrobed to briefs. At least that is what Win, Jim, and

John did. The temps were quite warm this spring day, and the boys got a little more comfortable than the average skier that day. A few celebratory beers encouraged the display. All in all, the Utah trip was a grand finale to my college years.

Billy Graham

I grew up in the Lutheran church, but my family identified as Christian more than the denomination. Belief in God was a given, and I honestly never doubted the God of the Bible being real.

St. John's Lutheran Church in Wilmette, Illinois, was rich in traditions but fell short on guiding kids like me from a basic Bible knowledge toward a conscious decision to accept Christ's death on the cross for the forgiveness of my sins. Unfortunately, my memories of the two years of confirmation classes in junior high are discussions about the Vietnam War. While our teachers were kind to give their time, I discovered that if your guide is lost himself, there is not much chance you'll ever get to your intended destination. I'm not sure today what our pastor back then really believed himself, but I can see now that he was not well equipped to instruct seventh and eighth graders.

Truth be told, my parents were a bit lost themselves. God was real, but beyond prayers at meals and church on Sunday, the impact of God in our family life was small and incidental.

In June of 1971, Bill Graham came to Chicago to speak at McCormick Place. Our church arranged for several school buses to drive anyone interested from the northern suburbs to Chicago's lakefront convention center to hear this world-renowned evangelist.

The Terrill and Getschow family went together along with many others. In the long walk from the bus parking lot to the large auditorium, I became separated from my family. While not explicitly deliberate, today I suspect that as a twelve-year-old boy, I didn't work that hard at following them. Wandering around the enormous setting, I found a seat by myself some thirty yards to the right of the stage. As my eyes wandered, I came upon my older cousin Mark a few rows in front of me. He too apparently had lost his family on the walk from the parking lot.

We sang some hymns before Dr. Graham began his talk. In his message, he explained that sin had separated us from a perfect God. The idea that I was a sinner created no objections from me. I had lived inside my own mind long enough to agree with that fact. Moreover, that God was perfect only made sense to me. God can only be perfect or not exist. There is no middle ground.

Continuing, he explained how Jesus Christ came down from heaven to die on the cross and that His death paid the price for my sins. My debt no longer exists if I only accept Jesus's death in my place. I had already done this privately myself some years earlier, and Billy Graham's message had served as a reminder of this to me. However, then he added something else that was new to me.

He explained that if one has accepted Christ as his savior, he needs to proclaim this publicly, and that could be accomplished here and now. He was inviting anyone to come forward to the stage and stand openly before men to proclaim one's faith.

I knew I wanted to go forward and stood up to begin the short walk. Trying to encourage the audience, Dr. Graham said, "Many of you arrived by bus today. Don't worry that the bus will leave without you if you come forward. The bus will wait for you." The idea of the bus leaving without me had not crossed my mind, but now that he said that, the idea was planted firmly in my anxious thoughts. I kept moving forward but was now sure the bus would, in fact, leave without me, unless when we were dismissed; I hurried back.

The beautiful hymn "Just as I Am" was sung as it always was at a Billy Graham crusade.

Just as I am, without one plea, but that thy blood was shed for me. And that though bidd'st me, come to thee, Oh Lamb of God, I come, I come.

Hundreds of people came forward along with me. Once at the front, Billy Graham led us in prayer. I now had formally and publicly proclaimed my faith in Jesus Christ as my Messiah. This was a pivotal moment in my faith walk that has continued as a journey of success and failure but most importantly of forgiveness and redemption. Each year, I more clearly see my weaknesses and do my best to surrender those to God.

When the service was over, I ran back to the bus, passing people left and right. I sprinted as if my very life depended on it. I found our bus deep in the parking lot. Climbing in, I discovered that I alone had arrived. For five to ten minutes, I sat by myself as my family and other passengers eventually came as a group.

However, for me, this was the way it should be. Faith in God is not part of a group decision. We need to stand on our own, making this commitment alone. Heaven is not somewhere we go because we are part of a group or what family into which we are born. The fellowship of believers, of course, is an excellent support to Christians, but in the end, it is between you and you alone with God Himself. So that is how it was for me. Alone with God.

Skateboarding

Brian Avery and I each owned a skateboard and loved the feeling of rolling down the street in our hometown. Our original skateboards of the late sixties were not the performance level of today's equipment, resulting in slower speeds, a rougher ride, and terrible falls triggered from just a small pebble stuck under a wheel. The wheels on my skateboard were a hardened clay that barely functioned.

We would typically skate together with our own boards but eventually realized it was more fun if we could go faster than our feet alone could propel us, leading to the combination of a bike and a rope and a single skateboard. Taking turns, one would ride the bike fast, pulling the skateboarder behind. We'd swing back and forth as if we were water-skiing.

One summer day in 1974, Brian was pulling me down Park Avenue when I saw my front left wheel break free and shoot off the left, leaving me on the remaining three wheels. As carefully as I could, I leaned into this pending crisis, riding heavy on the right side and intentionally crashing into the grass in the parkway. Fortunately unhurt, I assessed the damage and discovered that my board was broken beyond repair.

Now needing a new board, Brian and I drove to Evanston where we had heard there was a new skateboard shop. Walking in, we discovered that we had been living still in the sixties. Unbeknownst to us, the early seventies had brought polyurethane wheels, flexible boards, and highly functional trucks, changing the dynamics of this sport exponentially.

While Brian's old board still worked, we both walked out of the store with brand-new Fibreflex skateboards.

My Fibreflex skateboard

The ride was incredible! Beyond our wildest imagination, these boards were smooth and so fast and responsive. Our abilities leapfrogged with this new technology, and our level of fun climbed to new heights.

We went right back to the bike and tow rope idea, but this was not enough horsepower to satisfy our new desires. Brian's motorcycle would be so much better. Not only would it eliminate the effort of the bike rider but would be fun to either ride the motorcycle or ride the skateboard.

But where could we do this? Reasonably sure that the local police would not look favorably on this idea, we took to Indian Hill Country Club. There, within the club's property, was a private road not governed by the local police, or so we assumed. The road was also newly paved with the smoothest asphalt anywhere. We swapped out not just the bike but also changed the rope to a water ski rope with a nice handle to grip. Now we were cruising through the private road at twenty miles per hour. This was the epitome of skateboarding towing, and to our good fortune, no one in authority ever told us we could not do this, and we never had a bad fall.

We also went to the Wilmette beach as there was a fairly steep hill to cruise down with a long run out at the bottom.

Brian Avery at the end of a handstand run at the Wilmette beach

Here we would ride fast down the hill or practice tricks at the top of the hill in front of the Michigan Shores Club.

At the bottom of the hill, beach sand would accumulate from the wind, creating a less than stable support underneath. The worst fall I ever had was doing a handstand down the hill. I overextended myself, and my balance crossed the tipping point. In an effort to block my fall, I took my front right hand off the skateboard and reached to brace myself. Unfortunately, this left my back hand riding alone on the board, and immediately, gravity and my weight drove my left hand into the asphalt, dragging my knuckles

Tom Terrill at the top of the Wilmette beach hill

along the road. The skin ripped away on all but my pinky, leaving my hand bloody and in pain. Never again would I make that mistake; instead of seeing, the better choice was to tumble over and take my lumps that way. I still have some scars from that day decades later. We continued to have fun skateboarding and found friends, like Chuck Trotter and Jim Cameron, would join us too.

Chuck Trotter with perfect form on a handstand

Tom Terrill, age forty-two, still doing handstands on a skateboard

Ge-Ca-Wa

Six hundred sixty acres of land in the north woods of Wisconsin, this fenced-in paradise kept the property secluded from anyone other than invited guests, but it was full of wildlife. Registered as a licensed deer farm in Wisconsin, it had two lakes, three ponds, and deep woods everywhere. Deer, bears, porcupines, beavers, coyotes, turtles, badgers, and every kind of fish you could imagine. Bald eagles were regularly spotted overhead along with other countless birds.

Also, another four hundred forty acres outside the fence line were two additional lakes all privately owned by my uncle.

There were two cabins, each with two bedrooms and a semifinished basement in each. One was a game room, and the other was a dormitory with some eight twin beds and two bunk beds. All the kids slept in the dormitory while the adults slept upstairs.

Jenni Terrill on Canthook Lake circa 1998

A volume of books could be written about Ge-Ca-Wa by my uncle and his kids, but here I will share my memories.

Strawberries

I am a picky eater. I don't eat anything that has a bad name, looks bad, or sounds gross. I am suspicious too. Sweetbread sounds like something good, but then to discover someone is trying to trick you into eating some animal gland proves to me that I need to be careful what I put in my mouth.

This is me as an adult, so imagine me as a kid.

The Getschow and Terrill families had gathered at Ge-Ca-Wa in August of 1970 for some great Wisconsin wilderness fun and activities.

My parents and sisters were staying in the guest cabin. My uncle and aunt were in the upstairs of the main cabin along with my cousin Heidi and the Getschow summer girl, Dawn.

My cousins Mark, Kurt, and Brett along with my younger brother Jeff were downstairs in the dormitory. This room was forty feet long with a row of twin beds about two feet apart from each other. This room was adjoined by the unfinished part of the basement and the stairs leading to the kitchen.

One night, the adults went out to dinner in Hayward, some forty-five minutes away. This left Dawn in charge of the eight cousins. At bedtime, I was sent down to the dormitory with Kurt and Brett. Dawn was roughly seventeen years old, and Michelle and Mark were fourteen, so they were allowed to stay up later. The girls and my brother Jeff were allowed to sleep upstairs until the parents returned, so they were soundly asleep in the bedrooms.

This left Michelle, Mark, and Dawn awake in the kitchen playing cards. Well, Kurt, Brett, and I didn't really want to go to bed, so we tried to negotiate something of value to head down to the basement without causing a fuss. Brett lobbied for some strawberries to eat, and Kurt voted affirmatively. Strawberries? They meant nothing to me. A poor substitute for Skittles or some other quality candy for my refined palate. Being a junk food addict, fresh fruit was not something I would eat at age twelve.

Still, the deal was cut, and Dawn sent us downstairs with a giant bowl of four dozen strawberries. So down we went to our beds with Brettschneider holding tight to the bowl. Kurt and Brett slept next to each other with me on the other side of Kurt. These two popped one after another in their mouth, enjoying the succulent taste of fresh Wisconsin strawberries. They both willingly offered me to join their indulgence, but it just wasn't tempting to me. No objection on their part. It just meant more for them.

Some thirty minutes later, strawberries long gone and the three of us lying peacefully in our own beds, suddenly Brett started to moan. "My stomach hurts." Brett whined, causing his unsympathetic brother Kurt to laugh at him. "You ate too many strawberries, Brett, and now you're paying for it."

Brett's stomach acid mixing in a full belly from dinner and now two dozen strawberries added in for good measure was creating a volatile mixture that no eight-year-old could retain for long. Suddenly, Brett leaped from his bed and made a dash for the bathroom, but the distance was too great. Brett blew chow right at the base of the steps leading upstairs. A full load of red strawberries and stomach bile.

A few more heaves like a volcano erupting from Brett and Kurt's laughter changed to one of a sympathetic physical response. He too leaped from his bed and tossed his cookies (or strawberries in this case) alongside his brother. The two of them were creating a mosaic of barf patches all over the basement floor.

The sight, sound, and smell began to attack my now-fragile state of mind, and I needed to escape this basement vomitorium. I carefully got up from my bed, tiptoeing around the maze of semiliquid spew. But I was overcome as well. Having not eaten anything, I only got the dry heaves, but still, my body was convulsing, mimicking my cousin's but without any regurgitation. I made it to the steps without stepping in any of the puke and climbed up to a locked door.

Banging on the door to let me into the kitchen, I was met with a verbal no on the other side by Dawn who instructed me that it was well past bedtime and I would not be released. I was not sure what I said, but eventually, she succumbed to my plea and opened the door. I rushed into the kitchen like a lone survivor from the battlefield to tell my story.

Brett and Kurt too, now with empty stomachs and a feeling of relief, made their way upstairs. The basement was no longer habitable. Relieved to be upstairs, away from the smell, the three of us settled into chairs in the kitchen, exhausted from the ten minutes of intense action.

Dawn knew the bad news was that she was hired for just such events and the cleanup would be hers and hers alone. She descended the steps and masterfully cleaned the floor. I didn't know how she did it, but in my opinion, she should have been given an award for summer girl of the year.

My next experience with strawberries was ten years later at age twenty-two. I had not eaten one since that night, repulsed by the memory burned into my young mind. Standing in my grandmother's kitchen, I decided it was time to move past this block of never eating strawberries. I cleaned at batch and cut the stem with a knife and popped the strawberry in my mouth. Fearful that it might bring an adverse reaction, I stayed close to the sink.

I was OK. It even tasted good, so I had another and then a third. I wisely stopped here, knowing what too many could do. Today, I love strawberries and can tell the story without feeling a gurgling in my stomach.

Deer Hunting

Ge-Ca-Wa, being a fenced-in licensed deer farm, required a certain number of deer to be "taken out" each year to manage the population. I seem to recall roughly eighty to one hundred or so deer were living inside the six hundred sixty acres.

My first hunting trip was in the sixth grade. My father and I joined my uncle Lee and his two older boys Mark and Kurt for a flight up to Duluth, Minnesota, which was about an hour's drive to Ge-Ca-Wa. Lee's father-in-law, affectionately known as Popeye, joined us, as well as Jim Hendricks and his son Grant. The final additions to our party would be Bud Wydeven and his son Bruce, the next-door neighbors from the cottage at Lake Winnebago.

The ten of us took a long weekend in late October of 1969 to spend a few days hunting deer with bow and arrows. I had never been hunting before, and it sounded like a lot of fun. I think it sounded like fun because when I was asked, those inviting me were smiling and telling me how much fun it would be. When you're only eleven years old, I'm not sure one has contemplated the idea of ending the life of another living creature. Spiders, ants, and fish just don't count, but look what Walt Disney did with the movie *Bambi*.

So I arrived with excitement and a little trepidation. A stop at the local outdoor store to pick up bows for the boys and a quiver of arrows, both for target practice and hunting. No one would mistake me for a bodybuilder, as I was better known for a surprising lack of upper body strength. I'm not sure, but I think my bow was only a thirty-five pounds test. This meant that if I hit anything firmer than Jell-O, it might not penetrate the intended target.

On our drive from the airport, we stopped at a Ponderosa Steak House for a hearty meal of steak and potatoes. Of greater interest to me was the ability to place on my tray four containers of chocolate milk. I loved milk, and nothing beat chocolate. I was an honest kid that generally followed the rules, giving my parents little to worry about. My idea of testing them was to see how many chocolate milks I could place on my tray before being told to put some back.

Stomachs full, we left for Ge-Ca-Wa well into the dark of the evening. As we pulled up to the large gate with the Ge-Ca-Wa sign, the boys leaped from the rental cars and climbed over the ten-foot-high fence with only the headlights of the vehicles to show us where to go. This tradition fed into the spirit of adventure and freedom. We were climbing into our Shangri-la, and the ascent gave us a sense of earning the right to be there.

Once over the fence, it was opened for the cars to pass down the hill to the cabins. The five boys carried our gear and duffle bags into the cabin and down to the dormitory. I never went to camp myself, so five boys sleeping in the same room allowed me to experience the comradery of a group of boys. A long day of travel left everyone ready for sleep. My uncle explained that since there is no

TV in heaven, there was no TV in Ge-Ca-Wa. Instead, conversation and activity would rule the day and night.

The next morning, we woke up and went out in front of the cabin to do some target practice. None of the boys was very good with a bow and arrow, but we excitedly took our turns aiming for a bull's-eye and preparing for it to be a deer. After some twenty minutes of practice, we were ready for the real thing, and off we went on our first hunt.

A "drive" was explained to me. We'd take the two jeeps to the far end of the property and drop off five people to walk in the same direction some thirty yards apart from one another. This action would result in any deer pushing out ahead of the walkers and right toward the other five people strategically set up for the deer to pass right by them.

Steelhead Lake would be the first drive. A tall and steep hill runs from the dirt road at the fence line down to the shoreline. This covers one hundred fifty yards or so from the fence to the lake, creating a perfect squeeze guiding any deer right toward us. Those waiting for the deer were Bud Wydeven on the top of the hill. I was some fifteen yards below him, and Kurt and Bruce scurried down the hill with Grant trailing behind. Grant eventually went down the farthest virtually at the lake, and Kurt and Bruce stopped to talk some thirty yards downhill from me.

We had been dropped off at the top of the hill while the rest of the hunters drove on another half mile where they would park the jeeps. Spreading out thirty yards from one another, they began to walk toward our firing line driving any deer in our direction.

I was situated just fifteen feet uphill from a deer trail well positioned for when the drive would begin in ten minutes. The woods were thick with mostly hardwood deciduous trees, with some pines sprinkled in. Bud Wydeven lit up a cigarette. Knowing there was enough time before anything would happen, he was talking to me, passing on some tips on what to do if a deer came.

To my surprise, slowly ambling down the deer trail right toward me was a large buck with eight points. Bud did not see the deer and just kept talking. This was too early to be a result of the drive, so no one expected it. I, however, knew what to do. Slowly placing an arrow into my bow, I began to position myself for a shot once the deer got closer to me.

The woods were thick, so my best shot would be as the deer came right below me on the hill. Still twenty-five feet away, he kept walking on the trail, not aware of my presence and somehow not disturbed by Bud's low droning voice. I kept thinking to myself, *Bud, shut up! Can't you see this deer?*

The large animal walked on the trail ever closer, and I began to pull back the bow, preparing for a shot. My heart was beating so fast and loud I thought the deer must be able to sense my presence, but he paid no attention. The buck stopped just fifteen feet away from me, turned his head ninety degrees, and there we were face-to-face.

My bow was now fully extended and ready to fire. With no trees in the way, I had a perfect shot. Almost perfect. Right behind the deer, straight downhill were Kurt and Bruce, also utterly unaware of the activity. My mind was racing. If I missed the deer, I would be sending an arrow right at Kurt and Bruce with the slope of the hill, increasing the risk of striking one of them.

Frozen in place, I held the fully extended bow and kept hoping Kurt and Bruce would look uphill and discover my predicament. My mind was silently screaming, *Move! Kurt! Bruce! Move! Just a little. Get out of the way.*

They never saw it.

I couldn't shoot like this. My arms were beginning to quiver, and I knew I only had a little more time to hold this position.

There was only one thing I could do, and I did it. Breaking the silence with a shout "AHHHHHHH," causing the deer to bolt hard immediately, I turned, perfectly leading the deer, and let the arrow fly. Gracefully, the arrow flew right at the mighty beast when a twenty-year-old tree had other ideas. Thump, right into the tree. The deer kept running, never to be seen again by me.

Bud finally awakened from his one-way conversation to say to me, "Tom, did you see that?"

I turned around in utter amazement and with my mouth wide open trying to talk. I quietly said, "Yes," out loud, but my mind was spewing out words silently at a million miles an hour. *Yes, I saw it! What were you doing? Were your eyes closed? Why did you keep talking?*

My whole body began to shake as the adrenaline release was now having its full effect. Kurt, Bruce, and Grant never saw a thing. The drive failed to produce any other deer.

This introduction to deer hunting on my first drive blew me away. Thankful I did not shoot and kill my cousin or friend, I was also conflicted about my feelings regarding shooting the deer. Not until that moment had I really considered the idea of killing a deer. I'd never forget standing that close to a living creature, ready to end its life while staring at each other in the eyes. It was not some profound moment at the time, as I was wrapped up in the event itself and any deep thoughts emanated from a part of my brain not fully developed. It would take days, weeks, and even years for me to fully reflect on that moment.

Today I am content the way it played out. The drama ending without a strike seems right. Had I hit the deer, the odds are I would not have killed it but only injured it to the point that a gunshot from my uncle's revolver would have been required. Tracking a bleeding animal and knowing I was the one that shot it would not have sat well with me.

Don't get me wrong. I am OK with hunting and feel no disapproval toward my many friends that frequently hunt deer today. I just know that I like the way this story developed for me that day.

We gathered together to plan out our next location and decided to move just a little to the west. Arriving at the drop spot, we noticed a porcupine nest up in one of the trees. Porcupines can do quite a bit of damage to trees, and this troubled my uncle, generating the comment we'd need to kill this porcupine. Popeye noticed another and then another after that. My cousin Kurt started jumping up and down, saying and repeating, "Let's kill them all!" I gave Kurt a look and mimicked him, mouthing back in a teasing way, "Let's kill them all."

Kurt immediately knew how stupid he sounded and quickly hoped his actions would be forgotten. No such luck. Still to this day when Kurt and I are together at some point, one of us will eventually say that timeless phrase to the other: "Let's kill them all."

The next few drives produced no activity, and so we headed back to the cabins for lunch. On the drive back, I asked if there were ever deer on the island. The adults all laughed at my silly question and explained only in the winter when the lake was frozen.

Lake Canthook has a large island the shape of Greenland. Bruce and Kurt agreed with me that indeed there could be deer on the island, and the three of us hatched a plan. We quickly finished lunch, and while others were going back for seconds, we bolted to the pier and took off for the far side of the island. We pulled the boat up in the channel, and each took our positions. Bruce on the left, Kurt in the middle, and I would walk the right flank.

The island is roughly two hundred yards long and, like the rest of Ge-Ca-Wa, covered in dense woods. We walked a steady pace, not always able to see one another. The sound of breaking sticks and rustling leaves sent a loud signal to any animal that adolescent boys were on the move. Suddenly, I heard muffled shouting that sounded like Bruce. I stopped in my tracks, looked around, and quietly listened. Kurt started yelling, "Tommy get back to the boat. Hurry! To the boat. To the boat."

Without hesitation, I made a mad dash, but I was not sure why. Was there a bear on the island? What was wrong?

The three of us arrived at the same time, and Bruce jumped in the back of the boat to start the motor. Kurt explained that Bruce scared two deer on the island into the water, and they were swimming to the other side.

Kurt and I took positions in the front of the boat, side by side, while Bruce steered us toward the swimming deer. It was a race. Could two deer swim faster than a twelve-foot wooden boat with a three-horsepower engine? We were about to find out.

Puttering out of the channel, Bruce guided us on an intercept path with the frantic deer. Their heads just above the waterline, Kurt and I got our bows ready to shoot once we came upon them. I was not sure which moved faster, but the head start gave the deer a decided advantage in this effort. We could tell we would not catch them, but maybe we'd get close enough for a shot. As the first deer came out of the water, Kurt let his arrow fly. A long arc in the sky and the arrow fell harmlessly in the water some fifteen yards short. I gave it my best effort and saw my arrow land within a few feet of Kurt's.

The two deer climbed up on the shore and ran up the hill soon to be out of sight. We headed back to the pier to tell our story and prepare for an afternoon of hunting with the full group.

The afternoon was uneventful but still quite pleasant. Being in the wilderness contrasted my normal suburban upbringing. The chance to walk through woods, open fields, over hills, and alongside lakes and ponds without seeing a car, airplane, store, kid on a bike, or finely manicured lawn provided the tranquil break from a typical day. I relished the adventure and did my best to take in every moment of it. I think this is why I remember these events in such vivid detail. It was a special time for me.

Always being the early riser, the next morning, I awoke to two inches of fresh snow on the ground. I was not expecting this and thought I would take advantage of being the only one awake. I bundled up in warm clothes and grabbed my bow and arrow and headed out to hunt alone. I imagined myself to be a young Indian scout out to hunt for deer. I walked up the hill toward the gate and took the grass road to the right. I followed this seventy-five yards as the road peeled away from the fence line.

I found a small mound with a place to tuck myself in and hide from view. Here I would sit silently until an unsuspecting deer would happen upon my path, allowing me an easy victory. There I sat for some thirty minutes, getting a bit colder and colder as the minutes of inactivity passed. I lifted my head just over the mound to see if I could see the deer that must surely be coming soon. Nothing.

Back down into my hideout, I just needed to wait a bit longer. Another ten minutes passed, without a sound. Nothing. Finally, cold and getting hungry, I gave up and started the walk back to the cabin. The sun was out now, and the snow began to melt. I arrived back at the cabin to find everyone still asleep. I took off my clothes and climbed back into bed. My solo trip did not bring the triumph I anticipated. I think much of life is this way. Even when we go out to slay dragons, whatever our dragon of the day is, often there is little happening. It is just minutes passing by without much more than basic bodily functions of breathing in and out and eyes blinking.

Can I find peace and satisfaction in life in the quietest moments of nothing? The answer for me is yes, and I believe that moments like my solo effort have shown me the path. I've learned that every day is not the Fourth of July nor should it be. Like sleep and the rejuvenation, it gives; times of nothing happening also has a restorative practicality to it. I embrace this as a part of life.

Eventually, everyone woke up, and we prepared for the hunting that day. During the summer, there were two adopted fawns brought into Ge-Ca-Wa. Peppy and Bambi were fed with bottles by the cousins, and everyone grew attached to these two. They were set free within the fenced area with the other deer, and occasionally, they'd come around the cabins. Yes, we were hunting, but everyone knew that Peppy and Bambi were not to be shot.

We were getting set up for the drive, and Kurt and I were placed close by each other. We'd be with Lee, my dad, and Bruce. The others would take the jeeps out a bit farther and begin the march toward us. As the jeeps drove away, they frightened a group of four or five deer nearby, causing them to come bounding out of the woods into the opening at the grass road.

The early activity caught everyone by surprise as we frantically tried to find a shot with the deer leaping about us. A lone voice cried out, "Don't shoot. It's Peppy." Revealing his hiding place and waving his hands, Kurt gave his best effort to save his beloved friend.

No one else saw Peppy because Peppy was not there. We just saw fully grown bucks and did all acceptable targets. My uncle, frustrated by the lost opportunity, was now yelling too, but his anger was directed at Kurt. We all walked out from our hiding places and regrouped. This drive was a bust, and we needed to let cooler heads prevail. Once the others returned from a failed drive, we picked a new spot.

Just east of the bog, I got dropped off. My older cousin Mark was dropped off next. I wandered up a small knoll with a nice perch to see what was going on below me. Mark wandered back my way and was some thirty yards away but well below me down on the flats. Mark had no idea where I was nor that I was just watching him.

Sitting and waiting could get boring. Most of the time, deer were not running by, and so one was left alone with their thoughts. I could tell Mark was bored. He's pacing around and acting fidgety. Some ten minutes passed by, and I saw Mark take an arrow and place it in his bow. He pointed it here, then there, but not at anything real. He was just letting his imagination occupy the time of inactivity.

Suddenly, Mark shot the arrow right into a tree. No big deal. However, what happened next was the big deal of the day. Mark yelled out, "I got one!"

Huh? I pondered. *Got what, a tree?*

In the distance, Lee yelled back, "Atta boy, Marko. Where did you hit him?"

"In the neck," Mark replied.

Meanwhile, as Mark was pulling his arrow from the tree, Lee shouted out, "Did the arrow break off?"

From my roost, I watched Mark break his arrow and reply that yes, the arrow broke off.

"How far is the blood up the arrow?" Lee inquired.

Mark broke the arrow a second time to a very short length and shouted back that it broke high up. At this point, I started my descent down to where Mark was. Surprised to see me, Mark asked how long I'd been there. Telling him I saw everything, Mark, two years my senior, told me not to tell anyone.

When someone hit a deer, everyone stopped and began to walk toward the place where the deer was hit to start the tracking. With a good shot, a deer would drop quite quickly, but a shot in the side and the deer could run for a long time, requiring excellent tracking skills. Some four people wandered into where Mark and I were waiting, and the questions to Mark began. Mark explained the deer took off in this direction, and we began to follow.

Everyone else was continuing their walk when a shout from Kurt came. "I got one too! And it had an arrow in its side."

Unbelievable. Not to be outdone by his older brother, Kurt had now shot the mythical deer that Mark shot earlier. Lee, the proud father, shouted congratulations to Kurt, and now the tracking began in earnest.

We'd all come together with Kurt giving the update on the condition of the fictitious deer. There was no blood trail to follow, of course, but we walked anyways in the direction we'd been told.

This was getting silly. I kept looking at Mark with a face of anger and whispering that he needed to come clean.

"Never," Mark let me know, and so his charade continued.

I don't recall how long we did this dance, but way too long for me. Eventually, we gave up, and Lee figured we'd find the deer the next day.

We never found the deer, and Mark carried his secret to this day. I don't think Mark or I ever confronted Kurt on his lie either. So here and now, forty-five years or so later, I am now willing to spill the beans.

Brule River Canoe Trip

In 1972 during the early summer, a trip to Ge-Ca-Wa was planned to include an overnight canoe trip on the Brule River. The Brule is an unusual river in that it runs from south to north, emptying into Lake Superior.

Six of us would travel in two canoes as a father-son trip. My uncle would have his two oldest sons, Mark and Kurt, while my father would have me in his canoe along with my friend Bruce Wydeven from Lake Winnebago.

I had been in a canoe before but never on a river, and this adventure included camping out overnight. I loved the outdoors, but truth be told, I liked to sleep in a bed more than on the ground. Still, this sounded like fun and would be a new experience for me.

Kurt Getschow, Uncle Lee, and Tom Terrill leaving for the Brule River trip

Leaving the rest of the family back at Ge-Ca-Wa, we drove off in the van, towing a flatbed trailer with two canoes. The drive to our launching point was only forty-five minutes, and in no time, we had all our gear loaded into the canoes, and we were on the water. For most of the trip, the river ran slow, allowing us to enjoy the scenery of the north woods. A pleasant time of contemplation. I rode in the front of our canoe and my father in the back. Bruce sat in the middle seat, stuffed in with our sleeping bags, food, and tent tightly packed around him.

Rapids were small but fun, and I learned to "pry" in the front. This was where I would put my paddle straight into the water, leaning against the side of the canoe. When headed toward a rock, my job was to quickly pry the paddle, changing our direction to not run into the rock. This was new to me as both my father and my uncle could be heard yelling out to Kurt and me in the bow to "pry, pry"!

Moving through the first set of rapids had an element of pressure to perform, but in reality, it was quite easy. It had a thrill to it as the canoe accelerated through the water seemingly on a course of its own. The sound of metal scraping against the rocks as the canoe bounced around on our passage through the rapids took some getting used to, but soon it too seemed normal.

The first set of rapids over, we settled back into the slower-moving water. The 6–12 bug spray was essential in these quiet parts of the river as the mosquitoes were out in full force. We had a half-dozen rapids of a smaller size that built our confidence as kids, and I suspect my father and uncle felt like this would be an easy trip.

Toward the end of the day, we were planning to find a good spot to camp out, when we came to a much bigger and more extensive set of rapids. Feeling our oats, we confidently charged in but quickly saw this was going to be a challenge. Directions "to pry" were being called out, but with the noise of the white water, it was hard to hear.

"Look out!" I shouted as we hit a large boulder head-on, causing the bow to ride up a bit onto the rock itself. The swirling river pushed the stern of the canoe to the right, and before we knew it, we were sideways in the strongest part of the river. Being pounded by the fast-moving water, the inevitable happened, and we tipped over. Spilling the full contents of our canoe, including the three of us into the drink, we struggled to swim as our sleeping bags bobbed up and down in the rapids. Life vests that seemed silly to wear earlier now were a welcome part of my wardrobe.

"Feet first, boys!" my dad shouted, trying to guide us through this unplanned swimming exercise.

As I moved down the river, it seemed like more gear was floating that could have fit in our canoe. I then noticed my cousin Kurt was in the water too, as they experienced the same capsizing fate that we had.

I was never frightened. I knew we were safe, and in some ways, it was fun. The water was warm, and it seemed a bit like a water ride at Disney World. We just sat back and enjoyed the ride until the waters calmed down. I am sure my father and uncle were not as calm about the whole thing as they had the responsibilities that come with being a parent. I, on the other hand, didn't worry about a thing.

Now in calm water, we swam around, gathering up our scattered gear, and found ourselves in a small cove at the base of a hill that rose forty feet up from the river. My uncle directed us to start carrying the sleeping bags and tents up the hill to a flat overlook at the top. Climbing this steep hill was a challenge as the gear was now so heavy. None of our equipment was protected for such an event as our capsized canoes, so these cotton sleeping bags were thoroughly soaked with water. The hill was also quite slippery, adding to the effort of the climb.

I don't recall how long it took, but eventually, we had everything on flat and high ground. About this time, the one thing we didn't need started to fall from the sky. Rain. We couldn't get any wetter, and it seemed unlikely we'd ever dry off. The boys were sent to find dry wood, which was limited, to say the least. Still, somehow, a fire was started. To this day, I suspect some lighter fluid must have been used, but the flint rock and chard cloth that we learned how to use for a Boy Scout merit badge was all that we were shown.

Soon enough, we had a roaring fire. As we huddled around it trying to dry off, the rain continued to fall, so a permanent state of dampness seemed to be our fate. It seemed to me that sleep would be impossible even though it was dark and we were tired. However, I guess a fourteen-year-old boy can sleep even in such conditions as I did just that.

When I woke up the next morning, the sky was blue, the fire was still smoldering, and it wouldn't be long before we'd have bacon and eggs frying up in a pan. It seemed like when we capsized and then had the rain that the next morning would not work out well. But it did.

The funny thing is that we were all happy. Smiles and laughter and a sense of accomplishment were all richly bubbling up from the four boys. We were adventurers who had conquered the elements. Camping is an excellent way to bond. Something is sure to go wrong, and in the trial, our human nature is to move through the struggle together, committed to winning. As Mark, Kurt, Bruce, and I descended the hill to the water's edge, we knew that we had won. We had beaten the river that first day and night.

Day 2 would be a half day ending with our arrival at Lake Superior where the river emptied. Climbing back in our canoes and beginning the trip again felt good. The clear sky and ease of movement with the water's flow continued to foster positive feelings and sparked good banter from one canoe to the other. We traveled from calm water into some small to moderate rapids and back to calm water.

About two hours into the day, the river suddenly came to a stop. We pulled over to the side as the river seemed to flow into a marsh that looked impassable. Wondering how we'd get through this tangled mess of weeds, trees, and grasses, I waited for guidance. My dad said, "We are at the *portage*," a word I had never heard before. Looking around, I asked, "Where?" wondering what a portage looked like.

I learned this meant we could not pass on the water and would carry the canoes some five hundred yards on a narrow trail. This was arduous work, and I did my share of grumbling along the path. Had someone told me about this, I surely would have had second thoughts on the entire trip. All good and bad things eventually come to an end, and this too ended with navigable water that looked so good to my tired body. We dropped the canoes back in the river and continued on.

The water flow slowed as we approached Lake Superior. I was excited to swim in my second Great Lake and saw this as the culmination of the trip. My goal was to finish with a swim. We pulled up the canoes on the sandy beach looking out at the expanse of the largest of the great lakes.

I hurriedly ran off to a good section of the beach, free from debris to swim, and started into the water. I waded out up to my knees and could not believe how cold it was. My legs throbbed in the fifty-degree water, and I had my doubts. Still, I wanted to swim. No one else seemed to think this was a good idea, and instead, they were carrying our gear toward our truck that had been dropped off earlier. Alone in my resolve, I capitulated to reason and never went deeper than my knees.

At my age of fourteen, I was not as committed to seeing a goal through, especially if it was difficult to accomplish. My maturation in setting and completing goals was still in my infancy stage. The development of future accomplishment in my goals was sparked by some failures such as this one.

The canoe trip over, we loaded in the truck for a drive home. The boys climbed in the open bed with the gear, and adults were inside the cab. Today such travel would be frowned upon, but riding in the back of a pickup should be a part of every boy's life. The wind swirling around as we cruised down the country road offered a time of reflection. Too windy to talk in the open bed of the truck, the four of us smiled at one another, thinking about the last two days. Words were not required. In fact, the silence was better than talking. I'm glad I had this pleasure of riding in the back on countless occasions.

Life offers chances to partake in the ordinary and the extraordinary and those events in between. This in-between was well worth it. Had I never gone, I could not tell you what would have happened to me on those days, but with this experience, I have a memory that helps shape who I am.

Horseback Riding

If you don't own your own horse, the opportunity to ride is primarily limited to day trips with trail horses that are only interested in getting back to the barn as soon as possible.

In Ge-Ca-Wa, the setup was very different. My uncle brought in two to three horses that would stay for the entire week. A fenced-in pen an acre in size created the holding area for the horses, and an abundant supply of hay was placed right outside the enclosure.

Water was readily available from the nearby lake and plenty of willing kids to tote the five-gallon buckets if they got to ride the horses too. When we wanted to ride, we had to work, and the work was well worth it. Learning to saddle a horse, get the bit in its mouth and the reigns properly arranged was required for anyone to participate. The kids all thought it was pretty exciting and did not view this as work.

I never knew I was learning life lessons while they were happening. It was another gift to me to have this unique opportunity for a kid who grew up in suburbia. It is not easy to water, feed, and saddle up a horse. Heck, I was exhausted before I even got to climb up and ride, but the trade-off was well worth it.

Cody Terrill, age nine, riding his pony

An adult would lead the younger kids around the cabin area and down to the lake. The older kids, like myself, had the freedom to ride anywhere in the six hundred sixty acres of the fenced-in property. A typical loop was to ride up the road toward the gate and take a left turn following the property line until you were behind the cabins several hundred yards uphill. Then meandering down the hill toward the cabin and the lake to let the horses have a drink.

Part of the difficulty was going for a long ride when others were waiting to ride too, so the loop was a great way to get some quick laps in and then hop off to let another person take a turn.

Many years later as a father of my own kids, we'd return to Ge-Ca-Wa and again get to ride horses. One year, we had a pony along with the horses, and my son Cody fit perfectly on this little pony. As a nine-year-old, Cody took to this as if the pony was an extension of his own body. We marveled at how he could race around the cabin area weaving in and out of the trees, parked cars, and wandering kids. These two together made a great team.

My daughter Kate had her dear friend, Jackie Myers, with us and Jackie, and I went out for an extended ride one afternoon. We climbed the hill toward the gate and took the trail to the right heading out to the big field. At the top of the hill, Jackie asked if we could gallop them. "Of course," I enthusiastically replied, giving my horse a little kick. Away we went flying down the grass-covered jeep trail.

I was in the lead with Jackie right behind me and a little to my right. My horse stumbled with his left front foot, which sent me flying off the horse, tumbling into the grassy road. Fearful of being run over by Jackie's horse, I covered my head with my arms as I rolled to a stop. Thankfully, Jackie's skills were at the top of her game. She pulled back on the reigns as she saw me go down and veered to the right to steer clear of me.

Kate Terrill, age twelve, with Lake Canthook in the background

Remarkably, I was safe and had no injuries to speak of. I had never fallen off a horse before, and it gave me a bit of a wake-up call. Jackie and I continued our ride out to the field and back enjoying the sunny day.

I love to ride horses. I think it is a bit of the dreamer in me that fancies himself as a cowboy. But dreamer or not, being on the back of the horse is good for the soul. Something about the connection between man and animal has a strong positive effect. Moreover, the care these animals require allows for a proper transfer of work for reward. Not many things in life can accomplish all the benefits of riding a horse, and my life was blessed by the riding in Ge-Ca-Wa.

Fishing

There were four lakes to choose from when fishing at Ge-Ca-Wa. Canthook Lake was situated in front of the cabins and the most accessible. Steelhead Lake was within the fenced property but some ten minutes away on a rugged dirt trail. Outside the fenced boundary were Happles and Silver that required some heavy-duty four-wheel driving and a vehicle that you didn't mind subjecting to overgrowth dragging on the sides of the car during the approach.

The three out lakes each had a small boat turned upside down at the shoreline with oars and an anchor. Often, I would load a small electric motor and battery to be able to move about the lake slowly. As these lakes were surrounded by private property, you knew that you would be the only one on the lake fishing. My uncle initially took me to each one so I knew how to go on my own in the future. As an adult, I brought not only my son Cody to each of these but also my wife Jenni who loves to fish, a trait she inherited from her father, Joe Baer.

Most of my fishing, like everyone who visited Ge-Ca-Wa, was in Canthook Lake. One could fish right from the pier or take one of the several fishing boats docked in slips at the pier. As a thirteen-year-old, one day, I decided to fish from a canoe, something I had never done before. I took one of the canoes conveniently pulled up right next to the lake, flipped it over while depositing my already-rigged rod with my Hula Popper lure. No tackle box for this event. I had decided on a single lure, and my Hula Popper was it.

This lure floats and, when given a small snap from the rod, will pop a bit on the water's surface, drawing the attention of any nearby fish. I carefully guided the canoe toward the northeastern shore of the lake where some reeds were growing. I recall my uncle telling me this was an excellent place to catch smallmouth black bass, and that was my goal.

I had my canoe sideways to the shore and laid a cast toward the reeds, dropping it a few feet short. Reeling in, I gave the snap to my line, but nothing was there. A few more similar casts with the same result. I then threw one that went perfectly between two clumps of reeds but stayed in the water to not get tangled. I gave a snap and then immediately had a strike. The black bass was in shallow water, and his reaction to the lure caused him to break the surface and thrash about.

This action caught me off guard, and I learned too far backward, tipping the canoe nearly over. I overcompensated the other direction thrusting my body forward, which dropped me right into the lake. I hung on to my rod and grabbed one of the crossbars of the canoe, which was now sideways and full of water. Well over my head, I began to slowly swim the one hundred yards back to the pier, pulling the canoe and trying not to let go of my fishing pole. I did not know where the fish or my line was other than behind me somewhere.

Father and son fishing on Lake Canthook in 1988

It took a while, but I eventually got back to the pier where I was now able to stand up on a sandy lake bottom. I climbed up on the pier, leaving the canoe to sit, and started to reel in to see if my lure still had my fish attached. To my delight, the fish was still on my line. I reeled him in and landed him on the pier.

I figured this fish had been through enough of a crazy journey, so I released him back into the lake. He took off like a lightning bolt, presumably back to his home near the reeds.

Ge-Ca-Wa had hundreds, if not thousands, of guests over the years. I was blessed to spend time here as both a child and adult, and I feel so fortunate that my wife and kids were able to as well. They now have their own stories. For this, I need to thank Lee Getschow. My uncle was a remarkable man who left his mark most everywhere he went.

Lake Winnebago

As a baby, I was introduced to Lake Winnebago in central Wisconsin. My grandparents had a summer cottage on the north end of the lake where they stayed all summer long escaping the heat of Chicago. My mother and her brothers spent the summers of their youth at the family cottage on Firelane 8, and I, with my siblings and cousins, would spend part of our summers there as well.

As kids, my siblings and I loved going to the cottage. Not only did we get to see our beloved Nana and Baba but also to play with our cousins Mark, Kurt, Heidi, and Brettschneider.

The lake was huge but also shallow. While it is some thirty plus miles long and ten miles wide, it is only about twenty-five feet deep at the deepest spot. Being so shallow, the water was very warm, so we could swim and play for hours at a time without getting cold. The north end of the lake also had a wonderful sand bottom, and one could swim out one hundred yards, and the lake was only chest deep. It was an ideal lake for kids to enjoy the normal activities of a lake but also extra fun and games because it was so shallow.

My grandfather had a beautiful mahogany 1954 Chris Craft inboard with a three-hundred-horsepower engine. Because the draft on the Chris Craft was so deep, it needed to be one hundred yards offshore in the deeper water. He built a wooden pier about four feet wide but well over one hundred yards out into the lake. My grandfather proudly told everyone that he had not only the longest pier but the fastest boat on Lake Winnebago.

Looking north from the end of the pier in 1977

Built with seven bedrooms, the cottage allowed for high capacity. Curiously, we had but two bathrooms, which resulted in the rule that kids did not shower in the house. We bathed in the lake. Ivory soap which floats was essential and some Johnson's baby shampoo for the girls. (Boys didn't wash their hair before age twelve.)

It is essential to understand that the lake had sandbars at various points as one swam out from shore. So the depth of the lake varied from knee-deep to five plus feet on the way out to the end pier.

I have many wonderful memories of my time at Lake Winnebago or Appleton, as we called it for the most significant "big" city nearby.

Tom Terrill (left) and John Thompson (right) riding Jet Skis in 1977

The following is a collection of some of my favorite memories from Lake Winnebago.

Diving In

My heart pounded as I ran out of the cottage toward the lake. Continuing onto the pier, soon I'd be swimming in the lake, and with all the excitement my eight years of life could handle, I could see my cousins were already in the water.

My family loaded up the station wagon in July 1966, leaving our home in Kenilworth, Illinois, to drive to the cottage. My grandparents were there, and so were my cousins. We were eager to get to the lake, and the three-hour drive seemed to take forever. Some two hours into the journey, we finally passed the "ladies' prison" in Taycheedah, Wisconsin, which meant the southern end of the lake was just a mile or so away.

The ladies' prison was a landmark on our trip. As kids, we couldn't fathom the idea that a lady could go to jail, but we knew as we drove the long stretch of road parallel to a barbed wire fence that this place was real. We carefully looked through the fence, hoping to see a prisoner, but I never did. We'd ask our parents what offenses these criminals had committed to be there, hoping to hear some fantastic story, but they knew only about as much as we did. We had to settle for what our creative minds could imagine.

Leaving the correctional facility behind us, we now looked forward to the first sighting of the lake. We always drove the east side of the lake, and although it was longer than driving up Highway 41 through Oshkosh and Menasha, the view on the east side was majestic. Driving along Highway 151 and then 55, the road ran along a ridgeline where the hill on our left gently gave way down toward the lake, giving us an aerial perspective of virtually the entire body of water. My memory of this scene is vivid in my mind. Farm fields with red barns and the background of water glistening from the sunlight is one of my favorite sights as a child. I'm so glad we always took the long way.

As we turned off the highway onto Firelane 8, the excitement was overwhelming. Shrieks of "We're here! We're here!" came from all four kids as we drove down the gravel lane, across the railroad tracks, and onto the final stretch. Passing the other summer cottages, we looked ahead to see if anyone would be there to greet us. We pulled onto the grass of the large field to park and unpack the car.

It always fascinated me as a young boy that we parked the car on the grass. I never understood why the car didn't kill it, but lo and behold, grass was heartier than I understood, and this gave us the ability to park more vehicles without having asphalt or stones everywhere.

We carried our suitcases into the cottage through the back door and into the kitchen.

Greeting us were Nana and Baba, my mother's parents, with hugs and a joyful welcome. This was nice enough, but my childhood mind was focused on a single objective: swimming in the lake.

I went upstairs, quickly flipped open my suitcase, and changed into my swimsuit—no need for a towel or shirt. I flew down the stairs and out the front door looking for my cousins Kurt and Mark. I knew they would be in the water, and that is where I wanted to be.

I ran out on the pier and could see them in the water some fifty yards out. The lake is very shallow, and the sandbars come and go as you move out on the pier. The lake surrounded by farms created algae-rich water as a result of the fertilizer runoff. Therefore, the water is not clear at all. Maybe one could see two to three inches before the algae in the lake obstructed one's view.

When I got out to Kurt and Mark, my first question was "Are you standing?" All I could see were their heads just above the waterline. Everything else was under the water. If they were standing, it meant they were not on a sandbar and I could safely dive into the water rather than jump. They both said, "Yes, we are standing up."

In actuality, they were lying down on the sand bottom with their feet and bodies just under the surface and their heads sticking out. With this assurance, I dove from the pier three feet above the waterline into about sixteen inches of water. My arms out in front of my head crumpled as the force of my body hit the sand. My head followed quickly, diving into the solid bottom, as my chin rammed into my chest.

Everything went black. My whole body felt an electriclike surge from my head to my toes, and I struggled to move. Quickly, Kurt and Mark rushed over, knowing I must be in a lot of pain and likely in need of help. My neck hurt a lot, and I could not lift my head straight without significant pain. I swallowed a lot of water immediately after hitting bottom and was weakly coughing it out of my lungs. They helped me up and tried to explain that they thought I knew they were kidding. My tears were big, my neck hurt, and all I wanted to do was get out of the water.

What a terrible experience and shock to my system. I'm not sure I've ever had such a quick transition from joy and excitement to pain and suffering. Wounded, I walked back to the cottage to find the love and care that only a mother can give. My neck hurt for a few days but not enough to spoil the fun of the next week.

Only as an adult did, I realize how fortunate I was not either to die instantly nor fracture my spinal column and lose the ability to use my arms and legs like so many other young men and women had experienced in similar events. I guess my very young age likely helped avoid a more serious permanent injury. I never again dove into any body of water without knowing firsthand the depth. I also learned that I should never trust the smiling faces of my cousins without verifying. Lessons learned.

Fishing

I learned how to fish in Lake Winnebago. Taught by my father and uncle, I was raised with the assumption that all boys like fishing. As well, there was an expectation that we would eat the fish we caught. Well, I did enjoy fishing, but as for eating it, No, thanks!

As a very young boy, I was escorted out on the pier to learn to cast. I recall using a Dare Devil lure as the weight made the casting a bit easier than a lighter lure. I'd stand on the pier under the supervision of my father and throw a cast out into the lake. The speed at which to reel in was all explained while I was in the act. This active learning was great, and it was a bit fun too until getting a snag in my line. What a mess this could be. If I failed to have my thumb create the right amount of drag while the cast went out, the line would overspin, creating a tangle of fishing line. My dad would show me how to pull the loops up over and over again, releasing the snag. Curiously, I liked this challenge. I suspect this pleasure in fixing the tangle was what led me to become the go-to person in second grade for untying knotted shoelaces of my fellow students.

After enough instruction to learn on my own, my dad would wander back to the cottage, leaving me to experience this on my own. I enjoyed this alone time with my thoughts and imagination. I always was an earlier riser and often used this time to fish from the pier while everyone else slept in late. We most commonly caught bass from the pier. Once in a while, someone would pull in a walleye, but I was never so lucky.

I remember the first fish I caught from one of the boats out in the lake. It was a white bass. I had been out in the late afternoon with my dad, and we finished up at dusk. My first fish was the only fish I caught that day, and I was so proud to come in from the boat to show my grandparents, Nana and Baba Getschow. They had big smiles and gave the encouragement that I welcomed. I loved my grandparents, and their approval meant the world to me.

Most boys were taught how to clean the fish they caught to prepare for eating. Not me. I had no intention of eating any fish, and so I usually threw the ones I caught back unless someone else promised to clean it. I guess the thought of cutting it up seemed a bit disgusting to me, and I already knew how lousy fish tasted, so what was the point?

I loved going out in the boat to fish on my own. My fourteen-feet Crestliner with a Johnson nine-and-a-half horsepower gave me the freedom to escape out into the lake for my own adventure. Typically, I would troll, but sometimes I would use minnows or worms. Whatever was available. In all honesty, I was only a mediocre fisherman, never giving it the time and effort to become good. My younger cousin Brett was really the best fisherman in the family. Early on, we thought he was just lucky, and while there is an element of luck, he continually caught more and bigger fish than anyone in the family.

My fishing was more of a time of reflection for me. A chance to be with my own thoughts and figure out the perplexities of life through the eyes of a boy growing into a man. Therefore, I never felt bad coming up with a small catch or even getting skunked. I found my own success fishing with what I was able to work through on my own personal struggles. At least I tell myself that. Probably, I would have liked it better if I had the time with my thoughts and caught a lot of fish.

I fondly recall two memories of my fishing experience that I particularly enjoyed: catching minnows for bait and checking the bamboo poles left out all night at the end of the pier. Catching minnows was a lot of fun. A net about eight feet long or so with two wooden rods on the ends was the tool we used. With another boy on one end and me on the other, we'd drag the net along the sand bottom in ten to eighteen inches of water. Ideally, through a patch of seaweed, we'd lift the net to reveal the shinning catch of dozens of minnows flapping around in the net. We'd grab as many as we could with our hands and move them to a bucket. It was just so amazing to find what we could not see in the water with our eyes but was in fact down there.

Anyone would use these as live baits. I was happy to supply the minnows as this was just a lot of fun. The other memory I enjoyed was going out to the end of the pier early in the morning to see if any fish had been caught. In hindsight, this sounds very odd to me, but my grandfather had three to four bamboo fishing poles rigged into a clamp at the end of the pier. These were left overnight with a worm on a J hook. So if a fish took the bait, it would wait to be pulled in until the next morning.

I loved running out to see if any fish were awaiting their fate. To my recollection, about 20 percent of the time, there would be a white bass on the end of the line. I'd lift it out of the water and take the hook from its mouth and throw it in a bucket to carry in to show my grandfather.

Most of my fishing through age eighteen was on Lake Winnebago. Years later, I learned to fly fish with my wife Jenni, where again I found great peace standing in a river lost within my thoughts. Casting in a mountain stream with a fly rod and actively working the water was a whole new world in fishing and one I still enjoy today.

Postscript

As a boy, my father and uncle wanted their boys to all have the best equipment once we learned to fish. This meant a Garcia Ambassador 5000 red reel and a St. Croix fishing pole. At the time, I had no idea how good this gear was until forty-five years later.

My son Cody was living in Branson, Missouri, and asked if I could bring down some fishing gear for him to use. I grabbed my old tackle box and rod and reel and packed them in the car. Suspecting my fishing line was not good anymore, we went to the Branson Bass Pro Shop. I found a gentleman about sixty years of age to help us. When I pulled out my reel, he just froze staring at it. He couldn't believe what he was seeing and called over several of his co-workers to see this mint-condition classic reel. Everyone locked their eyes on this classic reel in amazement.

Then I pulled out of the case my St. Croix fishing rod. Again, utter amazement. I was told in no uncertain terms that I could never fish with these again. They needed to be under glass in a display case. It was suggested these were worth a lot of money to any collector of antique fishing gear. Jenni, Cody, and I just smiled and laughed like we were guests on the *Antiques Roadshow*.

The coup de grâce was my tackle box with classic original lures from the sixties. Just to see and touch these items made the day for four Bass Pro employees who lived for and loved fishing. Today those are all sitting in my basement still as I'm unsure what to do with them. Oh well, I guess I'll let my grandkids have them when I go to my reward.

Learning to Water-ski

For my eighth birthday, I got a fantastic present. We had dinner as a family, and then my dad asked if I was ready to open my gift. Of course, I was ready. What eight-year-old isn't ready upon waking up, and I had been waiting all day long. The entire family led me through the kitchen and into the foyer to our front door. I was told my gift was outside.

I opened the door, and there right before my eyes was a fourteen-foot aluminum Crestliner rowboat sitting on a trailer. At the back of the boat was a brand-new 1966 Johnson nine-and-a-half horse-power engine. I ran outside. "Is it really mine?" I asked.

My mom and dad explained that the motor was mine, but the boat and trailer were the whole family's. That was fine with me, as I knew the one who owned the engine would be the one controlling the boat. This was unbelievable.

We would bring this boat up to Lake Winnebago now every trip, which meant I never had to share access to a boat again. I happily took my older sister Michelle out for rides in the boat and even let her drive it too. My younger sister Kathy and even younger brother Jeff would have to wait a few years until they were old enough.

Like all sports, the younger one is when learning, the easier it is to accomplish. Water-skiing is no different. Lake Winnebago is well designed for young kids to learn to ski because of the very shallow water. We would start in waist-deep water with a family member in the water too assisting the beginner. If you fell on the early attempts, you had someone to help you get set for another try.

I mastered two skis fairly quickly and loved the experience. I got so comfortable that I no longer needed a parent supervising, so one of my cousins or one of the other kids that lived year-round at the lake would ski with me. I learned to drop a ski, which was a lot of fun, continuing to progress in this great sport. The difficulty in dropping a ski was that I couldn't yet get up on one ski. This meant we needed to pick me up out of the lake into the boat and go back and pick up the ski I dropped. This is a common practice, but the hassle was one I wanted to put behind me.

I needed to learn to get up on one ski.

The Seith family lived just a few houses down the shore. Steve Seith was four years older than me, and he knew how to get up on one ski, so Steve became my new best friend. Steve didn't have a boat and wanted to water-ski. I had the boat and motor and needed someone to drive the boat. It was a perfect friendship.

I was happy to drive the boat for Steve. He was a good water-skier and was fun to watch. I also felt special getting attention from someone that much older and athletic too. To get up on one ski behind a nine-and-a-half horsepower would seem impossible, but we had two things going for us. Being young, we didn't weigh much. The shallow lake gave a unique way to start.

Steve explained to me that we could stand in water up to our knees, but the boat would be out in deeper water to not have the prop churn in the sand. We got the boat ready with Steve standing in the knee-deep water on one leg. The other leg was in the boot of the ski with the ski held up to the water level.

Steve yelled, "Hit it!" and I turned the throttle all the way. The boat took off, and Steve began to hop on his free leg. The boat was pulling him along, and with each hop, the boat picked up more speed until finally he no longer needed to hop. He was up! Steve settled in, and I drove the boat parallel to shore heading east while Steve went out of the wake, back and forth. I marveled at his athletic prowess.

Steve finished his turn and told me I was going to learn to get up on one ski now. I couldn't believe it. Was that possible? I did not have the confidence myself, but I would never question Steve. He was clearly an authority on water-skiing after all.

Tom Terrill (left) and Bill Castino (right) ski tandem on Lake Winnebago

We set the boat up with Steve now driving and me standing in water up to my knees. Steve had told me I could do this, and I didn't have the nerve to fail. I yelled, "Hit it!" And Steve cranked the handle of the motor to full speed. I was hopping up and down and getting pulled forward. I just keep hopping and hanging on, and before I knew it, the ski was planing across the water. I was up. I did it. On my first try no less.

I was so excited. That summer, I skied a lot with Steve Seith. He encouraged me to push my own limits and to strive to improve. I never saw Steve after that summer and wonder where he might be today. I wonder if he knows how much he meant to me.

Each summer, I continued to water-ski on Lake Winnebago. My dad later bought a nineteen-foot Thompson with an Evinrude 55 horsepower on back. Friends from home came up to visit, and we loved to water-ski. Bill Fillion, Brian Avery, Billy Castino, and Chuck Caldwell, to name a few.

Parasailing

In the late seventies on my summer trip to Lake Winnebago, we were greeted with an innovative toy. But to call it a toy suggests it was something simple to manage and play with. In this case, it was anything but that.

My uncle Lee had purchased a parasail and many hundred feet of rope. This was new and exciting. Today there are specialized boats with a launch deck and a winch to let the line out slowly and reel it back in under a safe and well-managed design. As well today, it is expected that a trained crew is there to operate the boat and the parasail.

We had three hundred plus feet of uncoiled rope, the parasail, and some ten or so people ready to help. But we had no experience. No one really knew what they were doing, and being all males, directions were not required.

But who would go first? Mark Jiganti had been a high school gymnast with balance, strength, coordination, and, most importantly, a lack of fear. The perfect combination to take the maiden voyage.

Mark Jiganti strapped in for the first parasail of the year on Lake Winnebago

Mark donned a life vest and then the harness with the help of three guys trying to figure out which straps go where. Quickly, we discovered we had him wrapped up in what looked correct, but his leg straps were placed in such a way that it would not hold him. Had we not discovered our error, Mark would need to simply hang on with his own strength to avoid a three-hundred-foot free fall once aloft.

"Come on, guys, make sure it's right," Mark said with a little trepidation. Relieved to have found that error, we carelessly supposed everything else was correct. However, if you look in the picture above, you will notice the blue portion of the sail is off the ground lifted by inverted lines.

We walked out into the lake with Mark strapped in and six others holding the chute all carefully bunched together. My uncle was driving the boat with two spotters riding along. The three hundred feet of rope was secured on one end to the boat and the other end to Mark in the harness. With the line fully extended at the start, there is no ability to bail out. It's 100 percent go!

The slack in the rope was taken out, and Mark yelled, "Hit it!" The boat took off, and the six guys holding the chute threw it up into the air, hoping it would open properly. The chute filled to only 80 percent, thanks to our mix-up on the lines, but fortunately, it was enough. Mark's body quickly shot up two hundred feet high as the boat started to head west down the shoreline.

The launch required six people running while holding the chute.

From a distance, we all saw the error in the chute, but it was too late to do anything. Brian Avery, who was next, commented, "We are going to fix that before I go," which got a good laugh from the rest of us safely on the ground.

One big difference from today's parasailing back then is you landed in the water, not on a boat deck. It was a gradual decline with a skilled boat driver, but your body was still moving forward at about ten miles per hour when you hit the water. You were immediately dragged underwater even with a life vest, so you needed to take a big breath of air and hold on tight. Eventually, the boat stopped, and your head broke the surface, enabling you to take another breath.

Mark had a great ride and excitedly shared how cool it was with the rest of us eager to have a turn. Brian went next after we fixed the chute lines. No problems. I went after that also without incident. It was great fun to be that high, floating silently over the lake. I found it to be one of the more peaceful experiences of my life. Something about being alone, the wind in your face, and a view of the world that was quite unique from any other perspective make a lasting impression.

My uncle Lee was proud of his redwood pier. It went one hundred thirty yards (yes, yards, not feet) out into the lake. My friend John Thompson was always clowning around and had been ribbing Lee that he thought the pier was a veneer and not solid redwood. Lee was quite defensive. "John," he said sternly, "that pier is one hundred percent solid redwood."

John went second to last and had a great flight too. He was doing his imitation of Mick Jagger and his 1978 disco dance while in the air. My cousin Kurt went last. Streaking was a popular fad in the midseventies, but it had gotten a bit tired. It needed something new to bring life back to this novel trend. Kurt was a bit of an exhibitionist and was easily talked into doing a naked parasail. He took his suit off, and Lee could tell something was up by our laughter, but being three hundred feet away, he couldn't tell what.

Brian Avery and Mark Jiganti do backflips off the pier to celebrate their successful parasail adventure.

Lee shouted back, "Kurt, you'd better have a life vest on!"

Kurt responded, "Yes, Dad. Don't worry, I am wearing a life vest." Ready to go, Kurt yelled, "Hit it!" And we threw the chute in the air. Away he went with the first streaking version of parasailing. Again, once the ride started, there was no way to stop it, so Kurt flew for fifteen minutes above the north shore of Lake Winnebago proudly displaying his birthday suit.

Kurt landed, and like the kind cousin I was, I tossed him his bathing suit. The morning had passed, and we put the gear and boat away. Uncle Lee made his way in to grill up some lunch for everyone.

Kurt Getschow flying high above the lake but, this time, with his swimsuit on

We all came in to eat, grabbing a plate, and devoured our fill of brats, burgers, chip, corn on the cob, and potato salad. As we sat down to eat, John broke the silence. "Lee Babe, while I was parasailing, I flew right over the pier, and I could see from up that high that your pier is definitely veneer." As the laughter erupted, Lee just shook his head, unable to find a proper reply.

The Front Door

In the summer before eighth grade, I invited two of my closest friends up to the lake. Brian Avery whom I'd known since the age of three and Chuck Caldwell who moved from Los Angeles to Chicago a year earlier. Chuck's family had bought the house in Kenilworth, where my family lived. Suddenly, my bedroom became Chuck's bedroom. As you can imagine initially, I did not like Chuck for that reason alone. In short order, however, we became fast friends who enjoyed each other's company but also fought and argued like brothers.

Arriving the night before, Brian and Chuck awaken, ready for all the promised fun that comes with being at the lake. Unfortunately for me, a list of chores delayed the start of our activities. I had my morning work to do while Chuck and Brian skated scot-free as guests, without needing to lift a finger to help.

My cousin Kurt with Barron in front of the cottage in 1978

I'd be finished at ten o'clock and told them to meet me at the front door to the house. Ten o'clock arrived, and I was released from my list of chores. I went to the front door steps to find no one there. *Huh?* I wondered to myself, and I imagined that Brian and Chuck were off doing something fun and would eventually show up. Some ten to fifteen minutes passed, and still no one. Where could they be? Another five minutes, and it dawned on me they must be at the back door. I walked to the back of the house, and there they were, demanding to know why I was late! "What? Why are you two sitting at the back door?" I asked.

You see, at the lake, the front door faces the lake. The back door faces the road and the garage. Everyone at the lake knows this. Apparently, my friends had no idea. We argued which it was, but I knew I had the facts as well as everyone who lived on the lake on my side. An easy argument to win!

To this day, Chuck still claims he was right.

Fourth of July

I lit the fuse of the cherry bomb and ran behind the shed, waiting for the explosion.

To be at Lake Winnebago on Firelane 8 for the Fourth of July was a dream come true for any boy. My charismatic uncle, Lee Getschow, made sure of that. He would personally spend many thousands of dollars out of his own pocket for fireworks that he gave to kids to explode all day long.

On the morning of July 4, all the neighborhood kids would gather at the front door of the cottage, waiting for Lee to come outside. He was the Santa Claus of July 4. The kids were gathered around as he would hand out age-appropriate fireworks with thorough explanations of what was allowed and what was not permitted. But honestly, the rules were few, and enforcement was lax. Exactly the way a boy should grow up!

Punks were handed out to everyone, young and old. Punk is a stick with a corklike surface that slowly burns, enabling one to light a fuse for some thirty minutes. It looks a lot like incense.

Then the youngest kids (about age five to six) got sparklers and snakes. The seven-year-olds also got lady fingers, which were tiny firecrackers that made a nice popping sound but would not hurt anyone.

Eight- to twelve-year-olds got a further upgrade to the wonderful black cats. These are the traditional firecracker with which most people are familiar—great exploding sound and dangerous to have blown up in your hand. Lee carefully demonstrated how to set, light, and run for these middle-school-aged kids. Smoke bombs also arrived for this age group, which added a new dimension to the pyro that was coming out in full bloom in the neighborhood kids.

Thirteen years old and up found their arsenal fully loaded. In addition to all the younger kids' fun, add in bottle rockets, M-80s, roman candles, noisemakers, and cherry bombs.

It was a combination of Christmas and Halloween in that we had bags full of treats all handed out to us to go and have fun. And fun we had! The kids scattered in all different directions. Once I turned thirteen, I wandered out on the pier with my cousin Kurt and my friends Chuck and Brian. We'd stand on the pier lighting black cats and throwing them into the lake, trying to time the explosion to when it would hit the water. Too early meant it went out without exploding, and too late meant it went off too close to your hand. Sometimes we'd nail it perfectly where it blew up right at the water's surface creating a nice splash. This lasted for some ten minutes or so before we'd need to mix it up. I recall Kurt seeing a dead fish in the shallow water and giving it a look of a cigarette black cat. I turned away, not wanting fish guts blowing up in my general direction. Kurt was always good for pushing the natural limits.

Time to head to the field to see what new things we could blow up. On the way back, we passed by the mailbox on the post by the garage. I don't know if the mailbox was understood to be off-limits, but we certainly were not going to miss a chance to see if a cherry bomb could blow open the door. I don't recall damaging the metal mailbox, but I'm not sure I would have noticed much at that age in my wake of explosive destruction. A Coke bottle or two and we'd send bottle rockets into the sky waiting for the report. After a few dozen lit the proper way, it became time again to improvise. How far would it fly if we aimed it five feet high across the field? The answer itself did not really matter but more the experimenting itself.

The curiosity of a thirteen-year-old and the freedom to shoot off unlimited quantities of fireworks fostered a mind-expanding day of wonder. It also allowed the combined creativity or, better said, "creative destruction" literally of a group of adolescent boys. I don't think my uncle intended for this. He was just a boy at heart who never grew up—a rugged and masculine Peter Pan. However, I look back at this annual event as a right of passage for me. Each year, we were given more powerful fireworks, being able to handle them a bit more responsibly. The value of learning to be responsible without adult supervision while having unencumbered fun turns out to be a part of my maturation process. I learned from the mistakes I made and those of my friends but also learned how to think more creatively. Boredom could set in if we just did the same thing over and over, so we were forced to use our imagination.

We took small wooden boats we had made in the shop at Wydeven's house. Toy boats. Loaded them with toy army men and went back to the lake. We made a game out of our toys and fireworks, blowing stuff up and combining three or more black cats together to increase the explosion and adding in smoke bombs for special effects. It was all great fun.

Eventually, the last of the firecrackers were lit, and it was time to let our ears recover. Also, our stomachs. We never noticed how hungry we were until there was nothing left to blow up. July 4 was a time with plenty of food, and we gratefully filled our bellies with sandwiches, chips, and soda pop.

Now it was time to do a little work. While my uncle footed the bill for the fireworks, he did two things that were great lessons for me. First, he would send my cousin Kurt and me to the other cottages on Firelane 7 and 8 asking for donations for the cost of nighttime show still to come. For Kurt and me, this was a chance to become a salesman. We would knock on the door and ask for the man of the house. We'd explain that we were asking for voluntary donations to help cover the cost of the fireworks show. This was a great experience as it helped me get past a fear of asking for money. Not only did this help me in my future sales career but more importantly showed me how to ask for money as an adult for worthy charitable causes from friends, co-workers, and neighbors.

The second lesson was to allow people to participate and contribute even if they had lesser financial resources themselves. People don't want to be given things for free. Not really. Deep down, there is a desire to carry one's own weight. So while the donations might have added up to only 5 to 10 percent of the cost, everyone was given a chance to be part of the financing of this celebration. It was a way to honor and show respect for everyone. In Luke 21, Jesus taught about the widow's mite, and this experience of mine let me see firsthand people participating in various levels where the amount of money was not the important part. It was a chance to partake.

After a late dinner as nightfall set in, the big show was getting ready to take place. At the end of the pier, one hundred yards offshore, was set up the equipment for launching fireworks into the sky. Yes, a full-blown nighttime show just like one might see put on by city or park district around the country. However, this was a private show put on by my uncle and his team of willing co-workers.

Solid metal tubes to launch the fireworks were set up, and everything was carefully planned. After all, this can be hazardous work. Unlike today when electronic fuses and technology-driven launching improves safety, this was men and boys holding burning flares to light gunpowder-laced fuses. Sand was brought up on the pier as a fire deterrent, and of course, the lake itself provided the place to dive if something went wrong.

I never went out to the end of the pier to be part of the work crew. I preferred watching the show from the comfort of the lawn in front of the lake. It just made more sense to me to be close to the cute thirteen-year-old girls with the dark of night and the beauty of the colorful explosions lighting up the night sky.

My cousin Mark would join his dad. My father too was present at many of these launchings. Jim and Doug Bodway were always reliable assistants. One year, I recall something went wrong on the launch, and suddenly, explosions were happening on the pier. We could see the silhouettes of men diving from the pier into the water. Fortunately, no one was hurt, but the next day, I recall walking out on the pier to discover a gap between sections where the wood was gone.

Each year provided a similar but unique experience on the Fourth of July at the lake. With my friends and family, I had a lot of fun but also learned great life lessons. I didn't know it at the time, but with time to reflect as an adult, I can see that this annual celebration had an impact on who I am.

Camping Out

At about the age of twelve, we rarely slept inside the cottage anymore and instead chose to sleep in a sleeping bag out on the lawn near the lake. Here we could build a fire, sit around and talk, and relax to the sound of the waves on the lake while looking up at the night sky.

To be honest, at these ages, it was not about the night sky or the sound of the waves breaking on the shore. It was the fire!

I loved to build a campfire, and so did my cousin and friends. Together we would gather the fallen sticks and twigs for kindling and then get some logs from the woodpile out by the garage. There is just something about sitting by a campfire that brings out the best in a boy. It gave Brian, Chuck, Kurt, Jeff, and I a chance to talk about anything and everything.

Boys don't tend to talk about emotions and feelings, but the campfire setting allowed us to talk about our dreams and ambitions. We'd also share the things that we like. Music, sports, movies, and which girls we thought were cute.

Jeannie, Julie, and Linda were the three local girls that lived year-round within a few houses of the cottage. They would often join us for the campfire where eventually a game of truth or dare would start. This was more like spin the bottle without the bottle, which was OK with everyone there.

At young ages, these camping-out events took place in the front yard of the cottage itself. However, when we were sixteen and older, we instead camped out at a vacant piece of land on the lake about a mile away. My uncle purchased this lot, and in fact, we called it "the campsite."

Here we'd typically make our home base with tents in case of rain.

Colin Ambrose and Jeff Kopp at the campsite

This was not rugged camping in the wilderness. We had a toilet one mile away and food in the kitchen prepared by adults who were glad we were there. There were no bears, wolves, or mountain lions to be worried about and, in fact, private homes within fifty yards. However, it was an excellent time to stay up late and deepen the bonds of friendship with guys going through the same experience as you.

Forever etched in my mind are my happy memories of those nights sleeping outside and my love for those days and for the guys who shared the experience with me.

Brian Avery, Chuck Caldwell, Dave Shehan, Jeff Kopp, Colin

Ambrose, Scott Nelson, and Jeff Nielsen along with my best friend and cousin Kurt Getschow were all there with me. I could not ask for a better group of impact guys in my life.

During a four-year stretch, a second cottage was acquired. My grandfather had passed away four years earlier, and my uncle had bought out my mom's share in the cottage. I was often a guest of my cousin Kurt; however, the rest of the family missed the lake and hoped to be able to go up more often.

My father solved this problem by buying the cottage of Art Jones just ten doors down on Firelane 8. This cottage was very rustic. Not winterized, and the bedrooms upstairs had walls that only went up 90 percent of the way. This left a gap between the ceiling and wall, minimizing privacy if anyone stood on their bed and peered into the next room. We kids thought this was fun but also odd.

The Thompson

My dad also bought a nineteen-foot Thompson. A wooden boat with an Evinrude 55 horsepower outboard on the back. We picked up the boat in Menasha at a local marina and drove the boat across the north end of the lake to the newly acquired cottage. Most people had their boats on a hoist to lift it out of the water, but we did not have one for the Thompson. Another half-dozen boats were also anchored in the shallow water.

My dad did not like the idea of just one anchor, and so he purchased three of them. As we drove the boat into the shallow water, I hopped out of the boat in waist-deep water. My dad told me to dig a hole in the sand for the first anchor.

In the sand, if one quickly lifts and lowers their feet, running in place, a hole is created. I dug a hole about eighteen inches deep and dropped the first anchor in it. The sand quickly filled in the hole naturally. With a line secured to the bow on the boat and the anchor clearly and securely buried, this would be enough for most people.

My dad wanted to have additional anchors some fifteen feet to the east and west of the original center anchor. Thinking this was silly, I grudgingly dug the other holes and placed in anchors in each and secured it with another bowline.

Finally finished, we all waded in, leaving the boat to bob in the waves. The next night, a huge storm came in with gale force winds from the south. This created huge waves as the winds had thirty plus miles of lake to build upon. The morning after the storm, boats that had been anchored like ours had broken free and were smashed on the rocks. Even some boats in hoists were knocked over with the boats also destroyed.

One boat survived. Our Thompson hadn't moved an inch. It was right where we placed it with all three bowlines in place. My dad's seemingly excessive work turned out instead to be the right approach. In the vein of Robert Young in *Father Knows Best*.

The Adventures

Deadman's Creek

Freedom. It means different things to various people depending on their age, geography, religion, and color of their skin. To me, as a young boy at my grandparents' cottage, it meant a boat with a motor and the ability to go out on the lake anytime I wanted.

As a boy of eight, I would play with my two cousins that were of the same age. Kurt stayed in the same cottage, but my other cousin Glen stayed with his family and his mom's parents at the other end of Firelane 8. Glen, or Moose as he was affectionately known, lived only some ten miles away back in Illinois, but my memories of Glen are all up at the lake.

Kurt, Glen, and I would meet at the pier, ready for adventure. Some thirty-five yards out on the dock was our boat. A twelve-foot aluminum boat with a three-horsepower Johnson motor on the back. The boat rested on a sloped ramp of four planks that started three-and-a-half feet above the water and ended eighteen inches into the water. It was a common way to store a boat out of the water that anyone could easily slide it down into the lake with a little pushing and pulling. I walked down the ramp and hopped into the knee-deep water. Splashing the boards so the boat slid down easier, Kurt and Moose would get on each side of the boat, grabbing hold of the gunnels and pulling the boat down the ramp.

Once in the boat, Kurt would gravitate to the back, taking hold of the engine pull. Kurt liked to be in charge, so it was natural for him to take a position of authority. Glen and I climbed in and took our seats with Moose in the middle and me in the bow.

Today's adventure was going to be exciting. We headed west toward Deadman's Creek. Deadman's was a little inlet of very shallow water and a sand bottom down between Firelane 4 and 5. The name of this crick was enough to draw in any boy to explore, but most notable was what our parents and grandparents had told us. The sand inside Deadman's Creek was quicksand, which has swallowed up several unsuspecting victims who got out of their boats. At least that was what we were told. All the kids on the north shore of Lake Winnebago knew that Deadman's Creek was a place filled with danger and not to be taken for granted. How this story ever started, I don't know, but I appreciate the false myth created by someone and perpetuated by all the local adults. It was one of the mysteries of my youth, which made life more exciting.

As we cruised down the lake, we passed our other relatives' pier. George Buckley and his family were second cousins, and George was the mayor of Appleton, which was about as important as anyone could be in this neck of the woods. We passed by the end of the Buckley pier and waved to George and his wife Darlene sitting at the end of their dock. Any day the mayor waived at you was going to be a good day.

Seventy-five yards offshore, Kurt turned toward the opening to the creek. As we got within twenty yards, the water was too shallow to keep the motor running, so Moose took over at this point with the oars. Kurt tipped the motor up out of the water, and I leaned forward over the bow looking down into the lake.

Still, outside the creek, I could see the sand still looked normal, but as we penetrated the inlet, I asked, "Is this quicksand?" We didn't know. It seemed the same, but now we were clearly inside.

Glen took one oar out and pushed down on the sand. "It sure is hard," he said.

"Of course, it is," Kurt added, explaining that quicksand always had a hard layer on the top. I thought to myself that in the *Tarzan* show, it was very soupy, even on the top. I guess this was a different type of quicksand.

We moved deeper into the swampy water, which was all four to eight inches deep. The water was relatively stagnant, and the edge was thick woods right up to the water's edge. The three of us hung around for about a half hour, the whole time knowing that we were hovering over certain death if we fell out of the boat. Eventually, we circled back to the opening and crossed back into the lake. Safe now, Kurt lowered the motor, gave a tug on the pull, and turned our boat east toward home.

We had entered the most dangerous place on the lake and came out alive as conquerors. Conquerors as only eight-year-olds can be.

Sensenbrenner's

At about age thirteen, the girls who lived at the lake never looked cuter, and it seemed like a good idea to direct some of our attention away from sports and water activity toward them. Jeannie, Julie, and Linda lived year-round on Firelane 7, and so they were always there whenever I'd be up for a visit. I recall the first time we went to the Sensenbrenner estate about a mile east down the shore.

Most of the dwellings on the lake were summer cottages with a few year-round homes while the Sensenbrenner estate was some twenty acres or so with a huge mansion. The boathouse itself was a cement edifice bigger than most houses. At the lake's edge, they had a poured cement seawall of some four hundred plus feet, where it was less than ideal for tying up a boat. The property was a series of rolling hills leading up from the lakeshore to a fantastic overlook where the majestic home stood.

Professionally landscaped, the grounds had beautiful trees, flowering bushes, and beds of flowers, creating a serene and peaceful location, ideal for some young teenagers to stealthily enter for our own private event.

Kurt and I invited the girls to go on a short boat ride for a summer picnic on their manicured lawn. The girls would pack the food, and Kurt and I got a cooler full of ice and drinks. We hopped into a boat and took off on a beautiful sunny day.

Fortunately, we had a calm day on the lake, so we easily unloaded the food, drinks, and girls. With a long bowline, we secured the boat to a small tree and let the boat float some fifteen yards offshore.

I had never been on the Sensenbrenner property before. We walked past the boathouse and along their small harbor nestled into the hill. Acutely aware we were trespassing, we quietly meandered up into the estate looking for the ideal spot. I was very impressed with the condition of the grounds, and we were all a little nervous about getting caught. Julie mentioned something about guard dogs, a thought that had not occurred to me. Images of bounding Dobermans rushed into my mind, but all worry was for naught. No dogs ever showed up.

We found a spot of relatively flat ground under the shade of some large trees. This would do just fine. With a couple of blankets spread out, Jeannie reached into the picnic basket and started to pull out sandwiches for everyone. I passed out drinks while we let our racing hearts calm down. Clearly, no one was coming to chase us away. I'm not sure anyone was home, but the thrill of being where we were not supposed to be boosted the excitement of it all.

The five of us enjoyed a beautiful day and a couple of hours of pleasant conversation. What do thirteen-year-olds talk about? In our case, the girls asked many questions about what Kurt and I thought about life. It was a process of testing what could be said and what should be avoided. Mixed company was not all that common without parents or teachers nearby. We all enjoyed our time together and eventually headed back to the boat and home.

I went back to the Sensenbrenner property several more times in my life. Eventually, the home was dismantled and a new one built. When I look at an aerial view today, the property looks as well kept as ever.

High Cliff

On the northeast section of Lake Winnebago is High Cliff State Park. This is a small state park and a fun place to go. Only once did I go camping there, with my father, my uncle, and his older boys Mark and Kurt. Jim Bodway came along too. Jim was an in-betweener in that his age fell between that of the boys and the fathers. The entire Bodway family were local friends, and so Jim's attendance was natural and welcome.

We took a boat over to the park marina full of all our camping gear. After unloading the camping gear, my father took the boys to a soda pop machine to get us a drink. It was the first time I ever saw black cherry cream soda. Intrigued by the name, this was my selection that instantly became a lifelong favorite.

We took our gear up into the campsite and set up our tents. The boys then went exploring while my dad and uncle relaxed at the campsite. Jim had a plan to give each of the boys a special gift to remember our time. He cut three ironwood branches about the thickness of a broom handle.

With his knife, he stripped off the bark, revealing a bright white wood. Ironwood is very strong—hence, the name—and makes for a great walking stick. Jim carved our individual names into the three sticks and gave them to us at dinner.

I was so excited. It was about three feet long and perfect for swinging it around at just about anything. My name carved into it made it especially nice. The night of camping was uneventful but enjoyable nevertheless. The next day, we broke camp, packed up, and went back to the boat. The time with my family was fun, and High Cliff is a unique park, but the gift from Jim was what really stuck with me. I kept that for some fifteen years and always remembered the time I got it.

The fun times for a boy on the water is mostly when the water is warm; however, frozen water gives a whole new opportunity to get one's adrenalin going. The summer playground of Lake Winnebago turned into a magical white wonderland in the winter.

Snowmobiles

I was in the eighth grade when I first rode a snowmobile, and of course, my uncle led the charge on this outing. My uncle came to my house to pick me up for a weekend up north. My cousin Kurt and our mutual good friend Jeff Nielsen were already in the Dodge van, packed up and ready to go. Both Kurt and Jeff had been snowmobiling before, but this was my maiden voyage into the world of Arctic Cat.

On the drive up, we always stopped in West Bend, Wisconsin, about two-thirds of the way for some food at the A & W Root Beer stand. My uncle loved A and W and especially root beer in a frosty glass mug. I would get a small root beer and a cherry slushy along with some onion rings to go along with my "papa burger." Those cherry slushies would always give me the "frozen throat" headache, but I sucked them down like the sugar junkie that I was. I still love A & W and have extended that tradition to my kids.

We'd pull out of West Bend with another hour to go, but no one went to the bathroom there. That was because another twenty-five minutes down the road was the ladies' prison. When the trip was nothing but boys, a stop was always made to "take a leak" alongside the road. The goal was to hit the unattainable barbed wire fence some twenty feet away. The winner was whoever could pee the farthest. I'm sure this sounds strange today, but it was part of the silliness that adolescent boys find fun.

The drive continued up to the cottage, taking another hour. Upon our arrival, we quickly carried our suitcases into the cottage, got the heat cranked up, and put on our snowmobile suits. A warm and insulated one-piece suit to keep warm in the cold winter temperatures while traveling at sixty miles per hour outside.

We went out to the garage and the shop where some twenty plus snowmobiles were tightly packed in waiting for someone to fire them up. Kurt, Jeff, and I were more than happy to volunteer! The reason for so many snowmobiles was that Lee would bring two large groups up to snowmobile every year. The Troop 13 Boy Scouts and the youth group from St. John's Lutheran Church in Wilmette. This quantity would enable every boy to ride alone on his snowmobile.

Lee was ready to ride too, and he would take us out on a tour to show us where we could go and where we should not. These were early model seventies era snowmobiles, so nothing too fancy like today's versions.

Helmets donned, we cranked up the engines and started a single file out to the big field in back. This wide-open space was ideal for getting used to the throttle, speed, and turning. The field was well-worn with previous tracks from the neighbor's outings, and so there was little fear of getting stuck in a snowbank. After some ten to fifteen minutes of this, Lee could see I was comfortable enough to move on to some fun adventures. We headed down the Firelane and up the road toward the highway, but we took a turn at the railroad tracks. Lee shouted that we'd cruise down the middle of the tracks as it was unlikely we'd encounter a train. If we did, he instructed to be sure to leave the tracks for the ditch down below. No problem there. This seemed crazy, and if I saw a train coming at me, I had no concern about not getting out of the way but fast.

We were on our way to North Shore Country Club some three miles down the tracks. We took off about thirty miles per hour, single file with about thirty yards between us as I was bringing up the rear. It is quite an odd feeling to watch the steel rails out in front of you as you try to stay in the middle. After a while, I found myself feeling a bit mesmerized from the experience, and I went shooting off the tracks down toward the gulley. Luckily, I continued with my hand on the throttle, able to regain control of the machine and get back up onto the tracks. Beginner's luck!

No one saw me fly off or navigate back on. My heart was racing as my blood was saturated with a cocktail of adrenaline, testosterone, and norepinephrine. I didn't know if I was more excited or scared, but I knew I wanted more of this.

We arrived at the country club where the golf course was full of hills and vales with a thick blanket of deep snow. Lee again instructed us that if we got stuck, wait for a buddy to come to help you out but ideally don't stop unless you're on flat ground.

Kurt took the lead, with Jeff close behind. These two friends were as competitive as they could be with one another, and both wanted to show the other what they could do. I was a year older and maybe wiser (maybe just more cautious) and was happy to watch and learn from their mistakes. The four of us zigzagged up and down, traveling in every which direction. Kind of like the men in those Fourth of July parades with a fez hat on their heads and strange go-carts. Somehow they never crashed into one another, and neither did we.

This was fantastic. The most fun was busting through a snowdrift on the top of a hill and soaring into the air. You'd land some fifteen feet ahead, quickly throwing the snowmobile into a bank turn to do it over and over again. Lee would sit at the top of the hill and judge who would fly the farthest. With a broad smile permanently stamped on our faces, we repeated this routine a dozen times apiece.

Lee was ready to move on, and we went down to the frozen lake to buzz back to the cottage on a clear and easy path. We arrived back at the cottage at dusk, put the machines away, and went inside for dinner. Being winter, the sun set very early, shortening our first day.

We gathered wood for the fireplace and got a great fire going where we ate our dinner on the floor of the living room. That evening, we relived the successes and failures of the day, laughing and smiling throughout the night. We had so much fun that day, and we knew we had all day tomorrow to do it again.

The next day arrived with a fresh six inches of new snow, assuring an even better day. After a quick breakfast of cereal and OJ, we threw on our snowmobile suits and helmets and headed outside. The next-door neighbor Bruce Wydeven joined us, and my uncle's good friends Jim and Doug Bodway arrived too.

The seven of us went outside, ready to ride, and proceeded out to the lake. Each year as the ice expands, a "crack" in the ice forms, creating a giant ramp of sorts to launch a fast-moving snowmobile into the air for a soft landing (with the new snow) on the other side. As boys, we loved to jump this natural wonder. The seven of us did this a few times, but then Lee signaled to follow him.

Across the ice, we drove our snowmobiles following Lee to some smallish structure out on the lake. It looked like a toolshed as we got closer to it. Lee turned off his engine as did Jim and Doug, and they motioned for us to do the same. New to this, I was not sure what was happening next but obliged the request, and I walked over.

We went into the ice shanty, a small wooden structure designed for catching sturgeon. If you've never seen a sturgeon, this is a sight to behold. They often weigh in at 125 to 220 pounds. These are enormous freshwater fish that are caught during the winter. Doug fired up the heater while Lee and Jim gave a fresh cut into the ice. A rectangular-shaped hole about two feet by four feet had been cut into the ice which was some twenty inches thick.

Lee explained that we were going to fish for sturgeon. I asked where the fishing poles were, and everyone laughed. These are caught with a spear thrust into the water to capture this enormous leviathan. It was explained to me that we sit in this wooden shanty waiting for a sturgeon to swim by, and when it did, we could thrust our spear at it. Sounded kind of dumb to me.

I wanted to be sure I understood my options, so I said, "Let me see if I have this right. I can stand here with a spear in my hand waiting for a fish to swim by, or I can go outside and ride an incredibly fast machine across the ice at fifty miles per hour?"

Yep. That was the choice. The four boys flew back to our instruments of adventure and raced out across the lake. As I think back on those days of discovery, I feel fortunate not to have been born decades later when boys are given their daily pills to calm them down, when what they need is the chance to cut loose, screaming over a large body of frozen water at speeds no mother would approve.

Rules were not often followed, one of them being having every single snowmobile properly licensed and registered with the state of Wisconsin. Having twenty plus of these machines, only about five to seven were actually registered. One of the instructions given was that if you ever see the sheriff coming toward a group of boys, everyone should scatter in a different direction. This was to be done before any authority figure could come up asking for the proper papers. If they gave chase, we were to stop, but then it would only be one boy with one snowmobile. Then with a 30 percent chance of riding one that was legally registered. On one trip, this played out exactly as imagined, and only one boy was pulled over after the multidirection scattering; and he did, in fact, have a machine that was properly licensed. So the evasion plan worked.

On a different winter trip, my father and I drove up with my uncle and cousin Kurt. There was a big tent out on the lake off Waverly beach for a large party open to the public. There were one hundred plus cars parked on the lake and many snowmobiles. There must have been four hundred people for a big cookout and a festival of some type. We were in our truck and drove out onto the ice to get some bratwurst for dinner. My uncle and cousin went to get the food, and my dad and I went to get the drinks.

Now I need to interject here that my uncle had attended Notre Dame University where he played football, but more importantly, he was the boxing champion while a student there in Notre Dame's well-known Bengal Bouts.

My father and I had purchased the drinks and were carrying one in each hand toward a table where we would meet my uncle and cousin. I noticed a midtwenties man, apparently drunk, yelling and pushing around a young woman. My father shouted at the guy, "Hey, you! Cut it out now!" As this was happening, my uncle and cousin arrived to see the guy push the woman down onto the ice and start after my dad. My uncle stepped in and told the guy to back off unless he wanted more trouble than he could handle. The guy started to take a swing at my uncle who fired off two quick left jabs to the jaw of the perpetrator. He fell to the ice like a bag of cement. Wow! It all happened so fast.

The woman then rushed over to her fallen abuser and started hugging him and yelling at my father and uncle. I didn't know what to think at this point—perplexed, confused, stunned. I understood the inebriated guy trying to pick a fight with my dad and was repulsed by the abusive behavior toward his girlfriend. However, seeing her, the victim, rush to the abuser to give him comfort and aid made no sense. My fourteen-year-old mind could not process this apparent contradiction in behavior.

We finished our food and climbed back in the truck. I recall asking my father and uncle over and over why she would want to go back to the guy who abused her. They did their best to explain it to Kurt and me, but it just didn't sink in at the time. Still, I remember it like it was yesterday.

Closing Remarks

I was born into a family that went to the north end of Lake Winnebago in the summertime. My grandparents' cottage had mixed feelings for my extended family. My mother never really liked it that much while her brother Lee loved it more than life itself. Over time, this led to my family spending less time and my cousins spending their entire summer there.

Tom Terrill at the go-cart track in Appleton

As my cousin Kurt and I were very close, I often went up to visit. Taking the Chicago and Northwestern train or driving up with my uncle in his Dodge Charger. My family would spend the last two weeks of the summer to return after Labor Day when schools began. (As a side note, all schools should start after Labor Day still and let the kids be kids until then.)

My love of the water was born in this algae-filled lake in central Wisconsin. It was the best playground a boy could have, certainly the best for me. The opportunity was a gift to me that was part of the building blocks in the foundation of who I am today. Adventure, competition, the love of the outdoors, and a Tom Sawyer type of childhood all came to me here at the lake.

Valet Parking

1974 was a milestone year for my friends and me. That year, I turned sixteen in July and received the best birthday present of my life: my driver's license.

As we all know, a driver's license is a blessing and a curse, at least for anyone who had to buy their own gasoline or, even worse, purchase their own car. I only had to do the former, but still, without a job, gasoline was a significant expense.

Mark Jiganti was the hardest-working guy I knew in high school. He always found inventive and creative ways to earn money, and he only knew one answer when someone asked if he could do a job for them.

A friend of Mark's mother was having a big party in Winnetka, and they needed some young boys to valet park the cars. Mark jumped at the opportunity. When Mrs. Kerns asked Mark if he had any experience, he correctly said no but added that he had a friend with a motorcycle. This would allow us to get the cars faster than anyone else could. Mrs. Kerns thought this made sense, giving Mark the job.

Brian Avery had a Honda 150 cc motorcycle which he loved to ride around town. Mark knew this would be an ideal means of getting a valet back and forth from the home to the street. On Monday at school, Mark invited Brian and me to be his two partners. We immediately knew this motorcycle was the secret ingredient to a good valet job, even though we had never done this before. I asked Mark what we were going to be paid, and he explained that he didn't ask. Mrs. Kerns informed Mark we were not to accept tips, and instead, she and her husband would pay us.

Brian riding barefoot on his motorcycle

This family was a wealthy family living in an exclusive part of Winnetka, and we figured they were undoubtedly going to pay us more than we would deserve. We were pumped up. Giving up a Saturday night of high school social activities was an easy decision, knowing we were going to rake in the big bucks.

Ardsley Road was in the prestigious section of Winnetka, where the wealthy lived and we had a job parking their cars. Friday after school, we met at Mark's house to plan the job. It was as if we were robbing a bank the way we gathered around the table planning out the details. But truth be told, we didn't have a clue. Mark had a wooden board with small pegs and numbers 1 to 80 on it. This is where we'd hold the keys, and how great that it was already numbered! Mark's mom had some raffle tickets on a spool which she donated to the cause. Brian recommended we take tickets starting at 401 and give that to the first arrival. We'd just ignore the four and know exactly whose keys to grab.

We agreed that Mark would drive his car over at 5:30 PM to meet with Mrs. Kerns and get the lay of the land. Brian would pick me up, and we'd ride over together on his motorcycle arriving at five forty-five, allowing fifteen minutes before the first guests would arrive. This October night did not provide us with Indian summer temperatures, but instead, we had a cool forty-eight degrees. Riding the four miles on the back of Brian's motorcycle was so cold. My teeth were chattering as we turned off Green Bay road onto Pine Street. My yellow London Fog coat failed to provide any real warmth, and without gloves or a hat, Brian and I arrived needing to warm up.

Foolishly, we had not checked out the area in advance and discovered narrow streets and heavily wooded property obscuring the cars once parked. Realizing we could only use one side of the road, forcing us to expand the distance each successive vehicle would be from the party, foreshadowing problems yet to materialize.

6:00 PM arrived without a guest to be seen. Fashionably late appeared to rule the day; after all, this was the posh North Shore of Chicago where the smallest details would not be overlooked. Shortly after six o'clock, the first guests arrived, the sister and brother-in-law of Mrs. Kerns. Mark walked to the driver's door and opened it while Brian assisted with the passenger door lending a hand to the woman exiting the car. I meanwhile discretely climbed into the driver's seat and parked the car. Mark handed the gentleman the raffle ticket with 401 stamped on it, as I put the car in drive and deposited the car in the first spot available. It all started out so easy.

I strolled back up the driveway with the keys in my hands as the next car pulled in. This time Brian went to the driver handing him the number 402 ticket while Mark helped the woman out of the passenger seat. Placing the car keys on the number 1 peg, I watched as Brian drove the car out of the driveway. Warming up a bit with the activity, I felt quite confident that we had mastered this task. My mind wandered, thinking about the new skis I would buy with the money we'd split tonight.

We watched the third car turn into the driveway with the fourth and fifth right behind it. No worries. Mark took the first. I took the second and Brian the third. Our parents had taught each of us good manners, so we knew first to help the woman out of the passenger seat and let her able-bodied husband climb out on his own. We each got in a car and proceeded out the driveway. As we were leaving to park cars 3 through 5, each of our hearts sank, seeing a line of ten vehicles arriving while we pulled out.

There would be no one there to greet these cars upon their arrival. Mark parked his car and made a mad dash back to the house some one hundred fifty yards away. Brian and I did the same as the cars were backing up. Most everyone has seen the classic *I Love Lucy* TV show where Lucy is on the assembly line with the chocolates coming out faster than she can wrap them. This is what was happening with us, and we all had a sense of looming disaster.

Being young and frightened of screwing up, we shifted into running mode, quickly handing off the raffle ticket for the car keys. Yes, people were waiting, but they seemed much calmer about it than my racing heart. A crucial part of our plan required a smooth flow of cars arriving at a slow and steady pace. It was not working out.

We hustled back and forth, placing the car keys in order on the pegboard, which now filled up to number 45 when finally the pace started to slow to a manageable speed. The motorcycle was long forgotten as we needed all three of us to take a car when finally a lull gave us a chance to talk at the front door and debrief. Another car pulled in, and I took the lead in opening the passenger door while Mark went to take the car. We were now parking some four blocks away, which reminded Brian to fire up his Honda 150. Brian raced out to get Mark and hurried him back.

Suddenly, our original idea started to work as planned. Feeling a bit better, we quickly took the next fifteen to twenty cars with a back and forth on Brian's motorcycle. We were feeling great and knew we had this under control.

Eventually, the cars stopped coming, and the three of us took a deep breath to relax until the party would end and we'd start the process in reverse. This was when Brian asked an important question: "How do we know where car number twenty is parked?" Hmmmm. We all knew where cars 1, 2, and 3 were; but after that, it became a blur. Cars were parked down different streets and in a different order. I recall saying, "I think I can remember the cars I parked." I had a good memory and naively thought I could remember them all.

Back in 1974, cars did not have a key fob that you could click to have the horn beep or the lights flash. You just had to know where the car was. As for my memory, as the night settled in with the streets now dark, my ability for recall was sinking fast.

We knew we had a problem but figured when people would leave they would be spaced out a bit more than their arrival.

The first couple came outside and handed us their ticket. Number 403. Delighted, Mark, as our leader, took the ticket and went to get the car. He easily knew where the third arrival was parked. As Mark got the car, Brian and I glanced at the front door to see if anyone else was ready to leave.

That was when disaster struck. The wooden pegboard tipped over, releasing every key from its marked peg. Horrified, Brian and I rushed over as Mark, still unaware, drove the car into the driveway. We had a major problem. Not only did we have no idea where car number 20, number 33, or number 68 were parked other than "out there," we now had no way even to identify the keys to the owner.

Panic set in for each one of us as if we were in the boiler room of the *Titanic* and witnessed the gaping hole in the ship. Just like the inevitable sinking of the mighty vessel, our valet job was about to go down. The party continued while the band played on with the guests not aware of the impending doom. Their lives would not be lost, but we weren't so sure about ours.

Mark had a small wicker basket in his car, and we placed all the keys inside it. The next guest to leave came out handing us a ticket. Out of sheer embarrassment, we were barely able to talk and struggled to ask them to find their keys in the wicker basket. Confused and a bit put out, the man started to search for his keys. Upon finding them, he handed them to me, and off I started running into the street to retrieve his vehicle. But which car was his? I had no idea and no idea how to figure it out.

The streets were poorly lit, but that was the least of my problems. I jogged back up the driveway and told the man I did not know where his car was. Brian and Mark looked as helpless as I felt. There was nothing to do but turn over the keys back to the man and point to the streets, indicating that his car was somewhere out there.

He left his wife and went out looking for it. While he was gone, several more guests came out with tickets in hand, ready for us to retrieve their automobile. Mark started to explain the situation when the woman waiting for her husband piped in that we were useless and they'd all have to find their own car after rummaging around in this basket for their keys.

Disappointing someone is hard. Knowing you've let them down from their expectation creates a feeling of shame and guilt. More and more people came out to learn that they would have to find their own car. Standing around like the dolts we were, we had nothing to offer. It was a continuous line of grumbling and upset adults that lasted some forty-five minutes. We gave up and just watched it unfold before our eyes, too numb to talk with one another.

Finally, the last guests took the final set of keys. Too ashamed to communicate with the hosts, Mark climbed in his car while Brian and I vamoosed on his motorcycle for a freezing ride home.

We never asked for any payment, and none was offered. Getting nothing was, in fact, overpayment, which is what we always thought from the beginning. We'd get paid more than we deserved.

The Early Jobs

I'm not sure if I was born an entrepreneur or if I was molded to be one. My father managed the Chicago branch of a major New York Stock Exchange firm, and my mom was a full-time home-maker, so the self-employed bug was not from observing their choices. Growing up in Kenilworth, Illinois, meant your parents were affluent, and my parents were more than most. So a need for money was never an issue in my younger days, but earning money was a keen interest of mine.

My first work opportunity came as a third grader shoveling the snow from the walks of various neighbors. I had a coin collection as a kid, and most of my coins came from carefully sorting through rolls of pennies, nickels, and dimes. To do so, I had to have money to go to the bank and obtain these rolls of coins. Back then finding Buffalo nickels and Indian head pennies was still possible, but it took a lot of work. My income went to acquiring my supply of rolled coins.

In the fall, I went to the homes that were within a block walk of my home in four different directions and rang their doorbell. "Hi, I'm Tom Terrill, and I live at 125 Woodstock. I'm hoping to earn some money and would like to shovel your walk every time it snows this winter."

Most of the people were not interested, but six of them agreed to my proposal and hired me. I didn't realize it at the time, but these people already had someone that plowed their driveway and certainly shoveled their walk too.

I believe these kinds of people were more interested in the young man asking for work than what was the most practical thing to do. Today I try to model my own decisions of hiring young boys and girls for community tasks to the value of character development of the person as these thoughtful people did for me. I faithfully shoveled these walks for the next four years until we moved across town in the seventh grade.

Selling Coffee

My family started skiing on vacations in 1968, and we all loved it. My parents bought each of their four kids their first pair of skis and boots, but after that, we were on our own. As well, lift tickets were paid by my folks through eighth grade, but if we wanted to ski additionally with friends or once in high school, we had to pay the cost ourselves. The annoyance to my siblings and me soon disappeared after we were able to secure a way to earn money for these pleasures. A true gift from my parents to their kids was the understanding of making their own way.

I needed a new way to make money, and my father had a brainstorm. Coffee. The commuter train station shuttled the suburban businessman to their Chicago loop offices, and as they boarded the train, there was no opportunity to buy coffee. Just a mere two blocks away, my dad thought I could fulfill this need, although no one knew if there was a demand for coffee.

This was right up my alley. With some guidance from my parents, I went to the A & P and purchased the best-tasting coffee, which was their Eight o'clock coffee brand. Supplies of cream, sugar, and plenty of Styrofoam cups and lids. The remaining items for my new venture were sitting at home: two forty-cups percolators, two large thermoses, my brother's little red wagon, and a folding card table.

My mom taught me how to brew the coffee in these fancy percolators, and I put pen to paper and figured what price I needed to sell a cup of coffee to be profitable. Making my sign indicating twenty-five cents, I was now set.

At 8:30 PM the night before, I got the two percolators set up next to the sink with the coffee grounds and water all ready to go. Setting my alarm for 5:30 AM, I would come downstairs and plug them in, allowing plenty of time to finish. I'd dress, eat an early breakfast, and transfer the coffee into my two large Coleman thermoses.

In my brother's little red wagon, I pulled my gear the two blocks to the train station and walked inside. I found a corner to set everything up, laying my price sign on the table, and was now starting my second venture of being self-employed.

Surprise was the reaction from most of the businessman seeing this twelve-year-old trying to sell them coffee. Those that knew me came to ask what was up; I explained my desire to purchase a new pair of skis which got a good chuckle from many of the men. I think they suspected this effort was good for maybe a week.

"I'd like a cup," said Mr. Sivright, who took out a quarter and tossed it on the table. As I filled the cup, I nodded toward the cream and sugar. "No, thanks. I like my coffee black." Outside, I was calm, but on the inside, I was doing backflips and clicking my heels. The ice now broken, other men followed the lead of Mr. Sivright, helping my opening-day sales.

Between trains, the stationmaster came over to congratulate me on my idea and offered to store my card table in his office so I would not have to carry that each day. "Boy, that would be great!" I told him, appreciative of his words of encouragement and storage offer. After the fifth train, I came home in time to walk back and put everything away, then hop on my bike to ride to school.

That night after dinner, I again set up the coffee makers to repeat the process. Arriving at the station, I walked into Leo's office to get my card table. "Oh, hi, Tom. I have some bad news for you," Leo began. "I checked with the Chicago and Northwestern train administration, and they won't allow you to sell coffee on their property."

My heart sunk, thinking my career ended so quickly. Seeing the disappointment on my face and unhappy with senior management's decision, Leo said, "But they don't own the sidewalk. You could set up your table there, and they can't do anything about it." Leo had given me the answer and conveyed that he was on my side. I was back in business, defeating the lawyers of corporate America who only know how to say no.

Leo would still store the table for me, and I'd be outside on the public sidewalk adjacent to the station. My customers on the second day were all wondering why I was now outside. Upon hearing the reason, most of the men shook their heads at the silliness of the situation. This, however, was a blessing, giving me an obstacle to overcome and, in the process, strengthen the man forming within the boy whom I still was.

My sales were steadily growing to the point where I'd sell forty-five to sixty cups of coffee every day. Faithfully each day, I went through the process enjoying my experience and the fruits of my labor. As time marched on, the calendar came closer and closer to winter months when temperatures would drop below freezing, and the snow would fly. I wondered to myself, *Would my dedication wane? Would sales increase for a hot cup of coffee in December?* Time would tell.

For the most part, I worked every day that school was in session, missing only those days where it was pouring rain or temperature dropped well below zero. Standing outside in the dead of winter selling coffee to the commuters fosters perseverance. My resolve grew, allowing me to make it through winter into spring and right up until school was out. I had made enough money to buy a new pair of skis and still have reserves in my bank account.

My dad's idea had turned into a gold mine.

The operation was so successful that my sister Michelle wanted to join me for my second year. We agreed to split the work, which allowed us to add both earlier and later trains, thereby increasing sales. This partnership worked great in our second year. We both made enough money for an additional ski trip with my grandmother as the adult chaperone, and we each brought a friend along.

In the third year, I was now a freshman in high school, and my sister dropped out as my partner. At New Trier, the school day began with an "Advisory" period that consisted of any announcements from your homeroom advisors, the taking of attendance, and playing cards for twenty minutes waiting for class to being. It was a total waste of time.

My advisor was a young science teacher who rode his bike to school from Wilmette every day, passing by me selling coffee. He had seen me doing this every day for two years but didn't know who I was until I was assigned to his homeroom during my freshman year of high school. "Tom, would you be able to make more money if you didn't have to come to Advisory?" he asked.

"Why, yes. I could stay for two more trains if I didn't have to arrive at school until my first class," I answered.

"Then why don't we do this. If I see you selling coffee, I will mark you as present that day, and if you're not there, I'll assume you're home sick. If I need to reach you about anything, I'll tell you the next morning as I bike by." This was great. I thanked him for his willingness to be my ally and took him up on his offer.

Around the same time, Leo came and asked me if I had a younger brother. "Yes, Jeff is four years younger than me," I replied.

"I need someone to watch the newspapers as the men pay for them each day. Would your brother like the job?" I told him I would bring Jeff with me the next day and introduce him.

Leo's problem was that the daily newspapers were being paid for on the honor system, but too many people were taking advantage and lifting the paper but not leaving a quarter. All Jeff had to do was stand behind the table and watch the men. They still paid themselves or made their own change, but now they had to do this with a nine-year-old boy looking them right in the eyes. This ended the five-finger discount, and my brother was happy with the dollar a day he got for just standing there.

After three years, I retired from the coffee business, satisfied that I had started and finished my own venture. My time and money were well spent, leaving me fond memories. Jeff continued to work for Leo for several years until it was time for him to move on too.

Cleaning Gutters

Brian Avery needed money. Nothing unusual for a seventh grader with a girlfriend. Brian's father was one of the most observant men in our town, and he knew the gutters on his house needed cleaning. In his mind, he thought why should he pay someone to do a task if he had a son that could do it for free.

Brian was told the ladder was in the garage and to find a friend to secure the ladder while he climbed up the two-story house to remove the leaves and sticks that were blocking the free flow of the rain. I was the friend.

Upon finishing the task, Mr. Avery wisely instructed us that he was not the only homeowner looking to avoid a climb of thirty feet on a ladder and that many others would gladly pay a handsome sum for transferring the risk to a couple of twelve-year-olds.

We loved the idea and took to the streets with a plan to sell our services. It was quite simple. Brian and I together approached a home with lots of trees and rang the doorbell. Explaining that we would do the work of cleaning their gutters this fall and forty dollars was all it would cost. Most people said no, but many said yes, and we were well on our way to newfound riches.

We'd raise the extension ladder alongside the house and take turns climbing up while the person on the ground secured the ladder from below. Some homes we found the gutters were filled with wet and rotting leaves that stunk to high heaven. Other houses had dry and partially filled gutters.

We liked the work, and a typical home took a little less than an hour to complete. Splitting the forty dollars generated a very nice payment. Once again, I found myself in a position to sell our services and converse with adults about parting with their money. This experience was a common theme in my life and one I enjoyed. I wasn't born a salesman, but I certainly became one.

Brian and I enjoyed this job. Being high up and exploring visually, the roof of these homes was a unique experience. Some houses had a roof style that allowed us to leave the ladder and climb around on the roof itself. We loved this. Not only could we navigate up to the edge of the roof to clean faster but we also got to explore hidden coves and nooks that were not obvious from the ground. It was a new and exciting place for a couple of adolescent boys to discover.

I recall at the Thompsons' home in Winnetka finding a nice place to lie back on the roof and take in a little sun. Lying down with our hands behind our heads and our feet crossed as we relaxed on a slight incline hidden from view, Brian said, "Ah, this is the life." We were getting paid sixty dollars for this larger house, and there we were lying down on the job.

We felt a slight twinge of guilt for such an easy job, but then we'd remember Brian's father's point about adults not wanting to climb up that high. Any sense of our taking advantage of or being over-paid was quickly forgotten.

We continued these jobs each spring and fall for four years. Regular customers and steady money. It was a great way to have a spike in income twice a year. One of our jobs was next door to a classmate of ours from school who ran in a different crowd than we did. We were up on the roof when we saw him climb out a third-story window and onto his roof next door. Calling out to him, he was a bit surprised to see us. He smiled and explained he was checking on his "babies" which were his recently sprouted pot plants growing in the slant of the roof next to the chimney. We laughed too, thinking of the extent people would go to have their drugs.

The funniest and most memorable of all was our contact with Mr. Ryan. We did not know him or his kids at the time, but later, they all became good friends. Brian and I rang the doorbell to the Ryans' home and waited, but no one ever answered the door. So we left and went to the house next door where the Green family lived. Again, we did not know this family either. As we waited at the

Greens' door to open, a man walked down the driveway between the two homes and asked us what we wanted.

We looked up at the gutters of the Greens' home and told the man we'd like to clean his gutters for forty dollars. He said fine, and we should come back later that day. What we didn't know was that we were talking to Mr. Ryan, who had just authorized us to clean his neighbor's gutters. Brian and I continued making sales calls and planned to return later that day with our ladder to do the job.

Upon our return, we set up the ladder and started to clean the gutters. Now home, Mr. Green had no idea of any such activity and came out of his house to discover what was causing all the clatter. He began to yell at us, demanding to know what we were doing to his home. We explained that we were cleaning his gutters as he had agreed hours earlier. He denied any such agreement and insisted we leave his property. Perplexed, we packed up and left thinking this guy was nuts.

To a couple of young boys, Mr. Green looked a lot like any other man in his midforties, and Mr. Green and Mr. Ryan looked a lot alike. We were the victims of Mr. Ryan's great prank of mistaken identity. He knew the error and let it play out. A few years later, we became good friends with the Ryan family kids. I remember meeting Mr. Ryan then for what was portrayed as the first time. It took a few moments, but I put the details of the past together and recalled the odd incident with Mr. Green. I now realized what had really gone down that day.

We all laughed and forever remembered this funny event.

Sealing Driveways

I spent two summers delivering and installing kitchen appliances. That was the most physically challenging job I ever had, resulting in a personal commitment that I would no longer work for someone else. I wanted to be my own boss again and needed to find the right job.

John Thompson felt the same way as I did heading into the summer of 1978. We were close friends and kicked around the idea of sealing driveways. Heck, I knew how to go door-to-door to make a sale, and the skill level didn't look all that hard.

John had a natural ability in the "male"-oriented tasks, and this new challenge was quickly met with the confidence that John exuded. I researched finding a bulk supplier, settling on a company an hour away in Elk Horn, Wisconsin. Borrowing a flatbed truck from my uncle, we loaded up as many five-gallon drums as we could carry.

We printed up some flyers and started walking door-to-door. Before long, we had several customers lined up from our cold-calling and added a few family, friends, and neighbors that were pleased to help out with our entrepreneurship.

Thriving on the self-employed nature of the business, I found myself enjoying each day. The comradery John and I shared deepened our friendship. Much of the day was spent telling each other stories and jokes while we swept, poured, and applied the tar to the asphalt. There was a particular aspect of seeing the completed task I found rewarding. A clean driveway with a uniform coating gave an appealing look to the suburban property.

Sometimes we made mistakes from which we could not recover fully. At my uncle's home, John had been walking through the wet tar regularly. This was something we had always avoided doing, not wanting to destroy our shoes. But now he would carefully stay within the driveway knowing that his shoes would leave black tar marks should he stray from the asphalt. Somehow, he forgot and stepped out onto the concrete sidewalk leaving two tracks of his Converse gym shoes.

I tried to clean it quickly with some turpentine but to no avail. It was there until it wore off. I remember some five years later seeing the footprints still there while 90 percent of the tar on the driveway had long since vanished with time and weather.

We each made $2,500 that summer for our work, at a time when a year of college was only $5,000 to $7,000. Each of us contributed to the lion's share to our college cost assisting our parents, who generously provided the rest.

The next summer, John decided to take a pass on the driveway business, but I was still very interested. My college friend Ned Brickman had heard stories about how great an undertaking this was, and he decided to start his own in Milwaukee. I helped Ned get the start sharing the knowledge I had gained the previous summer. He too found it to be very rewarding.

I was still in need of a local partner when I ran into an acquaintance from high school, Warren Myers. He had already decided to start a driveway-sealing business with a couple of friends but needed someone who had experience. Our chance meeting formed the beginning of BlackSeal. A partnership of four. Warren told me about Jim and John, who would be our other partners, as we drove over to Jim's house. I never knew either one of these two previously and was a bit uncertain about having four partners. I feared the money would be too small once divided by four. Warren told me not to worry as Jim's family connections would get us some huge jobs.

Jim lived just a few blocks from me but in neighboring Winnetka. As we pulled into his Sheridan road family home, I had no idea whom I was going to meet. Walking in, I found Jim in the kitchen, making a sandwich. The meeting was mostly me explaining the process to Jim, John, and Warren. We'd all be equal partners, but as the only one with experience, I was the job site foreman in the beginning. This was fine with everyone, and we planned the next day to hit the ground cold-calling on local homes.

I did notice that Jim's house had a lot of National Football League memorabilia particularly related to the Baltimore Colts. The topic of football never came up that day, but as we left and I drove

Warren home, I asked him why there was so much football stuff in Jim's house. A bit surprised that I did not know, he explained that Jim's father Bob Irsay was the owner of the Baltimore Colts.

My family had season tickets to the Bears' games, and I thought that was a big deal. This guy's father owned a National Football League team. This was new territory for me. I was delighted to find Jim to be a very regular guy who was not self-absorbed with his family's high-profile business. That summer, we sealed many driveways, made plenty of money for everyone, and solidified new friendships. We rarely talked about football and instead spent our working time talking about rock music, girls, and where the next party would be—typical conversation for four college males.

Jim went on to become the Colts General Manager in his thirties and team owner when his father passed away. I remember the first time I saw Jim's name on the list of the Forbes 400 wealthiest people in the USA. I thought to myself I should have stayed in business with him.

Dangerboys

Growing up, skiing dominated the lives of my close friends. It was a love consuming many of us and one we shared with new friends who had yet to discover the joy of skiing. Brian Avery, Chuck Caldwell, Mark Jiganti, Jim Cameron, and I all had a devotion that penetrated our souls, driving many life decisions around how they would impact our skiing.

During one winter break in college, I was in Aspen teaching skiing at Aspen Highlands. The five weeks off between semesters gave me a chance to head to Aspen and continue the teaching I had done between high school and college. I would make money, ski for free, and get two days a week of skiing with friends.

On a day when I was teaching, my other four friends went to Ajax that day instead. At the time, an area known as Walsh's Gulch was an out-of-bounds area that held some excellent powder skiing. The problem was it was very avalanche prone, each year killing some unfortunate victims who triggered a slide.

While I was safely teaching a class of beginners at Aspen Highlands, some five miles away, Mark, Brian, Jim, and Chuck were riding up the Bell Mountain chairlift hatching a scheme. To get to Walsh's, one had to ride to the top of Ajax and cut under a ski area boundary rope, which at the time would result in your lift ticket being revoked if caught. The four decided they should go back and take a look at this area just to see it. Maybe they'd ski it; perhaps they'd just look and cut back to Gentlemen's Ridge, a run that set the ski area boundary.

Cutting through the woods and under the rope, my four friends were now treading into treacherous territory. Hearts pounding with a dangerous cocktail of excitement and trepidation, they found their way to the beginning of this open powder field. From the top, it looked beautiful. Untracked powder dropping over a steep ridge into the unknown looked like the bliss they'd hoped to find.

Standing there, the conversation shifted to how dangerous this was. They knew and spoke of the avalanche risk. That this might be the final run they ever skied if a slide was set off. A balance of thoughts to either take the challenge or to meekly head back into the safety of the inbounds ski area. The word that just kept coming up was "Danger."

Suddenly, Chuck shouted out, "We are the Dangerboys!" and he took off into the center of the run. That was all it took for Jim, Mark, and Brian to follow right behind him. Chuck continued to shout out the new clarion call, "We are the Dangerboys!"

They safely got to the bottom with a newly found moniker for our group of friends. From this point forward, our tribe would be known as "The Dangerboys."

That evening, the events of the day and our new name was shared with me. I loved it! So did all our friends back home in Chicago when they learned of it in the coming months.

John Thompson was the creative one of our group, coming up with interesting and unique ideas. One of which was wearing a fishing vest to social gatherings. John showed up at a Jackson Browne concert at Ravinia wearing a fishing vest, with a six-pack of beer stashed away in the various pockets. As John would finish one beer, he just reached into a pocket and pulled out another one. It was uniquely John but something I liked too. The next day, I went with John and bought my own fishing vest. The many pockets on the vest were perfect for holding items that would be fun to take out during a party. Toothpicks, gum, sunglasses, nail clippers, and, of course, beer. That summer, our friends all loved the novelty of the vest.

Interestingly, we found girls too were curious about the vests resulting in them coming to us to talk. This was the greatest value. Not only could we be fun and creative with our friends but cute girls we didn't know previously were now drawn to us. This was a winner!

John had bigger plans than just meeting some new girls. He wanted to make some money too. So John and I went into business together once again, this time making and selling the Dangerboy Vest.

Pre-Internet and the global economy in 1979, we began to research how to have vests made to our specifications overseas. Inexperienced and only twenty-one years old, we went by faith. We found an apparel manufacturer in Hong Kong, and our contact by letter was David Young. With specifications to our liking, we placed an order for one hundred vests at $14 per garment.

John and I called Mr. Young in Hong Kong before sending a money order for $1,400. We didn't know if we'd ever see our vests or our money, so a phone call seemed in order. I think the phone bill alone was some $30, and we discovered a man who barely spoke English but said, "You send money. I send vests." So we sent the money, and some three weeks later, our shipment arrived. Perfect.

We took out a classified advertisement in *Rolling Stone* magazine. Our key selling point was that the vest could hold twenty-four cans of beer. It could, but it was overstuffed, to say the least. The first check came in the mail to our PO box for $28.

The PO box continued to fill up with orders, and we were very excited. We took the next step of an ad in *Outside* magazine with a picture. John asked Rob Maine if he would pose with a vest full of beer for the ad. Rob had a great sense of humor and thought it would be a blast.

John Thompson with the check for our first order, giving the classic Thumbs-Up!

Unfortunately, the readers of *Outside* did not think much of our product and marketing. It was a total bust. I guess they didn't care about toting around a lot of beer on their outdoor adventures.

However, the *Rolling Stone* crowd still liked our product, and the orders continued to come in. We placed a second order with our Hong Kong supplier and seemed like we were on our way.

College, however, got in the way. At least that is the excuse John and I used as he headed back to Oxford, Ohio, and I to Madison Wisconsin for our senior year. While we liked the idea of being entrepreneurs, we lacked the commitment required to run such a start-up. This effort was more of a hobby as we both anticipated finishing school and accepting junior executive jobs with some yet-to-be-determined lucky company.

Dangerboys sat dormant postcollege and various career choices John and I made independent of each other. Eventually, John moved to Cincinnati while I remained in the Chicago suburbs. Nothing happened for years.

Now married with two kids and a suburban insurance practice in full bloom, I found little time to do anything else. Still, I thought about Dangerboys and the dream that we never really pursued. Sharing this with Jenni, she encouraged me to consider giving it another effort. In 1995, I did just that.

I developed a strategy to sell T-shirts and other similar apparel with clever sayings and graphics around adventure sports—activities that I enjoyed, such as skiing, mountain biking, and windsurfing. My long-term goal was to become a company like Patagonia, creating functional apparel for the adventure sports enthusiast. The T-shirts would be an inexpensive way to get the name out there and draw interest.

John Thompson told me he didn't want to participate but wished me success. I decided I could invest about fifteen hours a week to this endeavor and cut my insurance back to about thirty to thirty-five hours a week to free up some time. Jenni and I knew this would mean a financial hit to our income growth, but my heart was tugging me in this direction.

Like many entrepreneurs, I read Napoleon Hill's *Think and Grow Rich*. A classic book for anyone starting a business. This gave me some trustworthy guidance, including getting a board of advisors. Brian Avery was my longest and best friend. He too was an original Dangerboy himself, so I asked him. Ted Brown was one of my closest postcollege friends. His creativity, combined with remarkable self-discipline, made him a natural choice. And Chuck Trotter was the third. While he was always Chuck to me, he was better known as Charlie Trotter. World-famous restauranteur and chef who turned the cooking world upside down himself. We met quarterly at Chuck's restaurant, which meant at least we'd have some fantastic food while discussing the development of Dangerboys.

Ted recommended I meet Jim Courtright. A local creative wiz with advertising experience. Jim and I hit it off, and he took my vision and put it into practice. A logo, slogans, and graphic artwork. Jim was a genius who delivered exactly what was needed.

I researched the apparel market and soon became well versed in fabric, thread count, and fashion. At least well versed for a guy who still dressed the same way he did in high school. Blue jeans and a golf shirt.

Jim gave me eighteen graphic designs with the ability to customize a logo too. So with the Dangerboys name, I could add in the names of great ski resort towns in Colorado, such as Vail, Aspen, Breckenridge, and Winter Park. I selected a high-quality cotton T-shirt and a few silk screeners to do the artwork. I

Rob Maine "psyched to party"

also had an embroiderer to take care of the mock tees, Henleys, and golf shirts. With a supply of samples made and marketing brochures, I began cold-calling stores in Colorado.

I had set up some ten sales calls in the next week throughout ski towns out west. Jenni and I packed the car and took the kids out of school for a family trip in September to visit my sister Kathy and her family in Evergreen, Colorado. Her home would be the base from which I launch out each day on my sales calls.

Breckenridge was my first stop at Main Street Sports and Ski Country Sports. Main Street liked the Henleys with the Dangerboys name monogrammed in a scribble script font and ordered six shirts. I made a sale! Yes, it was only half-dozen shirts, but I had taken this new venture into an area I knew nothing about and made the sale. Ski County Sports was very interested in the ski-themed T-shirts where I'd customize the Dangerboys name with Breckenridge written underneath it in a silk screen logo with a skier in the O of Dangerboys. A smart touch by Jim Courtright.

Driving back the seventy miles to Evergreen, I was exhilarated by the sales and excited for the next day's drive to Winter Park.

My daughter Kate was nine years old. I invited her to accompany me on the sales calls that day, which to my delight she accepted. It would be about an hour's drive to Winter Park and one of three appointments there. The first appointment was a bust as the buyer did not show up that day as scheduled. *Oh well*, I said to myself, thinking it was their loss.

The next appointment went as scheduled with Kate at my side and me walking through our catalog with the buyer. However, they didn't share the vision and took a pass too. One more stop and then back to Evergreen.

In the early stage of my sales talk, suddenly Kate piped in, showing a shirt with a witty saying on the back, saying, "I really like this one. I think it will sell well." This utterly spontaneous interjection by Kate took me by such surprise that I said nothing and just sat there looking at her. She smiled while holding up the shirt and turning it from back to front and then to the back again.

I have no idea what the buyer was thinking, but I was flabbergasted. Kate had, without any encouragement from me, jumped right into the sale as if she had been doing this for some time. I loved her willingness to participate and her comfort at age nine, engaging with a buyer who was a complete stranger. The buyer said he'd think about it and let me know within seven to ten days.

Kate and I left Winter Park, and I could not stop smiling. While we did not make an official sale, I had something better—the thrill of seeing my daughter step into my world and contribute in a remarkable way. A moment I'll never forget.

A few days later, my most significant appointment of all was with Christy Sports in their Avon office. I met with head buyer Joy Lutton who purchased for both Christy Sports and the recently acquired Sport Stalker chain with shops in most of the major ski towns in Colorado. I felt so ill-equipped. This business was the real deal, and I was an inexperienced novice trying to impress professionals. Joy was kind to me and shared what she liked and what she didn't. In the end, she placed an order for stores in Breckenridge, Keystone, Vail, and Winter Park. Three different designs, all with our unique customized logo. This sale was the big one for me, and while I didn't know it then, it marked the beginning of the end.

While I kept dedicating time to Dangerboys, my insurance business kept growing and growing despite the limits of time I was giving to it. I couldn't do both. One would have to go. I didn't know it yet, but it was beginning to become apparent.

"The sale" to the store "buyer" achieved my goal. Not the purchase by the retail customer in the store. Over the next twelve months, I fulfilled orders and reorders. I continued to be excited by the idea of success, but deep down, the fire in my belly was fading. I was driven more by the "idea" Dangerboys than the sale itself.

I spent another eighteen months working on both Dangerboys and insurance and eventually let one go. Insurance was safe and predictable, and I was very good at it. Dangerboys was now over.

Out of Control

In 1973, the Eagles released their album *Desperado*. The songs followed an old Western theme, including a song about a cowboy riding into town to whoop it up, gamble, and let off a little steam.

The song is appropriately titled "Out of Control."

Teenage boys find a certain element of being out of control attractive. The rebellious nature coming out and revealing itself to both the person and to the peer group. I was no different from every other teenager in the seventies.

Here are some of those moments in my life.

Double Edge

In August of 1974, I walked into my English class. It was the first day of high school in my junior year, and I discovered my good friends Chuck Caldwell and Mark Jiganti were in the class. We were all excited to share a class and worked our way to seats in the back of the room. As the other students filed in, so did our teacher. At least we thought she was our teacher.

She introduced herself and explained that our regular teacher had taken ill and was hospitalized. She would be our interim teacher for a few weeks, but as she just learned this a few hours earlier, there would be no instruction this day, and we should treat this period as a study hall. Being the first day, we had nothing to study yet, so we began to whisper with one another.

Mark had been to Europe a few weeks early. Reaching into his pocket, he said, "Hey, guys, look what I brought back from France." It was a six-inch switchblade knife.

"Are you crazy pulling that out in class?" I whispered. Chuck was OK with it and asked Mark about the action on the blade opening.

Chuck had purchased several switchblades himself on a previous European trip and fancied himself as a bit of an expert. He learned that one "tests" the action of the blade by letting the dull side of the blade snap open on one's index finger.

Handing Chuck the knife, Mark said, "Check it out," thinking Chuck would just open it in the air. Unbeknownst to Chuck, this switchblade had a sharp edge on both sides of the blade. Opening the knife with his index finger positioned to take the blunt of the opening, Chuck released the blade which flew open, slicing Chuck's finger in the process.

"Crap, this is a double-edged blade," Chuck said as Mark and I watch his finger oozing blood. Mark and I were already cracking up when Chuck asked us, "Do either of you have a Band-Aid?" which made us laugh even more. What sixteen-year-old boy carries a Band-Aid with him?

The substitute teacher asked us what was so funny, quickly triggering our best effort at restraint. "Nothing," we said. Mark now had the knife again in his pocket while Chuck tried to stop the bleeding without much success. He then pulled out his wallet and produced a Band-Aid of his own, which he now remembered he kept in case he would ever need one.

This made Mark and me laugh all the more, which again caught the attention of the teacher. She had us move seats to separate the three of us but never caught on regarding the knife. This was my most memorable first day of school.

Greenwood Avenue Is Flooded Again

In the midseventies, the 500 block of Greenwood Avenue would flood after a hard rain. The storm sewers failed in this section of Kenilworth so that eight to ten inches of water would cover the street for one hundred yards or so.

My high school girlfriend lived on this street, so I was often there seeing firsthand this all-too-common event. One summer evening, the rains came opening the sky to a torrential downpour. I was with my friends Brian, Jim, and John a mile away at Brian's house when the storm hit, and we were trying to think of something fun to do.

We loved to water-ski at Jim's family cottage, and I kiddingly said we should water-ski on the street.

"We could totally do this, guys!" Jim said, with the enthusiasm for which he was known.

"What boat would we use?" John laughed.

I could see Jim's eyes light up on this idea, and I jumped in. "We can take my car and back it up into the water until the tailpipe is just above the water. Then tie a water ski rope to my trailer hitch."

"We can take an old pair of water skis and remove the skegs from the bottom," Brian added.

We set the plan into motion and stopped at my house for the old skis before driving back the two blocks to Greenwood Avenue. John backed the car into position while I walked out into the shin-deep water with the skis. Jim tied the ski rope on the car, and Brian carried it back to me.

"I don't know about this, Brian. The skis seem solidly stuck on the pavement."

"OK, lean way back and I'll tell Johnny to start slow."

I was worried about being yanked right out of the skis and falling on my face, so I appreciated the caution. We were navigating uncharted waters, and we all loved it.

Meanwhile, each of the neighbors was standing on their front steps, trying to figure out what we were doing. In the darkness, with only the streetlights to aid their vision, I could see they squinted their eyes as they pointed toward us.

"Hit it!" I yelled, and with a steady acceleration, John started to drive. My skis were dragging very rough on the street, but I hung on patiently waiting. Finally, the skis began to rise and plane on the surface. I was water-skiing on the road!

I waved to the local residents, and they waved back. It was surreal. Three-quarters of the way through the water, I let go and continued to glide on the surface. Eventually, I sank down nervously, waiting for the skis to come to a hard stop. When they did, my momentum ripped me from the boots, and I ran barefoot in the shallow water, trying not to fall.

Success!

We each took a turn and today proudly claim to have water-skied down a flooded street.

Wilmot Bombers

Sitting on the northern edge of the Illinois and Wisconsin border is one of the classic Midwest ski hills. Wilmot Mountain had nine chairlifts and a few rope tows with a remarkably low vertical rise of fewer than two hundred feet.

In high school, Wilmot was a familiar Friday night destination for many kids from the nearby high schools, including mine. At the time, the drinking age in Wisconsin was just eighteen, so the attraction to ski and drink beer made it very popular.

It didn't matter if someone was an accomplished skier or a novice to fit into our group that migrated the fifty-minute drive for an evening of skiing. Most of my friends were strong skiers anyway, but we brought along those who were ready and willing to learn or at least have some fun.

One night, we were particularly rowdy with a pack of some fifteen plus people. We were dominating the run with fast skiing, big air, and an attitude that this was our ski hill and we were in charge. About an hour before the 11:00 PM closing, it started to snow and snow very hard. Scott Stephens and I had been talking about jumping out of chair 4 shortly for weeks and decided that now was the time to do this.

We weren't crazy with a death wish but more the thrill of it. Toward the top of chair 4, the height of the chairlift was only about fifteen feet from the snow. We figured if we tossed our ski poles and slid around to hang by our hands from the seat of the chair, we'd only be six to eight feet from the snow. We strategized that if Scott and I went up the lift first and then had each successive chair with our friends, we could have about eight straight chairs evacuated in this silly prank fashion. Also, if so many jumped, we figured it would be too difficult for the ski patrol to nab anyone.

Scott Stephens and Tom Terrill doing a "spread eagle tip drop" in 1974

A little nervous, we loaded onto the first chair—Dave Shehan and Chris Dewey right behind us and Chuck Caldwell and Brian Avery behind them. The new snow kept falling, giving a soft landing for the soon-to-be jumpers. Scott and I were set and committed to fulfilling this task.

As we arrived at the selected low spot, Scott tossed his poles to the left, and I dropped mine on the right. Simultaneously as if we were a circus act, we grabbed the pole and slid around, so we were both hanging by our hands and now facing the chair behind us. Dave and Chris shouted a cheer of affirmation and prepared to follow suit.

Scott and I dropped at the same time, landing smoothly on the snow below. We grabbed our poles and moved out of the way for the next to have a clear landing. As Dave and Chris followed our lead, Brian and Chuck were ready as well. John Thompson and Jim Cameron were in the fourth chair, prepared to join the club. Those that had jumped began to shout to the successively arriving chairs to have those riders jump too. Mark Jiganti was riding with the first girl jumper, Peggy Shields. They both left their chairlift as everyone else had before them.

Now people we didn't know were arriving at the spot, and we encouraged them to jump too. To our surprise and delight, everyone was jumping and fortunately only at this low spot, so no one was hurt. Eventually, the lift operator stopped the lift, which ended the jumping. We all scattered in different directions as planned, with no one getting caught. We had succeeded in this teenage goal without anyone getting hurt.

The snow was now falling so fast and heavy that everyone was obscured by the air full of flying white flakes. We skied another ten minutes or so and then decided to call it a night. Our gang of lawless renegades went back to our cars still pumped up from the excitement of our jump that we were not ready to just drive home.

All this fresh snow was ideal for a snowball fight. At first, we started throwing snowballs at our friends, but as strangers arrived in the parking lot, they became our new targets. The snow was incredible for packing snowballs, and soon, the entire lot was filled with people engaged in an all-out war. Between throws, we took off our ski boots and packed up our gear in the car.

Dave Shehan flies over the jump while Scott Stephens photobombs the picture

As I climbed in the driver's seat of my family Oldsmobile station wagon, Dave and Chris decided to skitch out of the parking lot. Hanging on the bumper of the car, we fishtailed out into the snow-covered exit. As we approached the state road, Dave and Chris let go of the bumper, and I slowed down to let them jump in the back seat as we left the parking lot and began our ride home.

Phone Fun

Teenage years in the seventies were so different from today in many ways, but one of the most striking was the use of the telephone. Cell phones were yet to be invented by several decades, but everyone had a landline, and local calls were free.

My sister and I were using the phone more and more, which led my parents to get a second line. Tired of not being able to get through because one of us was on the phone talking with friends, the easy solution was the second line.

The technology was such that a phone could have either line, and the switch from one line to the other was made by turning a small knob on the phone ninety degrees. You'd hear the line click from one to the other and back again if you spun this knob back and forth.

One day while talking to a friend, I was playing with this knob, slowly turning it to the right. I knew if I turned it too far, it would terminate the call, but it was only a friend on the line, so I knew the consequence was just needing to call back. I was flirting with how far I could spin it without disconnecting my friend. The kind of thing kids do exploring boundaries any chance they had.

I got to a point where I heard a click. Simultaneously, I had entered a zone where I could still hear my friend talking but could also hear a dial tone. This was unexpected, and I asked my friend if he could hear the dial tone. Affirmative. This was new territory yet to be explored. What new practical jokes could be played with this information? I had discovered the Promised Land of Phone Fun.

We didn't really know yet what I had discovered, but as we tested out the ability to make a second call without disconnecting the first call, we learned we could make a three-way call. At first, this just seemed like a novelty with some level of convenience to connect with multiple people. Time would reveal additional value.

The next day at school, I shared my discovery with some friends. Some were skeptical of this claim, so a handful of buddies came over to my house after school to witness firsthand the technology breakthrough. Testing this out, we found we could quickly make one call and join the other without any problem by just holding the knob still. But now what could be done to cross into the world of practical jokes.

I thought how funny might it be if we could call two people at once and have them both answer the phone at the same time. If I remained silent, how might the conversation play out? Dave Shehan was a great friend who lived just three blocks away, and Barb Sivright, one of the nicest girls from our high school, lived a block away from Dave. They had known each other since grade school.

We called Dave's house first, and he answered the phone. I immediately hung up without saying a word and quickly dialed Barb's house. She too answered, as most sixteen-year-olds were inclined to do. I now knew they were both home, both close to the phone, and if I called again, they would likely both answer it roughly at the same time.

I called Dave's house and carefully turned the knob to obtain the next dial tone. Dialing Barb's number quickly, the plan was in action. Both lines were ringing at the exact same time.

Barb: "Hello."
Dave: "Hello."
Barb: "Hello?"
Dave: "Hello?"
Barb: "Dave?"
Dave: "Barb?"
Barb: "Hi, Dave! What do you want?"

Dave, at this point, had no idea what was going on. All he knew was that his phone was ringing, and Barb Sivright, who happened to be extremely cute, was asking him why he was calling. He couldn't say he wasn't calling as here he was on the line talking with her. He was baffled.

Dave: "Uh, well...uh...I was wondering if you knew about any parties tonight."
Barb: "Dave, it's a Tuesday. We have school tomorrow. There aren't any parties tonight."
Dave: "Oh yeah, I guess I forgot. Well, bye."
Barb: "Bye, Dave."

And they each hung up. We burst out laughing, trying to imagine what Dave was thinking and imagining Barb assuming Dave had lost his mind trying to find out about a high school party.

Jim Cameron had been dating a girl named Renee. Everyone knew this relationship was over, except of course Jim and Renee. Maybe this phone trick could speed up the process. I called Jim at his house and explained that we all knew it was time to end this relationship. While Jim agreed with me on the phone, he explained that he didn't know how to do it and that he did still have feelings for her.

"Jim, I thought of an idea that will help you."

"Oh, really?" Jim inquired.

I then made up a story about me calling Renee and tape-recording my call. "Yes," I began. "You see, I called Renee myself on the phone and recorded it. I'll play the recording, and when you hear her voice, you can break up with her as a practice. It's just a recording, but the practice will help when you do it live."

Jim said, "I don't know. This sounds kind of weird."

"Jim, give it a try. Here I will begin the tape recorder." In reality, I simply turned the knob, obtained the dial tone, and dialed Renee's house phone. "OK, Jim, shortly you'll hear the phone get answered. Once you hear Renee, my voice will end, and you begin."

The phone was ringing when someone picked up the call at Renee's house. "Is Renee home?" I asked. The person set down the phone, calling out, "Renee, some boy is on the phone."

While we waited for Renee to come to the phone, I quickly reminded Jim to jump right in as soon as she said hello.

"Hello?" said Renee.

"Listen, Renee," Jim began, "I think we need to break up. It's just not working for me."

"Jim, why are you saying this?" Renee asked.

Totally confused why a recording could ask Jim a question, he muttered, "Uh, uh, Renee?"

Now Renee was crying and said, "Jim, why are you doing this to me? I like you so much. I don't want to break up."

Brian, listening in, whispered to me, "Abort! Abort!" I quickly span back and forth the knob which disconnected both calls. We realized that this had gone too far. Our joke now had this poor girl in tears. About five minutes later, we called Jim and apologized. He still had no idea how this all took place, and I explained the discovery. The relationship did end between Jim and Renee. I never saw Renee again, and she had no idea of the backstory.

Quickly, this trick became widely known by everyone in our high school, and so the joke was played out.

Later in the school year, I was over at the Thompsons' house. John was someone I didn't meet until I was sixteen. Even though we lived in the same town, John attended Loyola, the local Catholic high school, but had just transferred into our public one.

John had his sights set on a particular girl whom he wanted to take out. I didn't see it happening and was sure she would reject his offer of a date. We were sitting in the den where John's father had his desk with a phone on it. John said he was going to go call this girl, but wanting privacy, he went down into the basement to talk on the extension there.

I decided to pick up the phone as John began his call to listen in. I had no intention of speaking but only eavesdrop on this personal call. As the phone was ringing, John said, "T-Bone, hang up the phone." I refused, having no intention of missing this.

"Hello?" the girl answered.

"Hi, Debbie. This is John Thompson."

Suddenly, I had a brainstorm. While John was speaking, I was as quiet as a church mouse. However, whenever Debbie spoke, I would breathe very heavily into the phone in a clear audible fashion.

John was making small talk with Debbie, building up the courage to ask her out, but the heavy breathing I did made John seem more and more creepy as the call continued.

I could hear John, with his hand over the phone in an intense and angry voice, whisper up the stairs toward me, demanding I hang up the phone. I still refused and instead kept up the heavy breathing the entire time Debbie spoke.

Finally, John did invite her to dinner and a movie, to which she politely refused while I kept panting into the phone. The call ended with John flying up the stairs to exact his revenge, only to see me running out the garage door and into my car for a necessary escape.

They never did go out.

My final phone prank was at a New Year's Eve gathering at my cousin Kurt's house. Kurt's side yard had a hockey rink, and the boys all came to play and hang out. Long after the skating was done, we were sitting inside the family room talking. About midnight, I grabbed the phone which had a very long cord from the phone base to the receiver.

I tossed the receiver to my favorite victim, Dave Shehan, while I kept the base unit and said, "I'll dial a random number, Dave, and you give whoever answers the business."

Dave was totally into the idea, and I immediately began to dial Dave's parents' home phone number. As soon as the phone was answered, Dave started shouting into the phone, "Hey, old man, it's New Year's Eve. What are you doing at home, you loser? Don't you have any friends, old man?"

Mr. Shehan, on the receiving end, said, "Dave?"

To which Dave replied, "Dad?"

The room broke out in uproarious laughter.

At this point, still controlling the phone base, I decided it was time to hang up, disconnecting the call. Hearing now a dial tone and knowing I hung up on his father, Dave flew out of his chair, shouting, "Terrill, I'm going to kill you."

I bolted from the couch and ran up the front stairs with Dave in close pursuit. Down the back stairs and outside, the chase continued with me just able to stay in front of a furious friend. Maybe a former friend. I didn't know yet. Eventually unable to catch me, the chase ended with both of us exhausted. Dave's anger subsided as he could appreciate the cleverness of the joke. We went back inside to join everyone else, without making additional calls.

All my phone calls were made on landlines as kids. My practical jokes came back to haunt me decades later, thanks to an inadvertent series of actions by my wife Jenni and her dear friend Susie Kelley.

The year was now 2014, and Michael and Susie Kelley were coming to our home for dinner. Jenni told me they would be arriving soon when her cell phone rang. It was Susie calling to say they were on their way and should come in five minutes.

I was upstairs to change clothes and clean up a bit from the day. Jenni, still talking to Susie, wandered upstairs while telling Susie she would see her in a minute. Haphazardly, Jenni tossed her cell phone on our bed and left the room. Of course, she didn't hit the "end call" red button but left the phone on. Not purposely, mind you, just without thinking.

Meanwhile, Susie did the same thing. Just stopped talking but didn't actually end the call. Moments later, Jenni saw their headlights pull into our driveway and called upstairs to me.

"Honey, the Kelleys are just pulling in. Please come downstairs."

I replied in a shout so she could hear me, "I'm on the toilet!"

Sitting in her car with her phone in her hand and thinking there was no call connected, suddenly Susie heard my voice coming out of her cellphone announcing I was on the throne.

Of course, I had no idea any of this was being transmitted. I finished up the task at hand and came downstairs to have Susie hug me and say, "I know what you were just doing."

So while there was no planning or scheming on anyone's part, I fell victim to a phone faux pas.

Climbing

Brian Avery, Polly Rutherford, and Tom Terrill sitting atop the Kenilworth Water Works

Starting at about age sixteen, my friends and I felt drawn to begin to climb things that were not meant to be climbed. This risk-taking was about defiance, but not defiance of authority as much as defiance of casualty. We didn't necessarily feel immortal nor immune from injury or harm, but rather this was a rite of passage: to do things that were dangerous yet not get hurt. To conquer things that seemed obscure and to act as if it was nothing more than a walk in the park.

I loved the Kenilworth Beach. The Water Works building stood at the east end of Kenilworth Avenue sitting on a bluff overlooking Lake Michigan. The east side of the Water Works had a wall with an architectural brick cobble ideal for climbing. It was an ideal first step into this new endeavor. Typically, we'd climb at night, when no one was around to report the activity to the authorities.

This three-sided building could also be safely climbed from the north side, which took a bit more effort. One had to run straight toward a concrete wall about ten feet straight up. We'd hit the wall full stride with an outstretched and elevated leg to leverage one's momentum straight up. This would allow you to grab the top of the wall and then lift yourself up in a pull-up. The ascent would continue from this level, but with the safety of a short drop if one slipped.

The south side posed the greatest risk. The climbing assistance was limited to a few outcroppings and had a full two-story fall if a misstep took place. I only climbed this once with Brian. Having accomplished it, there was no need to do it again, knowing the consequence for an error was at minimum broken bones.

John Thompson, Greg Stuhr, and Brian Avery climbing the east wall

Most of the things we'd climb were impulsive decisions when we'd encounter some structure and someone would just shift into climbing mode. At a movie theatre in Skokie, we saw a pipe running up the side of the outside wall. Just walking past it, Brian Avery and Jim Cameron took off without saying a word and started to climb it. We didn't have mountains to climb, but what we did have to scale we did because it was there.

Brian was the bravest of the climbers. Next to the movie theatre was a closed-down bowling alley with an archway at its entrance. This steel edifice was dirty, narrow, and had nothing to hang onto. Still, Brian scrambled up some thirty-five feet above the parking lot to take a victory seat long enough for me to snap a picture.

The most challenging climb of all was the old Kenilworth Water Tower. On the corner of Roger and Exmoor on the west side of town stood the old tower that rose some one hundred twenty feet in the air. The tank sat atop a steel structure of four legs that were roughly eighty feet high.

A ladder on one of the legs started some ten feet up, and it was easy to reach the ladder from the cross supports in the legs below. Brian Avery and I decided to climb the tower, so we reached out to two individuals who claimed to have done it before. Brett Johnson and Art Bergman were classmates of ours going back to kindergarten. The four of us met at the tower at 8:30 PM on a warm September night. Brian and I parked our car some five blocks away, so if the police showed up, we could hide and not have our license plate give us away.

Brett had a police scanner and thought the process through as if we were robbing a bank. A phone

Brian Avery atop the bowling alley arch in Skokie

call was placed to the police department where, in a disguised voice, Brett reported some kids were shooting off fireworks on the other side of town. As we listened to the radio scanner, we heard the dispatcher sending the patrol car well out of our way on a wild goose chase. Art was first, with Brett right behind him. They climbed quickly and were well on their way when Brian began his ascent. I was glad to be last as I was not sure I could make it to the top myself.

Art was quickly at the top, with Brett arriving shortly after that. Brian too succeeded in reaching the pinnacle of the water tower where they enjoyed a tremendous view of the Chicago skyline some twenty miles to the south. I, however, found myself frozen with fear just above the tree line. I could turn my head back over my left shoulder and see the lights of buildings in Evanston. That was good enough for me. Slowly and carefully, I climbed back down, realizing I had hit my mental limitations before acrophobia took over.

Safely upon the ground, I could feel the adrenaline coursing through my veins. My legs shook a bit with a remnant of nervous energy as I watched my partners in crime work their way back down. We were all happy with our level of accomplishment and quickly took off in case the law might be headed our way.

I never tried climbing the water tower again. It was just too high for me.

Shecat's Bar and Grill

Dave Shehan was a wild man. If there were a rule, he'd break it, but only if he could do so in a memorable fashion that would bring delight to others. He was a guy's guy who could be counted on to do something more than a bit edgy. Dave was a year younger than me, and a classmate of his gave a nickname to both Dave and his house. Shehan morphed into Shecat and the house into Shecat's Bar and Grill. The two names stuck, and Dave was proud of each.

I enjoyed taking pictures and trying to be smart in the process. With a play on words theme of Shecat and "chic" hat, Dave posed for the photo below in my front yard.

Dave with a skateboard, Mitzie the cat, a derby, and orange plastic glasses

My friendship with Dave took off in high school. He shared with me how his parents were pleased that Dave was hanging around with me as they saw me as a stabilizing influence in his life. We both laughed at that idea. As teenagers, we couldn't understand that concept at all.

One summer, Dave hatched a plan with Mike Stroud to hitchhike across the country. Mike's parents were on board with this idea, but Dave's folks would never approve of such recklessness. Still, Dave was committed to the idea. He arranged for me to drive them some thirty miles out of town onto the highway to drop them off. Dave called home from Mike's house to let his mom know he was leaving and he'd be back in a month or so. Unhappy with the call but unable to stop it, Mrs. Shehan reluctantly accepted that parenting is the hardest job there is.

When I dropped Mike and Dave off, I grabbed my camera to record their departure. "Hey, guys, I want to get a picture," I said. They were thrilled with the idea of the documentation. "I want to get the last picture of you guys alive," I jokingly said as I took the picture.

Mike Stroud and Dave Shehan next to my Chevy Impala on the beginning of their adventure

As legend has it, movie star Rock Hudson and a New Trier alumnus, as a high school senior, allegedly rode a motorcycle through the hallways of New Trier East. Dave took this story to heart and did, in fact, ride his motorcycle through the center hallway of New Trier East in 1977 on the day of graduation.

My favorite memory of Dave involved Shecat's Bar and Grill. In the fall of 1975, Dave sent word throughout our high school that he'd be having a party at his house that night. Dave was a popular guy, and everyone was planning to attend. I arrived with Brian and Chuck to find Dave's front yard full of high school kids, most of them on their way to a night of excessive beer consumption.

I walked in through the open front door and discovered a packed house. Hundreds of people had shown up, crammed into the living room, kitchen, and den. I wandered down to the basement where a couple of guys were handing out cold cans of beer to a long line of girls and boys. Trying their best to look cool, people were smoking, drinking, and socializing. The stereo was blasting the Who's teenage anthem song Baba O'Riley." As Roger Daltry's unforgettable voice powerfully sang out, *"Teenage wasteland, it's only teenage wasteland, teenage wasteland, oh yeah, teenage wasteland. They're all wasted."*

This would be the best party of the year, and it was only fitting that Dave hosted it at Shecat's Bar and Grill. Thirty minutes after my arrival, I still had not found Dave in the sea of humanity. I couldn't help but think this was going to be one big mess to clean up. Ashtrays were full of cigarette butts, but so was the beer-soaked carpet in the living room, equally full of discarded half-smoked cigarettes.

"Dave," I said, finally finding him in the living room. "This party is incredible. Everyone is here."

"Yeah, pretty cool," Dave replied with the satisfaction of creating a memorable night in New Trier history.

"Where are your parents?" I asked, expecting something like New York or Europe.

"Westmoreland," Dave calmly replied.

"What?" I said with astonishment. "Westmoreland? Your parents' country club! That's where your parents are? Five miles away?"

"Yep," Dave answered with confidence that this was not a problem.

"Are you insane? You'll never be able to get everyone out of here and clean this up in time. You're a dead man," I said, stating the obvious.

Right then, someone called from outside that the cops had shown up. Suddenly, Dave's confidence appropriately vanished as he glanced out the front door to see the Kenilworth police in his driveway with their red lights flashing.

Dave gave a call of warning to those in the house to hide their beer. But this was impossible. There were just too many people and too much beer with no place to stash it. Having not had anything to drink myself that evening, I walked out toward the police car to see what they were doing. As I got to the driveway, I saw an Oldsmobile 98 pulling in the driveway behind the police car. Dave's parents were home.

Remembering that they considered me a good influence on Dave, I thought I should go up and talk to them. "Hi, Mr. and Mrs. Shehan," I said with a smile on my face as if I were welcoming them to this amazing party.

Mrs. Shehan gave me a steel-eyed glare and sternly said, "Not now, Tom."

Oops! I had overplayed my hand. Suddenly, it dawned on me that my greeting sounded a lot like what Eddie Haskell from *Leave it to Beaver* would have said. Repulsed by my own bad form, I decided it was time to hightail it out of this budding fiasco. Brian and Chuck found me, and we hurried down the sidewalk to my car a few blocks away.

Dave's party was historic. In fact, there was a hidden genius behind Dave's plan. Not only would he throw the best party of the year and get caught by his parents and the police but he'd live to see another day. No one wanted to get caught in high school antics. Dave's brilliance and what really made the event memorable is that he did get caught. Dave was Steve McQueen on his motorcycle in *The Great Escape*. McQueen got caught, but man was he cool.

The Best TP Job Ever

Homecoming 1976 at New Trier East High School was a big deal, and a ritual of TP-ing the house of football players and cheerleaders was a tradition. Art Bergman was on the football team, and his girlfriend Anne Moloney was a cheerleader. Art was a friend going back to kindergarten, but in high school, we'd gone separate ways.

On Friday afternoon, John Thompson ran into Art in the grocery store with two carts completely full of toilet paper.

"Art, what in the world are you up to?" John inquired.

Art explained that he was going to do the best TP job ever and asked John to help. Unfortunately, John had a previous family commitment, but he recommended that Art reach out to me. Art gave me a call and asked if I could recruit some others to help. It sounded like fun, and I was free. Calling Brian and Chuck to tell them of the plan, they enthusiastically joined in. We all knew who Anne Maloney was, but really, she was just an acquaintance at best. One of four thousand in our large high school.

We met at 11:30 PM at Art's house and drove to the destination in two cars. Art had his auto loaded with one hundred rolls of TP, and Chuck drove his car with Brian and me. We unloaded the TP from Art's car in the driveway of the Moloney home and then drove around the corner to park the cars in an out-of-the-way location.

The street was quiet on this warm fall night. No one was in sight, and most all the lights were out in not only the Moloney home but the neighboring houses as well. Everyone had gone to bed. This home had some very old oak and maple trees dotting the front yard—branches twenty-five plus feet up in the air with the canopy topping out some eighty feet high.

Art took the first role and tossed it up to a large branch. A textbook throw unraveled the TP on the way up, as the balance of the roll crossed perfectly over the extended oak branch allowing the toilet paper to continue its unfurling process on the way down.

Immediately, Brian, Chuck, and I followed suit, hurling the TP as high as we could. Whispering affirmations to one another on the fantastic job drove us onward to complete our mission with a sense of purpose. We each had twenty-five rolls to deliver, and with each roll taking three throws to complete, it required a lot of arm strength. A little more than halfway done, a sense of giddiness took over after each throw. Laughter within our hearts and soul quietly erupted. The vision before our eyes was that of a living mosaic being created. We had already obscured the house from view in the street as we continued with another ten rolls apiece.

No cars. No late-night dog walkers. No lights were coming on inside. By the time we finished, a wall of TP had hung, completely blocking the house from view. The four of us stood side by side in the street, looking at our accomplishment. We'd never seen anything like it. No one had. We were proud and rightly so when we notice car lights three blocks away coming fast. The red flashing lights now came on, and we all bolted. Art and I ran south and into a neighbor's yard. Over fences and through bushes, we ran together for one hundred yards before we split off on our own. I kept running for blocks and blocks. I realized my best choice was to go the three miles home on foot as returning for a ride was tantamount to turning myself it. I got home exhausted and out of breath. I went to my room but could not possibly go to bed. My heart was pounding too hard and fast for sleep. However, I was alone—no one to celebrate with on our accomplishment.

Some thirty minutes later, a car pulled into my driveway. It was Chuck and Brian, who, to my delight, showed up to review the evening. Coming in the back door, we went to the basement where I shared that I ran all the way home without stopping.

Brian and Chuck did not run far as the police arrived. They dove into some thick evergreen bushes in the yard across the street and quietly sat there, not moving a muscle. They told me how the police car stopped in the middle of the street and two policemen climbed out of their vehicle. From only twenty yards distance hiding in the bushes, Brian and Chuck could each hear clearly the words from the two officers of the law.

"Look at that! Whoever did this job did it right," the first officer said.

"I've never seen anything like it before. This is the best TP job ever," the second officer added.

They stood there for some ten minutes just admiring the job. They weren't interested in finding the kids who did it. After all, it was homecoming, and these pranks were expected. Eventually, they climbed in their squad car and drove away.

Brian and Chuck waited a little longer and went to their car around the corner. They never saw Art, but his car was still there. We congratulated one another on a fantastic night. The affirmation from the police boosted our pride in the work all the more. It really was the best TP job ever.

Fifteen years later: I'm married with two kids and have a growing insurance practice. My physical therapist wife has a cardiac rehab patient in the insurance business, and he told her he'd love to meet with me. I agreed and set up an appointment to see if there might be any useful collaboration in our insurance businesses.

Mr. Moloney lives in Lake Forest, and I make no name connection as our TP job was fifteen miles away in Winnetka. After talking for some twenty minutes, Mr. Moloney asked me how my wife and I met.

"We went to high school together at New Trier," I said.

"Really. I wonder if you know my kids. I lived in Winnetka and have a daughter named Anne, who is about your age."

My heart started to race as a smile came across my face. Wondering what the statute of limitations is on a TP job, I started, "Do you remember homecoming of 1976? Your house was TP'd. Do you want to know the story about who did that?"

He didn't say a word at first. He just stared at me. He reached to an intercom and spoke into the mic, "George, get in here." His son, some three years older than me, walked in, asking what was up.

Mr. Moloney said, "This young man knows the story the TP job."

His son pulled up a chair, and I had both of their undivided attention. What fun it was to regale them with the details of the event and not worry about being arrested. Smiles and laughter filled the rest of the meeting. They loved learning the backstory, and I loved sharing it.

The Opel GT

When I was a senior in high school, my father impulsively purchased an Opel GT. This sports car looked like a Mini Corvette and was driven by Secret Agent Maxwell Smart in the final season of *Get Smart* in 1969.

While it was my dad's car, he took the train to work every day. My mom needed her station wagon, and so as the only other driver in the family, these wheels were essentially mine. I drove it to school every morning, and not having any classes until the third period, I didn't arrive at school until 10:05 AM.

Street parking was restricted until 10:00 AM, so I was able to park just one block from the school. In my high school of four thousand students, this was a luxury bestowed only upon me.

This white two-seater had a small storage area behind the seats with enough room for a large golf bag and nothing more. The four-speed manual transmission was fun to drive, but the coolest thing about the car was the headlights. Hidden from view in the hood of the car, they would roll out like a set of bug eyes with the push of a handle next to the gear shift.

Fall of 1974, I could be found driving around after school with one of my friends riding shotgun. At this same time, my father asked me to check and fill up the household fire extinguishers. These water-based containers were powered by compressed air and could shoot a steady spray of water some thirty feet. To refill them, all you need was a hose to add two-point-five gallons of water and a gas station air pump.

Loving practical jokes and pranks, I figured these fire extinguishers could play an exciting role in my life after school. The first effort was with Scott Stephens. As Scott sat in the passenger seat with the fire extinguisher on the floor between his legs, we drove toward the school at 3:10 PM.

Students were lined up, waiting to cross Winnetka Avenue as we approached from Abbotsford Road. The crossing guard would hold some fifty students while she waived us through making a left turn in front of the growing crowd. Scott pressed the handle, releasing a stream of water to the unsuspecting masses. Scott only shot it for five seconds before stopping as we continued west in front of the school. We were in the middle of a line of eight to ten cars, and it was confusing to the wet students what had happened and who did it. We took the next left to circle around the block and did this again. By the time we were back, a new group of unsuspecting students was about to get blasted.

Scott and I thought this was hilarious and shared with our friends this new prank. Several days in a row, we continued this practice, never being caught or identified. One day, Brian Avery was riding with me as we pulled the same trick. Brian was the number 1 trampolinist in the state of Illinois and saw a fellow gymnast on his motorcycle talking to a cute girl. We pulled up alongside and stopped to say hello. Just as Brian's teammate started to introduce us to the girl, Brian released the blast of water in a magnificent and effective dousing. The girl laughed as did Brian while I hit the accelerator to get out of there quick.

Unlike most victims, he had the means to pursue us, which he quickly did on his motorcycle. But what could he do? Yes, he was furious, but after chasing us for a few miles, he realized he could never force us to stop or get out of the car. We were immune from retaliation.

The single most memorable event in the Opal GT took place one evening at Tom Wilson's house. Tom's family owned a large estate off Locust Road in Winnetka. The private driveway was one-third mile long connecting Locust and Woodley roads.

Tom Wilson was having a party at his house; however, Tom required everyone to leave at 10:00 PM. As the time to depart arrived, no one wanted the evening to end. Dave Kuenzel suggested that anyone that wanted to continue the festivities do so at his house.

Many people had already left, leaving too many people for cars available. I had the Opal, but this was a two-seater. Scott Stephens knew some people could cram in the back for a short ride. I watched as Scott, Jeff Nielsen, Barb Sivright, and Denise Bernier climbed into the back. I would not have believed it if I didn't see it. The four looked like the fifties picture from *Life* magazine of teenagers jammed into a phone booth. I jumped in to drive while Chuck Caldwell and Brian Avery squeezed into the single passenger seat. We had seven people inside a car designed for two people.

"OK, guys, where does Kuenzel live?" I asked. No one knew.

"Well, we can't get there if we don't know where it is," I added.

Scott Stephens called out the window, "Hey, Shecat! Do you know where Kuenzel lives?"

Dave walked over the car. "How many people are in there?"

"Seven of us," Niely replied. "Do you know how to get there?"

"Sure, but there is no room for me in the car," Dave said.

"Climb on top and hang on," suggested Scott. Dave looked at me for permission to climb on the roof of my father's car.

"Sure, why not," I said.

So we drove down Tom's long driveway and turned south on Locust Road with our guide shouting direction and hanging on to who knows what. Fortunately, the house was less than a mile away, and we all arrived safely.

Postscript: This fire extinguisher trick escalated to when we loaded my cousin's van with four fully loaded fire extinguishers and rode around town blasting people. Finally, the Winnetka police caught on, pulling over my cousin Kurt and the five others in the van. While they took us to the police station, apparently this was not breaking any law, and we were released. The trip to the police station, however, signaled to us it was time to move on to something new, and we never did it again.

Missouri?

My history final was over, finishing the fall semester of 1979. Walking back to my fraternity house in the fifteen-degrees-below-zero temperature, I hardly noticed the cold. Distracted by my feelings, which were a mixture of relief from completing the semester and excitement for the ski trip I would be leaving on in just a few short hours. In addition to a whirl of emotion, I was physically getting weaker. Waking up with a bad sore throat that morning had become a focal point of my consciousness as each swallow gave an increasing level of discomfort.

In a matter of hours, Brian Avery would arrive in Madison driving his Chevy Capri, and we'd begin our cross-country trek to Colorado. I just kept thinking to myself that in two days I'll be skiing. I stopped and bought a Coke for the caffeine I required for our all-night drive and to soothe my aching throat as I finished the walk to my fraternity house in this bitter cold.

Organizing my ski clothes in my suitcase and cleaning up my room for my departure, I wondered if I might have strep throat. This really hurt.

Brian arrived, and I hustled my gear out to his car. I forgot about feeling sick as Brian and I were now embarking on our trip. Classes and tests were behind us, and mountains and snow were in our immediate future.

"Sorry, I've got some bad news," Brian said as I climbed into the passenger seat. "The car heater is broken," Brian revealed as I sat on the cold and rock-hard passenger seat.

Brian Avery skiing the bumps on FIS

"What? You're not kidding, are you? This car is freezing inside," I disappointedly replied.

The car fan could blow nothing but cold air. We started the drive, and quickly I began to shiver. The sore throat was rapidly progressing while my body struggled to keep warm. Brian pulled over after thirty minutes, and we both changed clothes. Donning long underwear under my corduroys now and a turtleneck, sweater, and down parka was required.

However, I took it a step further, putting on my ski gloves, hat, and even googles to cover as much exposed skin as I could.

Brian and I were driving down the highway in our ski clothes, trying to stay warm. Mother Nature did her best to thwart our plans as an Alberta clipper with thirty plus miles per hour winds came screeching down from Canada covering the Midwest. The temperature dropped to minus twenty-four below zero as we crossed the Mississippi River in Dubuque, Iowa.

I took over behind the wheel, and we pushed southwest toward Interstate 80. Brian and I had driven to Colorado together many times before. From early trips as passengers in our parents' car to many guys trips. Our first destination was Boulder to pick up Mark Jiganti who still had to complete his final exams.

The sunset before 5:00 PM as the temperature plunged. We arrived in Des Moines for a pit stop around 10:00 PM. Brian took his turn driving as we pushed on to the Iowa-Nebraska state line. I curled up, eager to get some shut-eye before my next leg of the drive. Drifting off into a shallow sleep, Brian pushed on with the winds curiously now at our tail.

Seventy-five minutes later, Brian broke the silence. "I can see the 'Welcome to Nebraska' sign in the distance."

Opening my eyes to see for myself, the letters on the lit sign came into focus. "Welcome to Missouri. The Show-Me State," the sign read. Almost midnight, our core temperatures below healthy readings, my level of clarity was about zero.

"That is so funny," I said. "Someone switched the sign as a joke." I honestly thought that was the only possible answer for this errant sign. Brian looked at me as if I was delirious with brain fever but didn't say a word. Instead, he took the next exit at a state line road and pulled into a lonely gas station. We both bolted out of the car and ran inside.

"Mister, what state are we in?" Brian asked, hoping somehow he'd say Nebraska.

"Mizzurra," he answered with an Ozark accent.

We couldn't believe it. We went to the map on the wall to figure out where we were. Apparently, we had driven straight south on Interstate 35 and were completely out of our way. I blamed Brian as he was the driver, but he did his best to deflect and claim I must have gotten on the wrong road in Des Moines before we switched.

Tom Terrill skiing the bumps on FIS

Either way, we were not where we should be.

Studying the map, we determined rather than fully retrace our mistake; we'd take a state highway in Iowa west to Nebraska. We left Missouri and began our course correction. No one else was on the road we took. It was too late at night, too cold, and too rural to have anyone else on this isolated state road. While Brian went to sleep, I drove, thinking about what else could go wrong. I wondered if this car could handle these temps, and if not, we could break down in the middle of nowhere. I started to reset the trip odometer at every farmhouse we passed so I'd know how far a walk we'd have just in case. Every ten to fifteen miles, we'd pass another farm, and I'd push the mileage counter back to zero.

Fortunately, we didn't have any more trouble and were able to pull into Boulder, Colorado, around noon. The arctic chill had given way to a typical Boulder day of sunshine and warm temps. Finding Mark's house, Brian and I walked in and crashed on a couple of couches to get some sleep. An hour or so later, Mark arrived. He finished his first final that day with one to go in the late afternoon.

The relief to be in Colorado was enormous, but my throat was feeling worse. I was confident I had strep and needed to see a doctor. I borrowed Mark's phone and called the University of Colorado student health facilities. Explaining that I was a student at the University of Wisconsin and visiting my friend, could I come in and be seen by a doctor. I'd gladly pay but really needed some medical attention. Unfortunately, they said no, as they only treated the University of Colorado students.

Mark's sister Jeanine stopped by for a visit. She was a year behind us and a good friend too. I asked Mark and Jeanine if they knew anywhere I could go to see a doctor. Outside of the university facility, they had no idea. Mark suggested I should go and just pretend to be him. Get treated for free and be on my way. Desperate for relief from this painful sore throat, I agreed this was a good plan.

Brian Avery, Mark Jiganti, John Stogin, and Tom Terrill skiing Ajax

So Brian, Jeanine, and I drove over with Jeanine as our guide. I would pretend to be Mark and get the care I needed. As the three of us walked into the clinic, we were telling Jeanine about our crazy drive the night before. Once at the check-in counter, I said. "I'm Mark Jiganti, a student here, and I have a bad sore throat. I'd like to see a doctor and get a throat culture."

"Of course," said the receptionist. "Let me check you in."

I felt relieved. Soon, I would be getting medical attention when she said, "Mark, what is your date of birth?" Panic set in. I had no idea. I gave a look to Jeanine that I needed help.

"September 20, 1958," Jeanine said. The receptionist curiously looked at us, wondering why I could not answer when my own birthday was. Jeanine was brilliant and continued, "He's my brother. He feels too sick to answer."

The receptionist reluctantly accepted that but then asked me if I'd ever been here before. Again, I looked at Jeanine for a clue, and she subtly shook her head no.

"No, I've never been here before," I said, answering for myself.

"OK. You can be seated, and we will call you up shortly," she finished.

The three of us walked over to some chairs to sit down and wait for my turn. While we were waiting, Brian and Jeanine were talking, and I just zoned out, staring into space. A nurse came over to us and said, "Mark?" I ignored her. My name is not Mark, and I don't answer to it. Clearly, she wanted someone else.

"Mark?" she said again, and once again, I ignored her.

A third time, she loudly said, "Mark?" to which I realized she wanted me. I jumped from my seat and asked if the doctor was ready to see me.

"Not yet, Mark. You said you've never been here before, right?" the nurse now asked.

"Right. This is my first time here," I confidently replied.

"Mark, our records show that you broke your arm last year and had surgery to repair it here. What is going on?" she asked suspiciously.

At this point, Brian and Jeanine stood up, and both silently walked out the door as if they didn't know me. They were not going to be caught in this scam.

"I'm sorry. I'm not Mark Jiganti. I am Tom Terrill. I'm a visiting student from the University of Wisconsin, and I'm quite sick. I need to see a doctor. Please can I see one?" I pleaded.

"No, you can't," she replied, and she turned and walked away. I stood alone. Sick, tired, and frustrated. I walked out to find Brian and Jeanine who were laughing at the confrontation that just took place.

I never did see a doctor.

Mark finished his final, and we drove to Aspen, where we met John Stogin, who flew in from Yale. My throat eventually got better, and we had a great ski trip.

Restitution

In the fall of 1983, I was a twenty-five-year-old newlywed setting up house with my bride Jenni. Everything was new as we began our lives together. One evening while driving home from work and listening to the radio, I heard Chuck Colson.[*] He had been with the Nixon administration and then convicted from the Daniel Ellsberg's psychiatrist office break-in. He was speaking on restitution. As many know, Colson had a change-of-life experience while in prison and had started a Christian organization called Prison Fellowship Ministry. He worked tirelessly for prisoners and their spiritual needs but also spoke on relevant topics of the day.

---

[*] Chuck Colson is often mistakenly referred to as a former convict in the Watergate scandal. This is not correct. He was convicted on a completely separate matter involving the *Pentagon Papers* and Daniel Ellsberg.

I recall listening to Chuck Colson explain that prisoners for their rehabilitation needed to make restitution to their victims. This made sense to me. Of course, they should. Our society had drifted away from victim's rights, and this acknowledgment sounded proper. In my self-righteous way, I silently applauded this concept as I drove down the expressway weaving in and out of traffic. Driving fifteen miles per hour over the speed limit, a pace I felt comfortable with while unaware of my own duplicity. All too often, convicts didn't really pay for their crimes, I thought, and this was a way to make it right.

Toward the end of the broadcast, Colson made a challenge to the listener (me) that there might be areas in one's own life where the concept of restitution was the appropriate response and that everyone should contemplate this idea. *Sure,* I laughingly thought. *Not me.* I was good. I hadn't been in prison and hadn't done anything to belong there either. Restitution was for the evil people in the world. Not the good.

Colson's message stuck with me though like a song that you can't get out of your head. I just kept thinking about this. But how did it apply to me? The next morning, I spent time reading my Bible and then praying. I decided to get this issue off my mind and ask God to show me if there were areas in my life where I needed to make restitution to others.

Immediately, the floodgates opened wide. I couldn't believe it. My mind filled with very specific things I had done that were wrong and needed to be addressed. Areas in my life where I had made supreme compromises and rationalized them as youthful indiscretions. Yes, I needed to make restitution too. I quickly wrote down my list:

1. Aspen Sports
2. the Winnetka Bakery
3. the Winnetka Fire Department
4. the parents of Hank Brown

December 1971, I was in Aspen, Colorado, skiing with my family. My good friend Brian Avery was my guest for the week, and we were enjoying ourselves skiing. Brian and I looked alike, dressed alike, and acted alike. We both walked into Aspen Sports in need of some toe slip plates that sold for two dollars and fifty cents. As we stood at the repair shop counter, we each had a twenty-dollar bill in our hands. We wore yellow wind shirts, and our hair was the same color and length. The repair shop employee came to the counter and asked what we needed. We both answered, "Toe slip plates." He looked at Brian and went back and got them from the shelf. As he came back, Brian paid him the twenty dollars and got seventeen dollars and fifty cents in change. The employee didn't realize that both of us needed toe slip plates. As he looked at me wondering why we weren't leaving, I said, "I need a pair too." He rolled his eyes and went back to the cabinet and got another pair. He handed them to me along with seventeen dollars and fifty cents in change and said something about getting back to work. As I stood there with my twenty dollars in one hand and the change in the other, I realized he had gotten confused about the payment and turned away. I slowly crumpled the twenty dollars into my hand and started to walk out with Brian. Once out of the store, I burst into laughter and explained to Brian what happened. We agreed to split the spoils in extra brownies and chocolate milk at lunch.

Now twelve years later, I knew what I had to do. I calculated what the present value of the twenty dollars was and called Aspen Sports asking if I could speak to the owner. I was only able to talk to a manager, but I shared with him how I had received something years earlier without payment and wanted to make restitution. I asked for the address that I could mail a check to Aspen Sports. The manager didn't seem to care much, but I needed to do this for me. I sent the check and continued on my list to the Winnetka Bakery.

In the fall of 1974, I was out for a drive and decided to visit my good friend and cousin Kurt. I went to his house, where he and his girlfriend were having lunch. As we sat around talking about the events of the day, Kurt's girlfriend mentioned that she was working at the Winnetka Bakery. I commented on how I loved bakeries, and that one was quite good. She suggested I should come by sometime when she was working, and we made a plan for Tuesday after school. We were both high school juniors but didn't know each other very well. I thought this would be an excellent chance to get to know her better. I loved smiley-face cookies too.

When I arrived and walked in, she saw me and nodded. The store was fairly crowded, and three to four girls were working behind the counter. As I waited my turn, I wanted to be sure that Kurt's girlfriend waited on me. As it was now my turn, I saw her grab a large bag behind the counter and come out front and hand it to me. I had no idea what was going on and asked, "What's this?" She responded that these were the baked goods I had ordered and already paid for and encouraged me to take them and leave. I was bewildered, but not enough to figure out I had a free ticket to the best bakery in town. I held my newly acquired goodies tightly and left the store. This was great. Once in my car, I opened the bag to discover a loaf of cinnamon raisin bread, blueberry muffins, and yes, there were three yellow smiley-face cookies. Oh, what a car ride home.

I visited the Winnetka Bakery for the next five Tuesdays, and each time, I received a bag full of special treats without any cost to me. It was free. Or so I thought at the time. Kurt and his girlfriend eventually broke up, and I thought better of continuing this trend.

Now in 1983, I realized it's time to pay a debt I had that until now I never gave a second thought. I called the bakery and asked for the owner. This time, I was able to speak to the owner, and I shared my story recounting the power of Chuck Colson's persuasive argument for restitution. The owner seemed interested but then told me he had bought the store about five years ago, years after my infraction, and that there was nothing for me to do. I appealed that he had bought a store that had an uncollected debt, and it needed to be paid. I sent him a check too and had another check mark next to the Winnetka Bakery on my list.

I was feeling right about this, but honestly, there was no magic. It was just a small sense of correcting a wrong. So much time had passed, and the people didn't seem to care. I had hoped for a more significant impact. Maybe the next call would lead to the impact I was looking for.

In 1971, as an eighth grader, a large group of my classmates hung out at night, wandering around our village. We had nothing to do and were hanging around familiar areas like our school. Our gymnasium was a large red brick building that backed up to an extensive blacktop area for outdoor activities. Someone in this gang of fifteen or so kids decided to make and throw several Molotov cocktails at the school. Now I had no idea what this was, but others did. As we meandered over to a nearby house of one in the group, I watched as a large vodka bottle was emptied and gasoline from a lawn mower can was replaced in the bottle. A rag was stuffed in, and this was repeated with another bottle. We walked back to the school, and I watched as someone lit the rag on fire and then saw the bottle thrown up high against the two-story brick wall. It smashed into flames, and the gasoline ran down the wall, lighting up the dark blacktop. We watched for about five seconds and then ran. We all scattered and ran from what was sure to be trouble. To my great amazement, there was no trouble. The gas burned up, and the fire went out. The bricks weren't going to catch fire, and we never wanted to destroy anything. We just wanted to see it happen. No police...no fire department. Just a bunch of broken glass that someone else would clean up.

This same event repeated itself three to four more times over the next year with the same results. No trouble and no damage other than the glass. Eventually, the thrill wore off, and we were done with it.

In 1975, at the age of seventeen, I was sitting around with eight to ten people, most of whom were older than me. Someone asked about the stories of the Molotov cocktails and if anyone ever found out who did that. I spoke up and said I was there and watched the whole thing. No one believed me other than Brian, who was there with me four years earlier and again this night. We shared how it wasn't a huge deal. It wasn't as impressive back then as we thought it would be.

Well, this group didn't believe me and said if it's no big deal, let's do it again. Foolishly, I agreed. We got some bottles, gas, and a few rags—one small and one large. We waited for dark and went over to the same location, our old grade school. We made sure no one was around as we didn't want anyone to get hurt or for us to get caught. We lit the rags, threw the bottles, and watched the flames burn on the brick wall. As in the past, it was all over in about thirty seconds.

This time though, a neighbor called the fire department and said the school was burning down. Never mind that it wasn't. The fire department did exactly what they were trained to do so well. They rushed out with multiple trucks to save the school. They arrived to find no fire. Just a bunch of broken glass and the charred marks on the brick wall.

Still, I knew this was trouble, and I did my best to hope it would all just go away. It did. It went away without incident, and I went on with my life.

Now, however, I had to make this phone call that had my heart pounding. As an adult, I can see how bad this was and how foolish my behavior was in this event. I had no idea what to expect, but I knew that the cost of sending out those trucks was considerable. I intended to pay that cost to the village of Winnetka and only hoped they wouldn't arrest me for my participation in this ill-conceived prank.

I asked for the chief of the fire department. I shared first about listening to the radio and now wanting to correct an event that involved the fire department. I expected a scolding on the phone along with details about the vast amounts of money I would need to pay. I deserved it and waited for it to come.

The chief was very kind. He listened patiently to me and then told me that this was long since over and not worth trying to open up. He refused to accept any money on behalf of the village and simply said it's over.

As I hung up, I felt so bewildered. I was relieved to not be in legal trouble, but I felt so incomplete on the restitution thing. I had written two checks and got a pass on the third item. I just kept thinking this was supposed to be a bigger deal. Maybe it was only a big deal to me. The others didn't seem to care and wanted to get on with their lives.

A little deflated, I now had three out of four items checked off. One to go.

In 1976, I was a freshman in college. Back then, long distance phone calls were expensive, and no one could afford to talk on the phone for long. I missed many of my friends from my hometown and wanted to connect with them. I decided to call Jim, who was at a nearby school some two hours away, but I didn't have the money to make the call. I thought that I should charge it to my parents' home phone. This, however, was no good because my dad would want me to pay for the call once the bill came in, and I didn't want to call him that badly. Suddenly, I thought of Hank Brown. I didn't know Hank. I just knew who he was. I had never spoken to him in my life—only one of nine hundred kids in our high school class.

Jim, however, was a friend of Hank's. In my twisted logic, I decided to make the call to Jim. Back then, one dialed 0 first and then the number. An operator would come on and ask what you wanted to do. I said that I wanted to make a third-party charge call and to bill Mr. Brown. The operator said OK and put the call through. Jim answered the phone, and I told him that Hank's parents were paying for this call. Like the naive selfish punks we were, we laughed and didn't give it a second thought. We spoke for a while and then hung up.

So this was the last one on my list.

I pulled out the phone book and looked up the phone number for the Brown family. I was a little nervous, as it was embarrassing to confess my actions and poor judgment of the past. I dialed the number, heard it ringing, and then…

"Hello?"

"Hello, Mrs. Brown?"

"Yes."

"My name is Tom Terrill, and you don't know me, but I went to high school with your son Hank."

"Oh."

"Well, Mrs. Brown, this is a bit embarrassing, but back in 1976, I made a long-distance phone call to a friend of mine who knew your son. I charged the call falsely to your family."

"Oh, I see."

"Yes, well, I was listening to the radio, and a Christian man named Chuck Colson shared how prisoners should make restitution to their victims. He challenged the listeners to evaluate their own lives and see if they too needed to correct wrongs. Mrs. Brown, I need to pay you for that phone call seven years ago. I have estimated the cost with interest, and I think I owe you one hundred dollars."

With a quiver in her voice, she said, "I can't believe what I'm hearing… You see, my husband has recently divorced me, and I am struggling financially. I have just been sitting here wondering how I'm going to buy food this week when the phone rang."

This was it! The moment I had been waiting for. I was stunned by her words. She wasn't sure about where she'd get money for food. *Is that possible?* I thought. I didn't doubt her; I was just shocked by the reality.

God had brought these sins of my past together for this one moment and had changed it into an opportunity to seek forgiveness from my victim and make restitution.

I finished the call making arrangements to mail her a check. I hung up the phone and started to cry. So many feelings rushed through my mind and body. Guilt, joy, amazement…so much more than I could take in.

I mailed the check, and that was my only contact with Mrs. Brown. I shared my story with Jenni and a few others, but mostly, I kept it to myself. I was still embarrassed about all these events from my youth but thrilled to have this final contact with Mrs. Brown close the chapter on my restitution.

I have thought about this often and feel blessed for getting the chance to correct my past.

A Day at the Lake

Springtime in Southern Illinois is just beautiful, and no one seems to knows this. So much of the state is flatland and open cornfields that it is assumed the entire state is like that.

In March of 1977, I was halfway through the spring semester at Southern Illinois University when some friends and I went out to Crab Orchard Lake for a swim. Fifteen or so of us loaded into four cars and drove the few miles to an ideal spot for swimming on this warm eighty-degree day. The water had warmed into the low seventies, and a swim was just what the doctor ordered.

Rick, Doug, Jeff, and I were the first ones in the water. Lori and Chari followed shortly after that. Lynnette stood at the water's edge, not wanting to get her very long blond hair wet. Maura and Cindy finally waded in with Kris close behind.

I loved the water and swam with everyone some one hundred yards or so offshore. Laughter filled the air, as we turned summersaults underwater, splashed around, and reveled without a care in the world. Classes, tests, and books were the furthest thing from anyone's mind as we treaded water in a circle of good friends.

After thirty minutes, some of the group started back to shore, and the group migrated back together, except for me. "Rick, I'm going to stay out a little longer and enjoy some solitude in the water," I told my good friend Rick Karpel.

As everyone went in, I just idly continued to tread water, occasionally going below the surface to immerse myself in this aquatic playground. I was trying to take in the beauty into my soul—something I didn't really know how to do as an eighteen-year-old. I'd look at the sun and then the water around me and, in the distance, my friends climbing out of the lake.

I was now ready to go in and slowly did a breaststroke with my head above the water. Without warning, just ten yards in front of me, rising up out of the tranquility of the calm surface was the head of a large snake. Looking right at me and me at him, we both were motionless for a moment.

My pulse rapidly increased as I slowly moved to my left. As I glided through the water left, so did the snake. Conceding the left position to the snake, I moved to the right, which the snake did too. I considered yelling out to my friends, but I was too far to be heard. And what could they do? No one had a boat. I went left again, and darn it all, so did this snake.

I thought to myself this was as bad as it could possibly be until the snake made his next move. He dropped his head and disappeared under the water, and I had no way to see which direction he was swimming. Petrified, I treaded water and gave a bit of a vigorous splash to the water immediately in front of me.

After a minute or two of this, which seemed like an eternity, I decided I had to swim in. So I very, very slowly began to swim forward. Each stroke preceded a hard push of water from my hands with a hard kick on the surface from my legs. I hoped the snake wanted nothing to do with me, and I wanted to be sure he knew exactly where I was so he would not accidentally bump into me.

I've never swum one hundred yards so slowly before or after, the entire time with my heart pounding so hard I could feel it in my throat. When I got close to shore, I could finally stand again and walked out of the water to join my friends who were playing Frisbee.

"Hey, Tom, can I give you a beer?" Doug shouted.

"Yes, that is a fine idea," I answered.

Madison

How I Got to Madison

My life often seems like a series of random events taking me to places never before considered. Skiing dominated my life as a teenager, and all decisions revolved around it. After taking a year off between high school and college to ski, I was now prepared to continue my education.

My great friend and gifted skier Jim Cameron was planning to transfer from a small Midwestern school to the University of Utah in Salt Lake, and I was going there with him. With acceptance letters in hand, we planned to live in a dorm together and ski, ski, and then ski some more. Sure, we'd have to take some classes, but we had a definite primary aim, and that was to ski.

In April of 1976, I returned from Colorado and a fantastic year of skiing without a penny to my name. My father had a significant business setback and told me he would not be able to provide any funds for my freshman year. Yikes! I had four months to work and save and then off to Utah. I had never been to Utah before, and somehow that seemed OK to me at the time.

But then Jim called me from Fulton, Missouri, and shared more bad news. He was not going to transfer but instead stay at Westminster College. Everything was falling apart. My interest in travel to Utah alone was at zero, and I was blaming everyone else for my situation. Asking Jim what I was supposed to do now, he recommended I apply to Southern Illinois University, a school I had never heard of before.

Aimlessly, I took Jim's recommendation, applied, and was accepted. My grades were weak in high school, and my test scores would have suggested I might not be able to fog a mirror. Still, I was accepted and decided that was where I would go.

I arrived with a chip on my shoulder and let everyone know it. My new friends in the dorm were all excited to be there, but I let them know I would be transferring to a better school. My goal was to seriously improve my grades and then head to either Notre Dame or Northwestern. Both schools' admissions offices had assured me that if my grades were a 3.0 at Southern, I would be accepted.

I made some great friends in Carbondale. Rick, Doug, and Jeff among them. Southern Illinois University was a party school and also a big illegal drug school. I had no interest in drugs but found I could not escape the influence and interest my friends had. Smoking pot was a multiple-times-a-day event. Before lunch, dinner, and at night, most everyone but me got high. To stay a part of the community, I became the guy who loaded the bong and cleaned out the seeds from the pot. I never took a hit and was not tempted. It was not my thing.

One day, I decided to blow away my friends. I took someone's pack of cigarettes and bummed one out secretly. Taking it apart, I hid the tobacco stash until the next premeal pot fest. Our room was full of the stoners that evening predinner, and I was loading up the bong. As everyone got high, I decided to pull my prank. No one could tell that I loaded the pipe with tobacco, but I then announced I too was going to get high. No one believed me as it had been months and months of me saying no.

I lit up the pipe and put my mouth to the bong and inhaled. Everyone watched in amazement, erupting in silly giggling of the stoned fools they were. I let them sit in their amusement for a few minutes and then broke the news. Much to their disappointment, I stayed pot free.

These were great friends, and they were not the degenerates I make them out to be. They just loved drugs and were wide-open to experimenting. One night, the campus was showing the Beatles bizarre movie titled *Magical Mystery Tour*. Eight of us decided to attend. Loving the music of the Beatles, it was an easy choice, but unbeknownst to me was a plan Bill arranged. Everyone but me would trip on LSD before the movie.

At this point, I was a bit jaded about the pot, but LSD was over-the-top. I learned of the plan the morning of the event and tried to convince some of my friends this was a terrible idea. I talked about chromosome damage they might be doing and birth defects they'd put upon their kids. I had no idea if any of this was right, but I did my best to sound convincing.

My efforts went for naught, and the seven of my buddies dropped acid in Bill's dorm room before we left for the movie. I remember Bill sharing how excited he was and that he would place the microdot in his eye as a way of getting it into his body. I shook my head in disbelief and knew my parents would be so disappointed to know the things my friends were doing.

We arrived at the campus theatre, and as the movie began, the LSD was taking its full effect on my friends. They were overwhelmed by the drug that they lost all sense of dignity and spoke out loud, making goofy comments about what they were seeing. Their drug-altered minds ruined the movie for me, and we all left well before it was over. Walking back to the dorm was a unique experience. Everyone knew who they were and that they were tripping, but coherence had abandoned them. Back at the dorm, I recall talking with Steve when he suddenly said, "Tom, your entire face just melted away." I had enough and went to find some friends in the dorm who were not strung out.

The next day at breakfast, they were recounting their wonderful night before on LSD. Bill smiled and said, "Tom, one day, I'm going to do you a favor and sneak some LSD in your food."

In the most severe and forceful tone, I replied, "Bill, if you ever do that, I promise that I will kill you. I mean it, Bill. Do you understand me?" Bill tried to explain that he was having fun with me, and I again reaffirmed that I meant it. His life would be over.

Bill never did, and I left Southern Illinois University with a good relationship with Bill and all my other friends. I knew I was never going back to school here. My grades came in with a 3.4, so I was confident I was heading to Northwestern or Notre Dame. The summer before, one of my work colleagues at the MidAmerica Commodity Exchange recommended I consider the University of Wisconsin in Madison. He went to school there and arranged for me to get an application.

I applied as a result but never took it seriously. To my shock and despite promises from the admission offices, both Notre Dame and Northwestern rejected me. I couldn't go back to Southern Illinois University because of the firm stand I had taken, so I would now be going to Madison. Again, I had never seen the school, but I spent so much time in the state of Wisconsin that I thought it would be OK.

In August of 1977, my parents and younger siblings drove me to Madison to begin the next chapter in higher education in my life. Here I met Ned Brickman and Jimmy Halpern who would be my closest friends those early years at Madison.

I had arrived in a different town for the third year in a row—Aspen, Carbondale, and now Madison. I was personally embarrassed at the way my life's track had played out, having as much direction as a corked bottle bobbing about the ocean. Well aware of this directionless feature in my life, I wanted to make a change but did not know what to do. It was at this point that I decided to major in history and political science, pointing my compass toward a future in Washington DC.

Backgammon

My father taught me to play backgammon in high school, and my love of numbers and odds made it a fascinating game for me. My parents gave me a beautiful cork-inlaid backgammon set for a birthday one year, which would be a source of diversion while in college.

Sophomore year, I met Ned Brickman. Ned and I hit it off immediately, loving sports, music, and backgammon. Like me, Ned had his own board, and we took turns playing games in his dorm room or mine. We played all the time, and I mean all the time. Twenty games a day was standard, and for a while, all spare time in the dorm was spent rolling the dice and moving the pieces around the board.

Playing so many games gave us a chance to mess around with crazy moves, pushing the limits of possibility as far as it could go. We also were so used to playing that the moves were made with lightning speed. After a while, we knew each other's game strategy so well we could almost make the moves for each other.

Every game consisted of rock music in the background. Whoever had home court picked the music from their album or tape collection. I learned a great deal from Ned about musical groups I had never heard of before and likewise shared with Ned my knowledge of rock and roll.

Backgammon fosters an environment to talk about the relevant topics of the day. Ned's father was a successful businessman in Milwaukee who was also quite conversant about politics and Israel. His knowledge rubbed off on his son, who imparted to me a point of view beyond the basics of the Middle East. These conversations would not have happened but for backgammon games, and I am grateful for my education on the side all while rolling dice.

Games were played with an open-door dorm room policy, so anyone on our hall could wander in and watch. Many did, which brought with it questions and comments. One game, some three to four people were hanging around watching the game. Ned hit an open man, putting me on the bar. Ned's board was strong, and so only the two and four points were open. As I got ready to roll, Doug said to everyone, "Oh, twos and fours are easy to get."

Well, this comment stopped the play as Ned and I were equally appalled and curious. I asked Doug, "Easier than ones, threes, fives, or sixes?" To which Doug said yes. Ned quickly asked Doug if he would play for money, which got a laugh but only from Ned and me. We looked at each other and realized no one else understood probability, which was so basic to each of us. Doug was a very bright guy, but when it came to odds, he didn't have a clue.

Side note: Five years later, both Ned and I were engaged to be married. Jenni and I traveled to Milwaukee for a formal party Ned's folks threw for Ned and Gayle. The guests were mostly the close friends of Ned's parents, so it was a party talking to people twenty-five to thirty years my senior. I left the crowded living room to find some elbow room where I saw a man sitting by himself. He was in a single chair in the foyer eating food he got from the buffet table.

Recognizing him, I stopped to talk and introduced myself. We shared some pleasantries regarding how we each knew the family and the state of the current weather when I decided it was time to shift the conversation to a mutual love this lone man and I shared: baseball. I told him a bit of my history as a fan and then asked him many questions, to which he gladly answered. This man, sitting by himself, was none other than the owner of the Milwaukee Brewers and future baseball commissioner Bud Selig.

Breaking Up a Fight

Langdon Street in Madison is where all the fraternities and sororities could be found, including mine. I was a Chi Phi.

When the Badgers had a home football game, large crowds flooded into Madison to celebrate not just the game but well into the night, and Langdon was the center of the activity. Alcohol flowed freely, and the percentage of people not under the influence was a minority by evening.

In September of 1978, I was walking down Langdon Street with a friend through large crowds of students on one of these nights when suddenly two guys were shouting quite aggressively at each other. The attention on the street was all drawn into this flurry of activity, including mine. The crowd formed a circle around these two who now had fists up ready to fight. The students were a mix of those just observing and others egging them on to fight.

I'm not sure what possessed me at the time, but I broke into the circle and began an oration that went something like this: "If Egypt and Israel can come together at Camp David and sign the peace accords* to not fight with each other anymore, can't we too as fellow students come together in peace and agree not to fight?" I then walked out of the circle as quickly as I walked in, not looking back. Walking with my friend who was stunned by what I just did, I asked him to tell me what was happening. I did not want to look but to keep a posture of "my work is done here." To both our amazement, the fight never happened, and the crowd dispersed. My friend asked me what I was thinking, and I had no answer but a big smile on my face.

Camp Randall and Badger Football

Football dominates the University of Wisconsin activities during the fall semester. The faithful followers of their beloved Badgers pack the stadium with the students occupying their section in the north end zone.

In the late seventies, the Badgers were not very good, typically losing a few more games each year than they would win. The fans, however, never left the game early, instead waiting for the fifth quarter when our incredible marching band would take the field for a celebratory show win or lose. For many, this was the best part of the game. The band would play crowd favorites, and the Budweiser song was the grand finale whipping the crowd into a frenzy.

On October 21, 1978, the number 9 Michigan Wolverines came to Camp Randall where 80,024 people filed in to see the game. My roommate Ned Brickman and I were in attendance, sitting just above the marching band seats in the student section.

Bloody Marys and screwdrivers filled the undergraduates during pregame warm-ups, which is a crazy way to start your morning. However, that was what the student body routinely did every football

---

*. September 17, 1978, the Camp David Accords were signed by Egyptian President Anwar Sadat and Israeli Prime Minister Menachem Begin.

game. There were also plenty of snuck-in libations to keep the blood alcohol level of the average scholar to a level of inebriation. In other words, the students were drunk.

Ned and I were there for all the fun but skipped the drinking part, so we were quite sober. Michigan dominated the game right from the get-go and went on the win 42–0. A complete humiliation for our team, but no matter. Our band was great, and everyone eagerly awaited the end of the game for the real fun to begin.

With just a few minutes left on the clock, the marching band vacated their seats and moved into the back of the end zone preparing for their postgame performance. With the score at 35–0, it seemed like the clock would just run out. Ned and I moved out of the crowded student section into the now wide-open seats from the departed band members. There we stood all alone waiting for the game to end when suddenly Michigan scored again.

The field crew tried to raise the net behind the goalpost used to secure the extra point kick from going into the stands. Their efforts failed as the marching band was obstructing the spot where the net rose up from the ground. The snap was made, the kick was up, and it was good, with the ball flying right into my hands.

I couldn't believe it! I had the extra-point ball, and it was mine. This football was going home with me. The crowd cheered as I raised the football, but immediately, a chant from the student section broke out. "Over…over…over" came the clarion call of instructions for me. Soon, the entire crowd of eighty thousand strong was shouting for me to toss the ball of our enemy's score out of the stadium. This sports tradition, to reject the souvenir of the visiting team's score, is common, but I had no plans to give this ball up.

I tucked the ball tight and shook my head to the crowd that no, I would not be throwing this ball out of the stadium. The chant continued, but now the drunken students were starting to move in toward me. The shouts demanded that I give up the ball, and the gap between me and these threatening fans was closing quickly.

Ned said, "Are you crazy? Throw the ball!" Again, I refused, but now I could see it was going to be a physical beating laid upon me, and I'd likely end up losing the ball. As the mob was within a few yards now, I whispered to myself, "Darn it all!" and turned and threw the ball up toward the top of Camp Randall. As the ball left my hands, the stadium erupted into cheers, and the threat to my well-being was over. I watched as the ball landed in the middle of the student section, where the next person continued the trajectory to the top. A few more throws and then the ball left the stadium.

The crowd went crazy. Meanwhile, the clock had run out, and the players left the field. Right on cue, the marching band began to play, and the party started. Yes, the Badgers lost, but everyone was having fun dancing and singing with the marching band.

My mind was still on my football. I knew that some lucky dude who was walking by the stadium watched the ball drop and picked it up. Somewhere some undeserving student was in possession of my ball.

However, at least I can say I was able to get everyone in the stadium to cheer for something I did.

Houseplants

In August of 1978, I drove to Madison to start my junior year at the University of Wisconsin. I had rented a three-bedroom apartment with my good friends Ned and Jimmy, and I was bringing up most of my stuff in my parents' station wagon, but I still needed to go back home for a second trip.

Upon unloading my gear, I headed over to the apartment of my friend Joel Fisch. Joel was two years behind me at New Trier and was starting his freshman year at Madison. I rode the elevator up and found Joel unpacking boxes with his roommate. Joel introduced me to Bob, whom I learned, like Joel and me, also went to New Trier High School.

Joel was an interesting guy. He was a gymnast in high school as was my girlfriend, and I got to know him through the gymnastics circle. Politics was an interest to Joel, and his persuasion was to the Democrat party while my ideology was firmly in the Conservative movement. This led to many theoretical discussions and debates about how to fix the world's problems. We shared a mutual interest in the well-being of Israel from both a Jewish and Christian point of view.

Joel, however, had an interest that was utterly foreign to me, and that was in houseplants. In Joel's apartment, he showed me his African violet and schefflera, which he had transported from home. How odd, I thought. I had never known anyone that had any knowledge, let alone interest, in plants other than my grandmother.

After an hour or so of visiting, I informed Joel and Bob that I was heading back to Chicago and would return the next day. This caught Bob's attention, asking me if I had room in my car for some stuff he needed to be picked up at his home in Winnetka. "Sure," I said. "I have a station wagon with plenty of room."

Bob gave me his address and said he had some plants in his backyard. Well now, this made sense why these two guys were roommates. Budding botanists must stick together, I figured.

I drove to my parents' home in Kenilworth and spent the night. In the morning, I packed up my remaining belongings before driving to Bob's parents' house. Bob had explained that his folks were out of town and no one would be home but to pull in the driveway and walk around back. I'd find the plants in the traditional orange-colored planters.

Bob's family lived in a substantial home on an acre of land. Pulling into the driveway, I felt a little awkward, not knowing this family. Even though Bob said no one was home, I thought I should ring the doorbell just to be sure. Doing so confirmed I was the only one there, and so I proceeded around the side of the house to the backyard to find the plants. Looking at the patio, I only found enormous stone planters that no one could lift. The backyard was large, and so I let my eyes wander to an overgrown section with lots of trees and bushes. There I could see the orange planters and headed in that direction.

Upon arrival, I discovered these were pot plants. Now it all made sense. Bob was a stoner, not a houseplant lover, and I had promised to bring these backs to Madison. Smoking pot was common among many of my friends and acquaintances, but I never indulged. It just didn't appeal to me, and the criminal element made it all the less attractive.

Foolishly, I started to carry the plants the long walk back to my car and loaded them in, believing I had to honor my commitment. These were big plants twenty-four to thirty-six inches high and took up a lot of room. Carrying two at a time, I had now placed about fourteen of these in the family station wagon when my imagination started wandering.

Here I was, a stranger to the neighborhood. The family was not home, and I was loading up my car with their possessions. I envisioned a neighbor calling the police to come and investigate. I could see the police asking me what I was doing with these, and my explanation would go something like this: "Hi, Officer. These are not my pot plants. They belong to a friend. I'm just loading them into my car to drive across the state line and deliver them, so you can see I'm completely innocent."

An image of me in jail popped in my head, and Bob would deny knowing me or anything about the plants. Finally, I awoke from the stupor of fulfilling a misguided promise and got angry. I unloaded the plants and carried them all back to where they originally were. Each step I took, my anger increased toward Bob. He had never told me they were pot plants, and my reputation and future were at risk.

I double-timed it, getting them all in the corner of the backyard, but I was not through. In my anger and self-righteous indignation, I began to tear the plants apart, being confident that each one would die. If the police showed up, it would be to discover me as an enemy to these plants.

I climbed back in my car and drove away at a reasonable pace, not wanting to draw any attention to me by people walking dogs or passing by. I now had a two-and-a-half-hour drive to Madison where the potential reality of getting caught sunk in. I was spared an awful fate. But how could I have been so foolish not to recognize this immediately? I was mad at myself too.

Upon my arrival in Madison, I went right to Joel's apartment and confronted Bob. His first sight of me brought a smile on his face, thinking his contraband had arrived, but quickly he knew this would not play out well. Shouting at Bob that he never told me they were pot plants, he nervously laughed, saying he thought I knew. When I told him I destroyed the plants, he was now angry, telling me I had no right to do so.

Who was this pompous jerk? I told him that he was inches away from me beating the crap out of him, and if he said another word about this ever, he would have more trouble than he could imagine. I stormed out and went back to my own rental house to settle down.

Over time, this story became a blend of humor and instruction. I can laugh about it today, including my own stupidity. The experience made me think about the choices I'd make in my life and potential consequences. I was fortunate not to have been caught at just the wrong time and hoped to share this experience with others to really think through decisions and actions before getting too far down the wrong road.

I first did so with a group of young boys at our church. They were sophomores in high school, and I shared the story with them. I believe the idea that an old guy like me was once young and had some of the same struggles and questions in life was meaningful. I wanted them to understand that sometimes in life, we need to anticipate problems before they arise. To create scenarios in their mind before they happened so they'd be better prepared when trouble came a-knockin'. I wanted my error in judgment to be a guide to them to think first and act second.

Mistaken Identity

In my sophomore year of college, I met a girl in my dorm named Teri, who was from Milwaukee. We hung out a bit and went on a few dates. After a few weeks, I was losing interest; however, she felt quite differently. Enough so that she was becoming a bit of a nuisance, continuing to pursue a relationship with me. I tried to be as nice as I could, but she had a hard time taking no for an answer.

Back at home, I had a friend from high school named Keri. She was a good friend and so much fun. We never dated but enjoyed each other's company. Keri went to college out east, and when she came home from college for Thanksgiving, she thought it would be fun to get a group together and go to a dance club.

Our family phone rang, and my younger brother Jeff answered it. "Tom, it's for you," he said.

I came into the kitchen and picked up the phone. "Hello," I said.

"Hi, Tom. It's Keri," said the cheerful voice. However, that was not what my ears heard. I was sure the caller identified herself as the girl from Madison named Teri.

"Oh, hi," I said in the most disinterested voice I could muster.

"How are you?" Keri asked.

"Fine," I said with a bit of annoyance in my voice.

"I thought it would be fun to get together," Keri said with her usual cheery voice, not realizing I was thinking I was talking to someone else.

"Where are you?" I asked.

"Here in Chicago," Keri said.

"What! You're here?" I said now with anger in my voice. I thought to myself, *Why has Teri driven down from Madison or her hometown of Milwaukee to Chicago? And now she's calling me. This has got to stop.*

"Look," I started. "I don't know why you're calling me. I did my best to tell you nicely, but you won't listen. I don't want to spend time with you. I don't like you. Please respect me and leave me alone," I said in a firm and direct tone.

Starting to cry, Keri asked me what was wrong. What had she done?

"Look, Teri," I loudly said, which immediately triggered an interruption from Keri.

"Tom, this is Keri. It's Keri. It's Keri," she just kept saying over and over.

Hearing this correction, I immediately started, "Oh, Keri. Oh, Keri. I'm so sorry. Please forgive me. I thought you were someone else. Yes, yes, I'd love to see you. Tonight. Let's get together."

Her sobs were now diminishing to sniffles of communication telling me she was OK and we'd meet that night at a common hangout place. When we saw each other later that night, I gave her a big hug and asked for her to please forgive me for my case of mistaken identity.

She now still likes to whisper to me, "Hi, Tom. It's Teri," whenever we see each other.

Ice-skating

I love to ice-skate. As a child, I built an ice-skating rink in our family backyard every year from sixth grade through my third year in high school. Friends would come over, and we'd skate, play hockey, and hang out.

In college, the best rinks ever were in Madison. There were several large frozen ponds maintained by the city. These were ten to fifteen acres in size and included hockey rinks. Rob Maine, Chuck Trotter, and I would often go out to these rinks for pickup hockey games or to skate around.

The rinks were well maintained, allowing large groups of people to enjoy the outdoor activity. People sometimes think cold weather forces one inside to avoid the elements, but in Madison, we embraced the cold and continued our lives.

Ice-skating is a remarkable sport and a joy to partake. Whether the graceful moves of a figure skater or the power and agility of a hockey player, the movement on the ice is truly unique. What other sport can you move backward at top speed and then, with a blade angle adjustment, redirect your motion in the opposite direction, carrying your speed the entire time? None that I know.

In my senior year of college, I returned from the semester break to have an unusually warm spell where several inches of rain fell on the two feet thick ice of Lake Mendota. This was followed by a fast-moving Alberta clipper where the temperature dropped to twenty below zero. This quick change froze the rainwater into a glass-smooth layer of ice across the entire lake.

A few of us took this unique opportunity to lace up our skates on the large lake and begin to skate in a long-distance run. From my fraternity house on Langdon, I was able to skate all the way to Picnic Point, some two miles in the same direction without crossing a blade track. Amazing!

The ice was several feet thick, so it was very safe, but my memory of breaking through on the golf course pond nine years prior had me a little spooked. The ice would make deep and loud noises as I traversed my path, occasionally shooting out lightning-shaped cracks to my right and left. The ice also had a combination of clearness and darkness. This was because below the ice was the darkness of the lake water while the ice from the fast freeze had a level of clarity, and so these cracks caused by my weight would shoot out a white contrast.

Rob Maine and Chuck Trotter, ready for some pond hockey

I had never experienced such a time before or since. This open window would soon close with the January snows covering the lake, taking away this opportunity. At the time, I didn't know how unique it would be, and I'm so delighted to have taken the time to enjoy this. In life, all too often now is the appointed time to partake, and to miss the chance is to have it gone forever.

Out on the ice was an odd structure too. We had two leftover hippies run for student government and win. They decided to do fun things with the money appropriated for student events. They built a papier-mâché but weather-protected Statue of Liberty à la the final scene of *Planet of the Apes*.

While I loved to skate and play hockey, I had only played pickup pond hockey. Never league hockey. I was a good skater and a pesky hockey player type that loved to go after the puck. My fraternity decided we should form a hockey team for the intramural university league, and I was ready to play.

Pat Corrigan and Tom Terrill on Lake Mendota, February, 1980

Ice time was terrible, and so our first game started at 11:00 PM. We were a ragtag group with about five guys who played hockey for their high school team. Chris was our team captain, and he coached me on some plays and formation, but mostly, I was a free spirit that went wherever I wanted. This didn't help our team as hockey requires functioning as a unit, but I had my moments of contribution.

In our second game, I was sitting next to Chris after a line change. I was curious about something and asked Chris if he was wearing a cup.

He sharply turned his head and said to me, "Are you not wearing a cup?"

"No," I said.

"That's it. You're done for the day."

I didn't argue the point, but I had not worn a cup in years and never for pond hockey. I had a helmet, mouth guard, and shin guards, which seemed like enough protection. After the game, Chris told me what a dumb move this was, and I would not play until I bought a cup. I took care of this the next day and assured Chris I was now ready. Still, I felt he was a little too cautious but respected his position as our team captain.

I was on the second line, and so the game started with me on the bench, but soon we'd switch, and I'd be out on the ice. Scott skated over needing rest, and I climbed over the boards onto the ice. I took just two strides when someone took a slap shot to clear the puck. It headed right for me and struck me squarely…in the cup!

The pain was intense. Bending at the waist, I set a glide path for our bench. Unable to physically function from the pain, I hit the boards and flipped over into my teammates. I struggled out the words, "Somebody, go in for me."

This direct hit was powerful and really threw me for a loop. I took the entire rest of the period off just recovering from the blow. I can't imagine what the result would have been without a cup, but I think I'd likely be singing soprano in our church choir.

We finished off our season as an average team. My league hockey days were through, and I went back to pond hockey. The next time I wore the cup was playing paintball ten years later. No direct hits there, but I was ready this time.

The Tollbooth

Growing up in Kenilworth, my family moved five different times but never left this small little town. In junior high, we moved to a house that was almost on the border of neighboring Wilmette. Just two homes separated us from the first home in Wilmette where the Kerns family lived.

Mike Kerns was my age, but as we didn't go to the same school, we were more or less neighborhood acquaintances. When I changed schools to Madison, I pledged to the Chi Phi Fraternity, where Mike was already a member. Mike's younger sister Lisa too attended the university, and the three of us often drove back home in the Kerns family VW bug.

This old classic vehicle had the appearance of a fun car to ride in. On the first of many three-hour trips, Lisa told me I could sit in the front passenger seat while Mike drove. I thought this was so thoughtful of her, and I accepted the offer. Soon, however, I discovered that no matter what the weather, this car sent a constant flow of heat into the floor space of the front passenger seat. It was unbearably hot, but it had now become my official seat. There was no air conditioner in the car, and a cracked window only gave nominal relief.

We always drove from Madison on Interstate 94 to Milwaukee and then turned south toward Chicago. Upon crossing into Illinois, we jumped on the Illinois Tollway. Almost immediately was the Rosecrans tollbooth, which at the time required a fifty-cent payment. Of some eight toll lanes, three were manned, in case you needed to make change, but the other five were automatic with a large catch basket in which to toss one's two quarters.

We made this journey many times over several years when a most unusual occurrence took place. Mike drove up to the automatic lane and stopped.

"What? Take a look at this," Mike directed Lisa and me.

Glancing where Mike was pointing, we saw the very large catch basket full of money. Massive amounts of change were packed into this basket that must have been three feet wide and a foot deep. For some ten seconds, we just stared at it, when suddenly Mike reached in his large hand grabbing as much money as he could. Throwing it in my lap, he hit the gas and drove off while we all shrieked with a blend of laughter and confusion.

The craziest part was that in addition to quarters, nickels, and dimes, there were dollar bills sticking out. In fact, the pile of loot that Mike snatched included a dollar bill and some ten dollars plus in change.

We all shared our theories as to why this oddity existed. I was sure it was a setup. It was either the TV show *Candid Camera* to see what people would do in such a circumstance or the police had set up a sting operation and we'd be arrested soon. This was my conclusion. Mike just laughed. He was confident that someone had purposely thrown in a rag to clog the machine and create a backup that would later be gathered as stolen money.

Whatever it was, I was confident we'd be pulled over by the Illinois State Troopers soon enough. But to my relief, no sirens or flashing red lights came our way, and we peacefully drove back to our homes.

An Internship

During my senior year in college, I began seeking in earnest a congressional internship. I typed out some 130 letters to various representatives and senators from multiple states and districts hoping to get an offer. These positions were nonpaid, so I'd have to have some money saved for living expenses and ideally find a cheap place to stay.

The response letters started to arrive, telling me that although I had an impressive résumé, they would not be able to bring me on board. The most exciting part of my résumé was a political reference I had of Don Rumsfeld. Secretary Rumsfeld was a high school friend of my parents and had met with me when he was CEO of GD Searle. I had sought his guidance for my political future and received some excellent advice.

After countless rejections, I opened a letter from Congressman Phil Crane of Illinois. I was extended an offer, to my great delight, and all I had to was accept it. I did so immediately and made my plans to head to Washington DC.

A grade school friend of my older sister lived and worked in Washington, and so I contacted her. She had a friend who lived in Arlington, Virginia, and had a basement room I could rent for a very nominal monthly fee. I moved in with Pedro in early May immediately after my graduation and began my work for Congressman Crane.

The work was overly simplistic. Initially, this was work that could be handled by a high school student, which discouraged me. I was opening the mail and sending back response letters to the constituents who wrote in. These letters were drafted in advance for every conceivable topic with a blank for the name and address. More than a bit disillusioned, I took these letters to the signing machine where I would insert a felt pen into the machine to sign the Congressman's name. There was no tally of the letters or their concerns. As far as I could tell, no one cared, and a simple message was sent back, suggesting that the congressman cared about the issue. Just a letter sent in reply, suggesting that someone cared, which was a complete lie as far as I could tell.

I learned that congressmen don't need stamps. If they sign their name where a stamp ordinarily goes, the mail will get delivered at no charge. A large stock of envelopes with a signature already affixed was available for the letters I was in charge of sending back. Bored with this daily routine, I decided to have some fun. I took a blank piece of the congressional stationery and inserted it into the IBM Selectric typewriter and began to type.

My first self-written letter was to my friend John Thompson. In it, the congressman expressed his admiration for my friend for his ability to consume large quantities of beer at frat parties. Several paragraphs of superlatives and inane comments later, I'd march off to the signature room. Signing the letter without much thought of how much trouble I would be in if caught, I'd lick the envelope shut and put the letter in the middle of the dozens of appropriate response letters I had already completed. I knew John would appreciate this, and the two of us would have a good laugh.

In the ensuing days, I sent similar-style letters to my friends Chuck and Brian, now no longer bored but excited about the humor they would find in these fake letters. My friends thought they were hilarious, and it fit the cavalier attitude we tried to display as twenty-one-year-olds.

Eventually, I was given some additional responsibility and was asked to research and write a piece for Congressman Crane to speak on the House floor on airline deregulation. In 1978, the airline industry had been federally deregulated, and my boss wanted a report on the result two years later.

Curiously, I never met my boss, Congressman Crane, which surprised me. He just was not in his office during the weeks I was in Washington.

In 1980, the congressional offices were not air-conditioned, causing the inside temperatures to rise quickly. Wearing a long-sleeved shirt and tie every day fostered an environment of sweat and discomfort.

One day about 9:30 AM, I was sitting at my desk working on a project. I got a whiff of an unpleasant odor and glanced around at my nearby co-workers. Someone had a developing case of body odor. I tried to guess who it might be when I thought I should clear myself and took a smell of my right armpit. It was fine. Then to the left where I discovered the source of the smell. It was me!

Somehow, I must have failed to get a good swipe of my Mennen Speed Stick that morning and now needed a quick remedy. I knew the temperature was rising and the day was still early. Getting up, I wandered down the hall to the men's room where I removed my shirt and tie using some soap and water to address the problem. Getting dressed, I returned to the office and began my work again. However, the lack of cool temperature made my armpit like a petri dish running out of control with bacteria. Within thirty minutes, the problem was back, and I needed a better solution.

A bad habit I had was to carry an empty wallet. That morning, I had no money and didn't have a credit card to my name. Most of the time, I was able to live my life just fine this way, but today, it created a problem.

Asking if I could take a break to go for a short walk, I left heading for a drugstore. Having no money, I formulated a plan justified by the need of the moment. Entering the Rexall Drugstore, I found an aisle with deodorant. I had a shirt button undone, hidden by my tie. Grabbing a can of Rite Guard,

I glanced to my right and left to see if anyone could see me. The coast was clear, and so I shook the can and placed it through the unbuttoned opening and sprayed the previously unprotected armpit.

I then took the can, popped the top back on, and placed it back on the shelf. I walked out of the store not being noticed for my purloined single spray and headed back to work. The problem was solved, and I was lucky enough not to be caught.

My housing situation changed when Pedro's job ended, and he moved back to Texas. Having no money and desperate, I contacted my sister's grade school friend to see if I could live in their basement for a week while I searched for an alternative place to live. They invited me on a Wednesday and said I could stay for the remaining six weeks of my internship. Relieved, I moved my few possessions the three blocks into their townhouse basement. Two girls shared this home, and I was so appreciative that I wanted to find a way to thank them properly.

That first weekend, both girls went out of town on Friday night, leaving me alone in the house. I decided I could do a thorough cleaning of the house, which was a bit of a pigsty. I vacuumed, dusted, and organized the living room and kitchen really well, but my masterpiece was still incomplete. The refrigerator was the most disgusting I'd ever seen. It was full of leftover Chinese food where the contents had gone bad with a hairlike growth covering the old rice. The milk was spoiled, having gone sour; and covered in mold were various cheeses. I removed the entire contents of the fridge, throwing away anything that smelled bad.

I then wiped down the inside where ketchup splatters and spilled wine had made the shelves sticky. Hours of work produced a sparkling clean refrigerator with only 10 percent of the contents retained.

Saturday night, the girls arrived home, and I was excited to hear the thanks I would get for this noteworthy cleanup. Surely, I had earned my way into their hearts, and my freeloading would seem small compared to the work I had undertaken.

I was in the basement reading when I heard them come in. I decided to wait to listen to the shrieks of joy before coming upstairs, but to my surprise, none came. Instead, about ten minutes later, one of the girls called me upstairs in a stern tone. She stood with the fridge door open and asked me where her scallops were. I was perplexed why no one commented on the fantastic and thorough cleanup and replied that I didn't know what scallops were, let alone where they were.

She whined that she had just bought those on Thursday and was going to cook them tonight. Explaining that I threw away anything that had mold or smelled terrible, they must be in the dumpster outside and that I was sorry. She stormed out, mumbling under her breath.

Confused, I went back to the basement. How was it they didn't notice the immaculate house and the transformed icebox? I spent the rest of the evening in the cellar, waking up the next morning to a summoning of my presence by my sister's friend. Hustling upstairs, I asked what was up. She told me that I'd have to move out as this was not working.

"OK. When do you want me to leave?" I asked.

"Within the hour" came the unsympathetic response.

Barely able to think, I asked if she could give me a ride to the airport, to which she said if I'd be ready to leave in thirty minutes. Flying downstairs, I threw my belongings in my suitcase and ran upstairs. I had an open airline ticket to return to Chicago and thought I'd try to fly home. Summarily dropped off at the airport, I watched as the girls sped away, never to be seen again. Fortunately, I was able to board a flight that left in an hour now on my way back to Chicago.

I called my cousin Kurt back in Kenilworth to see if he could pick me up at O'Hare, hanging up with just enough time to catch my flight.

To my parents' shock, I walked into the house early afternoon that same Sunday. Monday morning, I called into work to explain I wouldn't be in that day or any day after that. Embarrassed, I apologized for such short notice and was relieved to be forgiven by the person in charge of the interns.

I redirected my sights on a job in Chicago, ending my political career.

New Shoes

Now home from Washington DC, I was interviewing for a job in Chicago. My interest was with investment banks, where I hoped to line up a position as a stockbroker. The proper attire of the time was a three-piece suit, an impeccably tied tie, and black wing tips for shoes.

A trip with my father to Johnston & Murphy made sure I selected the right shoes. Dressed for success, I rode the train downtown for three scheduled interviews. As I traversed through the streets of Chicago's Loop from one appointment to another, I found the unbroken-in leather irritating my tender feet. Upon completion of the third interview, my feet were killing me from the blisters caused by these hard leather shoes.

I was struggling to walk the five blocks back to the train station as I passed the Sears Tower. Unable to go any farther, I took my shoes and socks off, rolled up my pants, and walked barefoot back to the train. Oh, the looks I got from people passing by. Fortunately, I saw no one I knew in this embarrassing but necessary situation.

As I climbed into the train, the conductor told me I'd have to put my shoes on. I showed him the blisters under my ankles, to which he let me pass and asked me to do my best to hide this fact. I got back to my hometown of Kenilworth and continued barefoot the two blocks to my parents' house.

Ever since then, I am careful to break in any new footwear before venturing outside.

Wolf River

Just north of Keshena in the Menominee Indian Reservation, the Wolf River flows with an evenly dispersed pattern of rapids and calm water. People from the area have taken rafts, kayaks, and inner tubes down these waters for decades.

The Troop 13 Boy Scouts from Kenilworth, Illinois, made an annual pilgrimage the first weekend in June to camp out and run the rapids in truck-tire-sized inner tubes. Led by my uncle Lee Getschow and his faithful scout leaders Charlie Barnes and Art Bergman, some fifteen to twenty-five high-school-aged boys were preparing for an adventure of a lifetime. At least in their young lifetimes.

Lee was famous for having special friendships wherever he went. I never knew how, but he had a unique arrangement with the Menominee Indians, allowing us to camp out right along the river on the reservation. Non-Indians were never permitted on this private government-sanctioned land without permission, and permission was given to no one. No one except my uncle and his Boy Scouts.

For most boys, scouting ends with the eighth grade, but if one elected to continue with scouting in high school, the benefits were enormous. Trips like this one were only for the "senior scouts."

We assembled the tents, dug a firepit, and laid out the food when we arrived at the campsite. Mosquitoes were everywhere in these deep woods, and insect repellant was a necessity. Not just for the mosquitoes but also to minimize the wood ticks. Blue jeans, a long-sleeved shirt, and a hat were a given unless you wanted to be the blood donor to these thirsty insects. I recall one year deciding to count the wood ticks that I would pick off my body during the day. When I hit twenty-five after only ninety minutes, I gave up counting.

My friends and I loved this rafting trip, and every year, we continued to make the trip. Brian Avery, Jeff Nielsen, and I would drive up to meet Kurt who lived in Green Bay.

In his sixties, my uncle became very ill with cardiac myopathy resulting in a heart transplant. When it came time for his first trip after the operation, I arranged for a large group of our friends to come as a surprise to both our friend Kurt and his father, Lee. Along with Jeff and Brian, I was able to get Jeff Kopp, Jeff Wilder, Peter Moles, Colin Ambrose, and Greg Stuhr. The nine of us came for a reunion trip with one another and to express our appreciation to Lee for his years of leadership in scouting.

Greg Stuhr testing the waters at Duckness

Wet suits are essential this time of year as the water is cold, and in the inner tube, you will get wet for sure. This year, the water was running at record levels resulting in some of the rapids being at dangerous levels. With extra caution, we ventured out on the first set of rapids, which generally are quite tame. This year, the additional water volume made them all the more exciting, which got everyone pumped up.

Our system was to "run the rapids," climb out of the river, and jog back up on land to do it all over again. Each set of rapids would be run three to five times before moving down the river in a truck to the next set. This was an active trip, and so the slow float between rapids would be avoided.

Down the river we went, arriving at my favorite rapids named Duckness. Here we leaped in feet first with just our Converse gym shoes and wet suit to protect us against the rocks. One would stand on a rock ledge and then leap out into the white water, which would quickly carry you down the river. The turbulent water was so much fun to travel through sliding some seventy-five yards to the calm water below. There we'd sprint back up the trail alongside the river to leap in again. Duckness gave us all such a thrill that leaves an impression of a lifetime.

Moving down the river, this time with our tubes, through the calm water we'd float through the Dells of the Wolf River where the cliffs climbed up sixty feet along the water's edge. This narrow chute provided fast-moving water with a broad and deep pool at the end. At this point, we'd pull over on the eastern side of the river and climb up the cliff. A path could be followed to store your tube and walk out to the edge of the cliff.

Now was the time for bravery. One could jump off a low spot of only ten feet or so. Nothing more than high-dive height in a community swimming pool. But there were two more launching points— one of about twenty-five feet and another close to fifty feet from the river below.

The high school boys were all very excited and took their cue from our group of veterans. Kurt quickly went toward the fifty-foot ledge while Jeff Nielsen warmed up with a leap from the twenty-five-foot level. Brian Avery stepped out onto the ledge after Jeff and did a beautiful swan dive into the water. Brian was a high school trampolinist who felt at home, flying through the air. Kurt and I looked at each other from our respective perches and jumped at the same time.

Lines quickly formed from each level, but with most kids opting for the twenty-five-foot jump. I was old enough that I didn't have anything to prove, and so I stuck with my comfort level at the twenty-five-

Tom Terrill and a senior scout taking the plunge

foot drop. After my third jump, I noticed two freshmen who were now dry. Clearly, they were not comfortable with this leap and were nervously watching everyone else, hoping no one would notice they had not jumped.

Peer pressure gets people to do stupid things. Almost all my poor decisions in life were ones I would not have made if I was alone. That said, peer pressure can also help encourage one to push a bit beyond their comfort zone, and this is a positive result.

I walked over to the two boys and asked if they wanted to jump. Nervously, they both said yes, but I could tell they were afraid. Telling the boys they did not have to jump but that if they did it just once, they would always have that experience. I was confident they would not be injured and that this would help each of them in confronting more significant obstacles later in life.

They walked with me to the twenty-five-foot jump and hung out at the end of the line. With an upfront view, they could see boy after boy making the leap. I was verbally encouraging them without trying to push too hard. Each of them got to the front of the line and leaped. I recall the first boy when he came up from below the water surface with a huge smile on his face and his shout of affirmation to his friend who then took off into the air.

This brief moment in time was my opportunity to influence these boys to grow. Just like water and fertilizer for a plant, boys need the right ingredients sometimes to become the man they are on the inside.

We continued our adventure down the Wolf River finishing at Big Eddie's rapids. Everyone loaded up into the vehicles, and we headed back to the campsite. We took off our wet suits after a long day and started a fire to cook dinner a bit later. My friends and I, however, had decided not to spend the night again camping and to drive back to Green Bay to hang out at Kurt's house.

Just an hour away, Kurt had a large home with plenty of bedrooms for our group. His wife and kids had gone on their own weekend getaway, leaving us for a boys' night to end our weekend.

Kurt had ordered a stretch limousine to pick us up and take us to dinner and then out to the various bars in Green Bay. This way we'd not have to worry if anyone had too much to drink and safely drive a car. For me, this was not a concern as I had long ago given up any alcohol, but still, it made the parking and travel quite easy.

When friends who have not seen one another in a while get together, they often revert back to the behavior of the past. Retelling stories of the earlier triumphs in life, we were all trending in this direction as the evening progressed. We went out for a nice steak dinner and a few beers. From there we move on to a sports bar to socialize, watch some games on TV, and drink a bit more beer. Sometime around 10:00 PM, I was now tired and ready to go back home. Brian and Greg agreed, and we told everyone we would take the limo back home and then send it back for the rest of the group.

Happily, the three of us got back to Kurt's and climbed into bed. At midnight, I was woken up by Colin Ambrose, who asked me to come downstairs to see if Jeff Nielsen needed to go to the hospital or not. Confused, I threw on a shirt and walked downstairs to find Jeff's head in the kitchen sink and Kurt with the sink's faucet sprayer flooding Jeff's head with water.

I see Jeff had a large gash in the top of his skull, and immediately I said, "Yes! Jeff must go to the ER as that will require a lot of stitches." Both Kurt and Jeff didn't want to go, however, and I kept asking them why.

While the limo was driving the three of us home, everyone else came outside some twenty minutes later ready to leave, but the limousine was not back. That was when a gang of some fifteen motorcycles pulled in the parking lot. Kurt was a good street fighter. He was the Chicago Golden Gloves boxing champion at age seventeen beating out young men in their twenties. Here we went reverting back to younger days.

Kurt walked up to the leader of this gang and started verbally insulting him, trying to pick a fight. It did not take long before Kurt and the gang leader were throwing fisticuffs back and forth, eliciting everyone else to join in. Jeff Nielsen and Jeff Wilder dove into the action too as a full brawl was breaking out.

Jeff took a hard right to the jaw, knocking him backward onto the ground where his head met directly with a concrete parking block. Right then the limo pulled into the parking lot where the boys all scurried in, shouting for the driver to hit the gas. Tires were screeching out onto the street as everyone was whisked away safely. As they pulled away, a dozen police cars came screaming into the area to arrest those involved.

Kurt and Jeff were sure if they showed up at the ER, the police would arrive too with some silver bracelets for the boys to try on. Being arrested was not on the weekend agenda; however, I was concerned about Jeff's health. Eventually, they agreed to go to the ER, where Jeff received many dozens of stitches. Told not to go to sleep that night in case of swelling or a concussion, Jeff stayed up while I went to bed myself. Jeff would fully recover, and no one got arrested.

The next morning, I came downstairs and read the paper while eating breakfast. I read an article about the new movie called *Apollo 13*. The woman reviewing the film shared how she had been on the movie set and confessed she felt more interested in meeting Tom Hanks who played the leading role than Jim Lovell, the astronaut whose story was told. I thought to myself, *How shallow. Meet the real person or the one portraying him? If given a chance, I'd meet Jim Lovell.*

Guest Speaker

In the early nineties, I joined the local Rotary Club, where I was able to meet other businessmen and businesswomen in my community. Rotary is a service club which requires the highest standards of moral and ethical conduct from its members. Each week, an invited speaker would attend to present some interesting topic. The members invited these speakers, and everyone needed to take a turn to bring someone.

It is challenging to get interesting speakers, and often these are at the level of the local dog catcher or county recorder. My aim was to bring the most captivating speakers, and my first one would be a layup.

Charlie Trotter's was the best restaurant in Chicago. Honestly, it was the best restaurant in the United States at that time, and Charlie (Chuck) was one of my closest friends. He came to our Rotary luncheon and blew everyone away. His notoriety was epic then, and we had to move our lunch into a large hall for the many additional guests. My first speaker was the best in years, and I felt quite pleased.

However, now the bar was set so high, and I was not sure how to top it. I made a list of famous people that I thought I might somehow get to come and speak, and Jim Lovell was on that list. Captain Lovell was the commander of the Apollo 13 mission that captivated the nation and the world when a malfunction in space risked their safe return. I knew the Lovells lived in neighboring Lake Forest, but I had no connection at all. Still, I set my sights on Jim Lovell, and I had a year to get him.

Jim Lovell maintained a local business office in his home, and I was able to track down a phone number. Nervously, I dialed his number from my office, trying to think what to say. His secretary answered the phone, appropriately screening all calls. She told me that he was out of town for several weeks, and she asked how she could help me. I explained that I was hoping he would be a Rotary Club speaker for me in about nine months. Name-dropping, I mentioned that Charlie Trotter had just been my guest and how Jim Lovell would do a great job. With a polite tone, she conveyed to me that this was extremely unlikely, but I could call next week and that she would ask him.

As a child, I loved watching the Apollo launches and splashdowns on TV. I recall being both fascinated and worried about Apollo 13 with their unfortunate mechanical problems. As an adult, I purchased the hardcover book and familiarized myself with all the details of this historic moment in our country's space program. This was a fantastic story that would be a delight to hear in person.

The next week, I called back and got the answering machine. I dutifully left a message and hoped for a return call. No call came, and I waited another week to call again, this time reaching his secretary. She explained that she had not been able to ask him yet, but I should call next week. This went on for five months where every Tuesday afternoon I would call to either be told to try again next week or to leave a message never to be returned.

I got so used to getting nowhere that my nervousness was long gone, and the calls were routine. One Tuesday at 4:50 PM, I was ready to go home from work and started to pack up my things. I reached for the phone and absentmindedly called the number expecting an answering machine at this hour.

As I held the phone to my head, suddenly it was answered, and I heard a man's voice say, "Jim Lovell." I panicked and quickly blurted out, "Commander Lovell, my name is Tom Terrill, and I wanted to catch your secretary."

"She's not in. Can I help you?" he replied.

"Oh yes, well, I…uh…you see…I was, uh, hoping you might be willing to be my guest speaker at the local Rotary Club luncheon."

"Well, I don't really do that sort of thing. And do you think anyone would be interested?"

"Yes, people will be extremely interested. I had Charlie Trotter speak [name-dropping again] a few months back, and I think you would be as interesting as he was."

"Well, OK. If we can schedule it, call my secretary tomorrow, and she can set it up."

"Thank you, Commander Lovell. I really appreciate it."

We hung up the phone, and I was doing a jig in my office to celebrate. I can't say for sure, but as I walked out of my office to my car, I think my feet were hovering about twelve inches above the ground.

The next day, I called back to get this scheduled. Speaking to his secretary, we set a date for three months later, which would be perfect timing. I did, however, have a question, and I told her that I was not sure how to properly address him. I explained that I called him Commander Lovell, and was that OK?

She then said to me, "The people that were on the Apollo mission with him can call him Commander Lovell. Were you on the Apollo mission with him?"

"Uh, no."

"Then you call him Captain Lovell."

"OK," I said, somewhat embarrassed.

We set the date, and I was thrilled. My father-in-law was in the navy during World War II. Joseph Winslow Baer was a blimp pilot that escorted ships out to sea, looking to see if any German U-boats were in the area. I invited both my wife Jenni and her father Joe Baer to be my guests at the head table with Captain Lovell.

A week before, I was invited over to Captain Lovell's home to discuss the upcoming event and make sure all arrangements were in order. While I was a bit starstruck, I was still able to carry on a coherent conversation and enjoyed my one-on-one time with him.

The Rotary luncheon set a club record for attendance that day, and we needed to have two adjoining rooms merged into one large banquet hall. It was my job to introduce a guest that needed no introduction. Still, I knew precisely what I would say.

I went back to that Sunday morning in Green Bay when I read the newspaper account about the movie critic more excited to meet Tom Hanks. Sharing with everyone what a treat we had to meet the real person Captain Jim Lovell rather than the actor who played him on TV. Thunderous applause welcomed Captain Lovell that day, and he delivered a marvelous speech. Afterward, everyone wanted to come and shake his hand and extend their appreciation for his service to our country. Humbly, he downplayed his part, and eventually the event ended.

Some twenty years have passed since then, and I often see Captain Lovell walking his dog near the Lake Forest Beach. I ride my bike there in the morning and will give him a shout-out, saying, "Good morning, Captain Lovell," as I passed by. He kindly gave a wave and a hello to me, not knowing how much I appreciated his generosity to me back then and enjoy how this story played out for me.

Charlie Trotter's

While the restaurant Charlie Trotter's was world-renowned and its celebrated chef-owner changed the world of fine dining forever, for me, it was simply the place I could go to see my friend Chuck and enjoy time with him.

Chuck thrived on entertaining, and food was a conventional means for him to do so. In high school and college, he'd host dinner parties for friends where he did all the cooking. All of it. I did not attend the first few events, and when I did finally arrive, the meal served was an Israeli peasant dish, as Chuck described it. Who thinks like that? Well, Chuck, of course.

John Thompson, Jenni Terrill, Chuck Trotter, Janet Avery, and Brian Avery

When he opened the restaurant, he had various ideas for the name, including "Zelda" after F. Scott Fitzgerald's wife. Settling on his own name was the right choice as his name did epitomize food and wine and a complete fun-filled dining experience.

I met him in high school when he was a punk freshman. Brian Avery was the best trampolinist in the state of Illinois, and Chuck was up-and-coming in gymnastics. Leaving school one day, Chuck came up to Brian and said, "So, Avery, you think you're pretty good on the tramp, huh?" Brian just shook his head, saying nothing.

"Who is that?" I asked Brian with a tone of disgust.

"Trotter," he began. "Ignore him. He's nothing." And Brian was right at the time. He was nothing to a couple of sophomore boys.

Time passed and people changed, and in that process, he became one of my closest friends. His parents always called him Charlie as did his co-workers and people who met him after he opened his business. Many childhood friends also switched to calling him Charlie later in life, but for me, he is forever my friend Chuck.

The Dessert Wave

Everyone who went to Charlie Trotter's for dinner felt special. In delivering a unique experience to each person, Chuck was able to penetrate his guests' emotions, leaving them overwhelmed with joy. In the first year or two, Jenni and I came to the restaurant every three months, and on our fourth trip to the city, we witnessed three memorable occurrences. It was July 30, Jenni's birthday, and we were coming downtown to spend the night after dinner.

Chuck's first wife Lisa was the hostess on this Friday evening, and we were dining upstairs at a table overlooking the bar area below us. In the early days of Charlie Trotter's, one ordered off the menu. As we opened ours that evening, it said right across the top:

Happy Birthday, Jenni.
And don't worry, we'll find something for Tom to eat.

Customized menus were not yet standard, but here we had a shout-out right at the onset. Recognizing her birthday was a big hit with Jenni, and my finicky eating being pointed out brought a good laugh to each of us.

About halfway through our dinner, Chuck came up and joined us, wishing Jenni a happy birthday in person. The stains on his chef's white uniform gave evidence of a fast-paced kitchen, and he looked a bit of a mess. After about five minutes of the three of us laughing and yuking it up, Chuck told us he should really get back to the kitchen and promptly left. Knowing just how busy he was, we were grateful for this time to connect, brief as it was.

An older impeccably dressed gentlemen was dining with his wife, and their table was just ten feet from ours. As Lisa was doing her rounds, he pulled her aside. "Young lady, my wife and I have come to eat at Charlie Trotter's because we were led to believe we'd have a world-class experience. And this table, right there next to us, had their friend, the kitchen help, in the dining room with them. This is unacceptable."

"Oh, you mean Charlie? That was Chef Trotter with his friends," Lisa explained.

The man was not sure what to think. Chuck was so young, as were we that it just didn't fit in his paradigm of thinking. Jenni and I laughed quietly with each other, understanding his confusion.

Dessert menus were brought out, with a dozen selections that looked wonderful. We each ordered something and agreed to share it. Chuck was a practical joker, and having known us since high school, he enjoyed any opportunity to embarrass his friends.

Some activity started to occur at the entrance to the dining room, where many of Chuck's waiters were gathering and whispering among themselves. Neither Jenni nor I could tell what was going on, when suddenly they marched in in unison, each with a large plate in their hands. Silently, we watched as twelve desserts were placed on our small table. All our table appointments had to be removed from our table to make room during this fast-paced delivery.

We were stunned and speechless as Lisa walked up to our table and said, "No one has ever ordered every dessert on the menu. Good luck eating it all." And with a pleasant smile, she left our table.

I couldn't help but notice a scowl of displeasure on the impeccably dressed man. We were just not up to his standards, and Chuck's funny prank made us look like a couple of rubes that accidentally ended up at this fine establishment.

Jenni and I, however, loved it. We took a bite here and a taste there. We passed plates back and forth. We gobbled up some and ate most of the others. We left the one with lemon alone. We don't like lemon in our desserts. It was a bit like a feeding frenzy of driver ants devouring its prey.

We couldn't eat it all, of course, and as we succumbed to the sugar overdose, Chuck arrived again at our table. He had just cracked himself up with this practical joke that he could barely talk without a bout of self-interrupting laughter. The merriment was contagious, and the three of us smiled at one another as our communication was mostly through our laughing.

Eventually, we all regained our composure and spent another few minutes catching up. "Chuck, I think you'd better stop at that table there," Jenni recommended. The prim and proper older couple would need some TLC to make sure their evening ended well, and no one could turn on the charm better than Chuck.

This was the first time Chuck did the dessert wave. At least that was what he told me, but it was so much fun that it became the typical experience for all his guests. Not typically twelve plates full but enough to share and enjoy with one's friends and family and give the right touch to the culmination of a night at Charlie Trotter's.

Ping-Pong

In 1979, I played a lot of Ping-Pong. My friendship with Chuck Trotter had grown significantly, and I found myself at his parents' home in Wilmette a great deal the summer before my senior year in college. On a whim, Chuck and his brother Tom moved their family Ping-Pong table from the basement to the backyard. There were no more low ceilings, tight spaces, and musty smell to be reckoned. Instead, we had sunshine, an unlimited ceiling, and the ability to dive and land on the soft grass. What fun!

I stopped over one afternoon to find Chuck and Tom playing Ping-Pong outside. We had a blast in this new setting, and I was quick to join in on the fun. Hours later, the excitement was still as intense as when we began, and it continued day after day throughout the summer. I loved it.

While my Ping-Pong skills improved dramatically, I also got to know Chuck much better. Hours hanging out each day will do that. From that summer on, part of my ongoing relationship with Chuck involved Ping-Pong, and we'd strive to play any chance we got.

Fast forward a half-dozen years and Chuck is now the celebrated chef and owner of Charlie Trotter's. The best restaurant not only in Chicago but in the whole country. His success led him to expand by buying the building next door, and while formulating plans on how to develop the building, he purchased the most important piece of furniture for this empty space—a Ping-Pong table.

My office at this time was just thirty minutes from the restaurant, and I would come down to see Chuck and play Ping-Pong in the early afternoon. We did this several times a month. When Chuck's first marriage was ending, we had lunch every Wednesday. We'd play our match before I went back to the office, and he'd head to the kitchen to prepare the most dazzling night of superb dining for the lucky ones with a reservation at his eponymous restaurant. At least that is the way he would have described it.

Several years later, my office receptionist told me that Chuck was on the phone. "Hey, Chuck," I started. "What's up?"

"You'll never guess who was in the restaurant last night," he replied. I asked for a hint. He offered, "He holds an unbreakable record in sports." I thought for a moment. Our mutual love of the Chicago Cubs made me sure it was baseball, but what record? Joe DiMaggio's fifty-six-game hitting streak was untouchable, but he was no longer living. Hank Aaron was the lifetime home run king, but it seemed unlikely he would have come in at this point in his life.

Then I figured it out. "Orel Hershiser!" I proclaimed, recalling he set the consecutive scoreless innings record of fifty-nine in 1988.

"Yes, you're right," Chuck said. "And he's coming in to play some Ping-Pong in thirty minutes."

Sheepishly, I asked, "Can I come?" wondering if I could enter this game among leaders in the respective field.

"Sure. I was hoping you could," Chuck encouragingly told me.

"I'll be there in forty-five minutes," I said, hanging up before I even finished my sentence. I grabbed my car keys and wallet and ran past our receptionist. "Gone for the day!" I yelled as I flew out the door.

On my drive down, I had enough time to think through my arrival. I never had to think about arriving much of anywhere, but I didn't want to look or act starstruck either. Also, this was Chuck's turf and his game. I was clearly the third wheel, and I needed to respect my lesser role.

There was a spot to park right in front, usually reserved for the valets in the evening but open to my car now. Bolting out of my car and racing up the stairs to the studio kitchen, I momentarily forgot my plan to be cool. However, I quickly recovered and stopped myself before going inside.

Chuck Trotter in Captiva, Florida, in 1984 visiting Tom and Jenni Terrill

I stood outside the door to catch my breath. For fifteen seconds, I just stood there, deliberately slowing down my breathing and mental pace before I opened the door and walked in. A game was in progress with Chuck on the far side of the table and Orel just a few yards from me as I entered the room. Keeping my distance until the point was played, Chuck spoke up, "Orel, I'd like you to meet my friend Tom. Tom, this is Orel." It was first names only. I already knew his last name, and he had no need to know mine.

"Nice to meet you, Tom," Orel said, and I responded in kind. They then went on to continue the game while I quietly watched from the side. When the game was over, Orel suggested Chuck and I play a game. Chuck and I did, but this was one game neither one of us wanted to play with the other. The whole point was to play Ping-Pong with this Major Leaguer.

After my game with Chuck, Orel came in replacing me and played Chuck again. Now we were all sufficiently warmed up and started to play for real. One of Chuck's kitchen staff appeared and said, "Chef, I was wondering if you and your guests would like the kitchen to prepare some food for the special occasion." Chuck gave some recommendations that I don't remember now and didn't understand then. The fare served at Charlie Trotter's was so far beyond my comprehension of the simple turkey sandwich on rye that I typically had for lunch.

"So do you play much Ping-Pong during the season?" Chuck asked Orel.

"Yes, we have a table in the Indian's clubhouse and get some good games going," Orel said.

"Who are some of the best Ping-Pong players?" Chuck asked, curious about others in this select group of professional athletes.

"Well, let me think about that," Orel began. "Kenny Lofton is very good. And so is Albert Belle. But some guys are terrible."

"Terrible?" Chuck queried. "In what way?"

"Well, with some guys, I don't use a Ping-Pong paddle, but instead I use a CD case," Orel explained. "One guy is so bad I have to play him using my shoe." We all laughed, imagining how bad that unnamed athlete must have been.

As Chuck and Orel's game ended, two of Chuck's staff came in with several plates of delicacies. One of them described what they were carrying in and that this would be served to the restaurant's guests that night. We left the Ping-Pong table to indulge. I could not use enough superlatives to describe what it was like to have dinner at Chuck's restaurant, but to dine while playing Ping-Pong with a sports celebrity amplified the afternoon to a level I had never experienced before.

Mike Stearns, Rob Maine, Chuck Trotter, Joel Fisch, and Tom Terrill at Charlie Trotter's one evening

Immediately, a bottle of wine was opened to match the food we were enjoying.

After a short while, Orel looked at me and asked if I would like to play against him. No question ever asked had a more obvious answer, and so we went back to the table.

We warmed up a bit and then started to play. Ping-Pong is a deceptive game as you can feel as if you are about the same ability with an opponent, but then the score ends up 21–7. As we played,

I was a bit tense and rigid initially but soon felt at ease. On his second set of serves, Orel paused, looked me right in the eye, and said, "Here it comes." I didn't know what this meant, and it struck me as odd. Then he reached back in some unfamiliar motion and sent a serve that bounced high over the net and looked like a gimme point for me to take with an easy slam return. However, when the ball bounced on my side of the table, it shot off in a direction that seemed impossible and was completely unreturnable from the position I had placed myself.

"How did you do that?" I asked. My question went unanswered, and he returned to a standard style of serve. My mind was still back on that point, wanting to know how he did that serve. Realizing I needed to get my mind back to the present, I set it aside for now. I served, and Orel returned it to my backhand side with a slightly elevated hit. I took advantage and crushed the ball with a backhand put away.

"Hey, nice backhand slam," Orel said. At that moment, I was not sure if I was prouder of the fact that I hit a ball he failed to return or that he complimented my backhand. Either way, I was feeling terrific! Yes, I was losing by a mile, but I felt so good about that moment. Orel took back the serve, and on his second serve that set, he once again paused, looked across the table into my eyes, and said, "Here it comes."

Trying to get ready with this warning, I still was bewildered by the action on the ball. Once again, the ball bounced clear away from my paddle, and I failed even to touch it. What was he doing? I knew not to ask. He wasn't going to tell me, and Chuck was just laughing. The game ended 21–7 with me on the losing end; however, losing never felt so good.

We were all having a great time, each in his own way. Chuck thrived on being a host and relished being able to provide an atmosphere of sport, friendship, and exquisite dining while interacting with a top professional athlete. Orel took great pleasure in the fine dining, comradery, and competition while interacting with a top professional chef. I had better-than-a-front-row seat. I was on the stage with these two celebrated men, and while I was a top insurance broker, that didn't seem to matter to anyone, so I kept that to myself. And yes, we all enjoyed the Ping-Pong.

After many more games and hours of fun, the afternoon culminated with a smackdown challenge. "Charlie," Orel began, "I'm going to play one more game, and I'm going to beat you with my shoe as my paddle."

"Oh, you think so," Chuck replied with a laugh of incredulity.

"I don't think so. I know so," Orel said without cracking a smile. While I'm sure it was for show, we saw the Bulldog, as his former Los Angeles Dodgers coach Tommy Lasorda called him. Orel proceeded to remove his gray leather loafer, place it in his right hand while taking a stance ready to serve. "You ready?" he asked Chuck.

"Son of a…" Chuck whispered, barely audible while shaking his head back and forth. "This is not happening," he said as Orel served the ball. The volley went back and forth with Chuck taking the first point. The game continued, playing fairly evenly as the score built to a 20–20 deuce.

Needing to win by two, this game came down to a dead even level of skill. Except one man was playing with his shoe. Orel took each of the next two points and won the Game 22–20. He placed his shoes back on and came to shake Chuck's hand. It was all in good fun, and good fun we had. "Tom, it was nice to meet you," Orel said while shaking my hand.

Chuck went back to the kitchen to get ready for the dinner guests coming that night. Orel went back to his hotel, and I drove back home while reviewing the events of the day in my mind. It was a beautiful day indeed.

The In-laws

In 1979, Peter Falk and Alan Arkin starred in the movie *The In-Laws*. It was a funny story about the parents of the bride and groom, and one side was more than a little bit wacky. This made for some funny scenes and an enjoyable movie, which I laughed heartily at in the theatre.

In 2003, a remake of the movie was released, this time starring Michael Douglass and Albert Brooks. Much of the movie was filmed in Chicago, and when celebrities were in Chicago at that time, they would pull every connection they could to dine at Charlie Trotter's.

One of my largest clients had sold his business for an extremely handsome sum and wanted to celebrate the event. "Tom, can you get us into Charlie Trotters?" Bill asked.

"Sure, Bill," I responded. "Tell me what you're thinking."

"I want to celebrate the sale of the business, and I was thinking Ramona and I would host Jenni and you along with your mom and dad too. What do you think?" At this time, the reservation list was four to six months out for the general public, and Bill hoped to open some champagne much sooner than that.

I put in a call to Chuck and told him what I needed, and he rolled out the red carpet as usual. He told me to pick any date and time we wanted, and he'd see that it would happen. I went back to Bill and worked out the details for a night that worked for everyone.

Jenni and I had enjoyed ourselves at Charlie Trotter's many dozens of times and never paid for a meal. Chuck wouldn't have it any other way. This time, however, I explained to Chuck that it was important that we get a bill. My client was rightfully proud of his business success, and a free meal would cheat him out of his ability to pay for this expensive evening.

The six of us arrived for our seven o'clock reservation. "Mr. and Mrs. Terrill, we are so glad to see you once again," said the doorman as we came in the restaurant. The staff knew the names of my clients and my parents and welcomed them as if they were all old friends. This first impression set the tone for an unforgettable evening, and we all felt eager for what would soon unfold.

As we were escorted through the dining room and toward the stairs, I was thrilled. I preferred the upstairs and the dining room in the back. As we walked to our table, we noticed a group of six nearby. There sat the actors Michael Douglass and Albert Brooks. Four women accompanied them; none of them appeared to be their wives. Each of these women was considerably younger than the male actors and looked like the stereotypical arm candy of Hollywood celebrities.

We sat down to our lovely table, and before we could blink, the sommelier opened a bottle of champagne and filled our glasses. Raising his glass, Bill made a toast to start off the evening. One of Charlie Trotter's best waiters came to our table to again welcome each of us by name and see if we had any food requirements or preferences before our meal would begin.

"I would like to see a menu," Bill said.

"I can, of course, bring menus for the table, but Chef Trotter has requested that he be allowed to select your food and wine tonight. I think you'll be quite pleased with his choices," our waiter recommended.

"Done!" Bill enthusiastically answered for everyone. Our waiter inquired if anyone had any food allergies or had anything that was off-limits from our food preferences. Completing the formalities, we sat back and waited for the multicourse affair to begin.

My client was a bold man who spoke his mind freely. "I think I'm going to go ask Michael Douglass why he isn't out with his wife," Bill suggested in all seriousness.

"No, Bill, don't you dare," replied his wife Ramona while the rest of the table laughed at the idea. But I knew Bill and was reasonably sure he might just do it unless he was firmly persuaded otherwise. At just the right time, six servers appeared all with some delicacy for each one of us. The plates were placed with synchronized precision as our waiter described in minute detail what each of us was about to enjoy.

For a moment, the other table with the two movie stars was forgotten about as we marveled together at the explosion of new tastes tantalizing our taste buds. "This is fantastic!" said my father while my mother commented, "I have never tasted anything like this before." The funny thing was that it was hard to remember what we were eating other than the word "sesame" was thrown in the fanciful description.

Immediately, our plates were cleared as we finished our last bites, and another round came our way. The portions were always small, but when twelve plus plates are placed in front of you during the evening, you don't leave hungry.

Bill again brought up the topic of the nearby table and that he really wanted to know where the wives were while these two guys were out and about with four exquisite women. I feared this heading the wrong direction and tried to change the subject. Right then, Chuck entered the dining room. The entire area went silent as Chef Charlie Trotter himself appeared. The eight tables in the room all were expecting this and watched in anticipation as he headed toward the Hollywood table.

Hollywood was expecting this too. Such prominent celebrities required attention, and attention they would have. But instead, Chuck walked right by without saying a word and came to our party of six instead. "I hope everyone is having too much to drink," Chuck jokingly said as he arrived. He gave Jenni and my mom hugs and then introduced himself to Bill and Ramona.

He stood holding court for some five minutes when he said to our table, "You know what? They don't need me in the kitchen right now," as he signaled a busboy for a chair. "I'm going to join your group if I'm not imposing."

Chuck sat down and began to tell stories of times in high school and college with Jenni and me. Stories with just the right amount of embarrassment to get a laugh from everyone, including me. Our waiter brought over another wine glass and poured it until Chuck said to stop. "I'm going to stay until my glass is empty," he proclaimed, which lasted for thirty minutes.

At the end of the one-half hour, our gracious chef friend excused himself and left for the kitchen. He exited the only way he could, which was to pass by the Hollywood table. However, there was no stop on his agenda, and once again, he passed by without a word.

"That is fantastic!" Bill said with delight in his voice. "Charlie Trotter just spent thirty minutes at our table and then snubbed Michael Douglass and Albert Brooks. I love it. I just love it!" Bill continued. I was pretty surprised myself. Chuck was such a good host that I knew he would have to take care of a personal appearance at some point, but a message was delivered loud and clear. There was one table in this room that was more important than any other, and it was ours.

The evening continued with oohs and aahs and laughter stories aplenty. The night was a complete success and one that we all remember well. I suspect Mr. Douglass and Mr. Brooks remember it too.

The Undesirables

One summer evening, Jenni and I went to Evanston to have dinner at the Davis Street Fish Market. This popular restaurant was in the same space as the former Evanston mainstay, the Dominion Room, where I worked as a busboy during my freshman year in high school.

Joining us were great friends Howard and Jean Wiley Miller who were in town from Cleveland.

Jean and Jenni were best of friends since junior high, and I first saw Jenni and Jean simultaneously when they excitedly discovered they were in the same English class freshman year at New Trier. It was my first class of high school, and I sat quietly watching from my desk as the other students arrived. Jean crossed into the room and let out a squeal of delight as she ran to Jenni and sat on her lap. These two friends made such a commotion that I couldn't help but notice. I remember thinking to myself, *What would I do if one of my friends tried to sit in my lap?* Quickly, I dismissed the thought, as no two guys I knew would ever do that, which just confirmed to me that women are mysterious and there is no need to apply logic to understand them.

It was a beautiful summer evening, and after dinner, the four of us strolled through the streets of Evanston. Like Jenni and me, Jean too was a high school friend of Chucks. "How is Chuck's restaurant doing?" Jean asked.

"It's doing great. We should go there now for dessert," I enthusiastically said, thinking this was a brilliant idea.

"Can you just go there for dessert?" Howard asked.

"No," Jenni answered, giving me a look that this idea was a dud.

"Jenni's right, he doesn't just serve dessert to the public, but he will for us," I confidently said, trying to sell everyone on this idea. It was just a twenty-five-minute drive, and the evening was still young. Too early to call it a night.

Jean and Howard wanted to go but graciously deferred to Jenni and me. I was so persistent that Jenni finally capitulated to my determination. So off we went, enjoying the drive down Sheridan Road before turning onto Lake Shore Drive at Hollywood. One couldn't help but hum the Aliotta Haynes Jeremiah song "Lake Shore Drive" while cruising downtown on a warm summer night:

And there ain't no road just like it, anywhere I've found. Running south on Lake Shore Drive heading into town. Just slippin' on by on LSD, Friday night trouble bound.

And then that very song came on the radio, which was remarkable timing. As we drove down enjoying the summer night, everyone caught my enthusiasm for dessert and a chance to visit with our distinguished friend. I pulled up to the valet stand, right in front of the restaurant, and we all hopped out, heading for the steps of the front door of Charlie Trotter's.

"Tom, I'm wearing blue jeans," Jean noticed, concerned about how underdressed we were.

"No problem," I assured Jean. "It's Chuck's place. He can let us in," I continued, unfazed by the obvious, a trait I seem to have always possessed.

We walked in and moved toward the hostess spot, looking for Dona Lee, Chuck's mom. However, she was not working this night. I looked around and didn't recognize anyone working, so I went to the bar and said, "We are old friends of Charlie from high school and want to have dessert. Would you tell him we are here?"

I had never before used the name Charlie. Never. Moreover, what I didn't realize at the time was that some people that really did not know Chuck from high school would claim they did. Mistakenly, they would use the name Charlie trying to get him to come out. This error in the name was a sign to his staff that the patron was not legitimate.

"I'm sorry, sir, but do you have a reservation?" he asked.

"No, I don't, but Charlie is really a good friend. I'm down here all the time. Please tell him Tom Terrill is here. He'll tell you we are OK." He left politely but never actually found Chuck and returned telling us we could not stay as we didn't have sport coats.

"I knew it," Jenni said. "Let's go," she continued as she headed for the front door.

"No, wait, Jenni," I said in her direction while then turning back to the bartender. "What is your name?" I asked.

"Troy," he replied.

"OK, Troy, I understand you're just doing your job, but let me write a note to Charlie telling him we stopped by." Troy agreed but said the other three must leave while I wrote a quick note.

"I'm outta here," Jenni said, wishing I knew when to give up. Jean and Howard followed Jenni and were standing by our car still at the valet stand.

I took a pen and piece of paper and quickly scribbled:

Hey Chuck,

Jean Wiley is in town with her husband, Howard. Jenni and I thought we'd pop in for some dessert on a whim, but Troy said we are not dressed appropriately. Maybe another time.

Tom

Chuck Trotter and Jenni Terrill fixing dinner, Captiva, Florida, 1984

I handed Troy the note and walked out to meet up with everyone else. Apparently, the note found its way to Chuck who dispatched a messenger with a sense of urgency. As the valet was finding our car keys, the door to the restaurant flew open, with a different employee calling out to us.

"Wait!" he shouted. "Please come back in."

"Troy said we couldn't stay," Jenni replied with an air of refusal.

"I'm trumping Troy," he responded, imploring us to return.

"No, it's too late now," Jenni continued. I forgot how hard it was to get her to date me in the first place, and her offended stubbornness was a large mountain for this errand boy to overcome.

"Jenni," Jean said with a tone that only a childhood friend could give, "let's go in."

And so in we went. Four places were cleared at the bar while we had a mini dessert wave brought out to satisfy our mutual long-suffering sweet tooth. Chuck came out shortly after that and had a good laugh with us about the almost-near miss. We shared some old stories and told some new ones, continuing the friendship.

I never used the name Charlie again to refer to my friend.

In Memory of Chuck Trotter

Professionally, I have a hectic season. The fourth quarter of the year is just crazy for anyone in the health insurance business, and I find my free time virtually nonexistent.

On Monday, November 4, 2013, I was in my office when my cell phone rang at 3:44 PM. I looked at my phone and could see it was Chuck Trotter. I was so busy and really had no business taking the call. We had spoken a lot on the phone over the last few months, mostly about the political landscape, and on the fourth ring, I decided to take the call.

"Chuck!" I started. "Nice to see your name on my phone."

"Tom, how the heck are you?" he responded. "I have an idea. We need to start the Illinois chapter to get Ben Carson elected president. What do you think?" We both admired Dr. Carson and hoped he could get some of his ideas into the mainstream politically.

Chuck Trotter on a cold Thanksgiving at Lake Michigan

I laughed at the idea, knowing I didn't have the time and he wouldn't make the time.

We talked about our friend Chuck Caldwell who was recovering from recent surgery and what Jenni and I were doing.

When I hung up, I looked at my phone, and we had spent exactly one hour talking. It was time I didn't have to give, but I have always tried my best to override the tyranny of the urgent in favor of the relationship. I was smiling, thinking about how I valued our friendship.

The next day, I had an appointment first thing in the morning. When it was over, as I walked to my car, I opened my e-mail on my phone. I had two e-mails that in the subject line just said "Chuck." Neither would open properly, and so I decided to wait until I got to the office.

My son Cody had been working with me for just a few months, and when I walked in, he was waiting in my office. "Hey, Dad, did you hear the news about Chuck Trotter?" Cody said.

Imagining some new honor had been bestowed upon him, I thought nothing of the question. "No. What news?" I asked.

In a soothing voice, Cody said, "He died, Dad."

I froze for a moment, not believing it possible. "What? Where did you hear this?" I asked with a broken and quivering voice.

Cody said, "It's all over the news. He was found dead in his home this morning. He never woke up."

I walked to my desk, sat down in my chair, and wept. Uncontrollably, I sobbed while my son tenderly put his hands on my shoulders and back.

Chuck Trotter at the Kenilworth Beach on an early summer day circa 1979

The news stunned me, and the raw emotions came forth like a fountain of sorrow. After thirty minutes, my tears stopped as my body couldn't handle it anymore.

Opening my e-mail, I saw the e-mail from Mark Jiganti in Colorado. He had heard the news on the radio but wasn't sure it was true. I called Mark on the phone, and we had a somber discussion on this tragic news.

E-mails and phone calls started to flood in from friends. I called Jenni, and we both cried on the phone. Words could not express the shock and pain. Some calls I took, others I could not. I focused on those from our high school and college days as we processed the news together.

People from across the country began making plans to fly back home to Chicago to pay respects to our dear friend. The funeral would be well attended and more about his life as a chef, restaurateur, and businessman.

The childhood friends gathered first at the Michigan Shores Club in Wilmette the night before the funeral. There we celebrated his life. We shared stories about Chuck and laughed more than we cried. I had some letters Chuck had sent to me in college with a short comic play he wrote that involved most everyone at the event that night. It was fun to see his humor, and some of his lines could only be read now that he was gone.

Chuck at Mark and Ronnie Jiganti's wedding in 1984

I miss Chuck and his zest for life but rejoice that I knew him and shared a friendship full of happy memories.

What's in Your Medical Records?

I was born with excellent vision, a genetic gift from my mother and father. Therefore, I never had a reason to see an eye doctor, that is until I had a melanoma on my leg in 2006. Having been fair skinned and, with my childhood, having had frequent sunburns, I always imagined myself to be a good candidate for skin cancer. Lo and behold, at a routine exam with my dermatologist, I learned I had a melanoma on my leg. Very high up, in fact, so high that I never had any sun exposure here.

My doctor told me I should get a thorough eye exam because one can have a melanoma in their eye and not know it. This was enough for me to schedule my first eye exam. I got a referral from a friend, called the eye doctor, and went in for my appointment.

Now this first appointment required me to fill out all the typical forms and information. I also spoke with the doctor's nurse who had more questions than I could imagine. She went on and on. Eventually, I was in the doctor's chair and began the full eye examination. Two and a half hours later, I finally left the doctor's office. I could not believe how long it took, but I was glad to get a clean bill of health.

Two years later, the doctor's office called, suggesting I should come back in for a routine follow-up exam, and this seemed like a good idea. I arrived for my second ever appointment with an eye doctor, again greeted by the very engaging nurse asking about my health, family, and what fun plans I had for the summer. Eventually, I was brought into the examination room and met with the doctor, where we went through the usual steps in the eye exam. After about fifteen minutes, the doctor was called away and said he would be back in about five minutes.

During my wait, I had nothing to do, and so I began to look around the room for something interesting. Behind me and over my shoulder, I noticed a computer screen and saw my name: Thomas Terrill. Taking a closer look, I could see it was a copy of my medical records regarding my previous eye exam. Everything was typed out, with numbers that were meaningless to me. Still scanning over the screen, I noticed something handwritten on a large blank space in the scanned document. In all upper-case letters, I saw a six-letter word: "TALKER."

What? They had labeled me a "talker" and placed it in my file! I was shocked. More than that, I was upset. I've been known to get a little gabby, but who were they to make it a part of my medical file?

The rest of the appointment, I was resolved to only give yes or no answers. I have never been so tight-lipped in my life. I was committed to showing them I could zip it up as good as the next guy and prove them wrong.

Now when I'm taking a long time to tell a story and someone tells me to speed it up, I respond that I can't speed it up; you see, I'm a talker, and I can prove it. It's part of my medical file.

Flight to Hawaii

In March of 1998, my family took a trip to Hawaii. Departing from Chicago, with a change of planes in Los Angeles, our final destination was Maui. Jenni and I decided to indulge ourselves and upgrade with miles to first class. The long day of travel seemed to beckon us to the luxury promised in first class, and we quickly succumbed to this temptation.

Kate and Cody, however, would not have such luck and were banished to coach. Our friends kidded us that we were selfish, but in truth, the kids had a great time in the back of the plane without parental supervision.

Uneventfully, our plane landed in Los Angeles where we changed planes with a short one-hour layover. Our kids were excited to cross off another State of the Union that they had now set foot upon, even if it was ever so brief.

Ready for another round of silly excessive service, Jenni and I boarded with the kids. We turned left once on board for our first-row first-class seats while the kids turned right once again toward coach. A dish of warm cashews was delivered with an offer of a cocktail to help acclimate us to this enormous airplane seat. Difficult this flight would not be, at least, so we thought.

Once we left the security of land behind and had only blue ocean below us, we encountered some pretty bumpy turbulence. The captain announced that he expected this for some time, and he was right. Two-plus hours of shaking and rattling while the seat belt sign remained on left us feeling less than enthusiastic. The flight attendants kept the drinks coming for all those in the eight rows of first-class seats.

The seat belt sign remained on, but the number of libations poured and consumed necessitate a trip to the bathroom for many of our first-class companions. Jenni and I kept waiting for the turbulence to end and the seat belt sign light to be turned off to no avail. Finally reaching my breaking point, I unbuckled, left my seat, and went to the lavatory. Locking the door while being shaken back and forth by the bumpy air, I discovered the floor of the bathroom was quite wet with urine. The conditions made good aim difficult, and those that had gone before me had failed miserably. Disgusted by the sight, I braced myself and was mostly successful in hitting the target.

I came back to the seat to tell Jenni about the poor and rapidly deteriorating condition of the bathroom and encouraged her to go now while it was bad but not unusable. Taking my advice, she journeyed into the land of damp and sticky bathroom floors. Jenni came back quickly, shaking her head back and forth and muttering under her breath just how disgusting it was.

Our front-row seats now became the viewing stand for all others who came behind us. We knew it was only getting worse with each additional visitor. After eight or so people had gone after us, Jenni nudged me to glance at the man waiting outside the bathroom door for his turn.

"Look at that guy's feet," Jenni said to me. He was barefoot! We both stared at the guy's feet the entire time he waited. Casually dressed with his long hair parted in the middle, he had a look that said "I'm from California" all over him. He came out, and I watched him walk back to his seat in the last row of first class on the other side of the plane. We couldn't help but keep looking at him and imagining his bare feet exposed to the urine of a dozen or more people.

Eventually, the rough ride smoothed out for the last hour, and we arrived in Maui, ready for some Hawaiian sun. We met up with our kids and walked to baggage claim when we ran into some friends from home who happened to be on our flight. They were in coach and didn't realize we were on the same plane.

"Where were your sitting?" Kimberly asked us. We explained that we rode in first class. "You did! Did you see Jackson Browne? He was on our flight too in first class."

"What? Are you sure?" I asked. I was a huge fan of Jackson Browne, finding significant meaning to his lyrics in my life, and had seen him many times in concert.

"Tom," Jenni said as she figured out what I had not yet, "Jackson Browne was the barefoot guy!"

Jenni was right. It was indeed Jackson Brown standing barefoot as he entered into the lavatory. He had come to Hawaii, the papers reported, to join Bonnie Raitt for a concert on Maui.

I felt sad for him and cringed again, thinking about that bathroom. However, more than that, I wished I knew he was there. I would have gone over to him and quoted the ending lines from my favorite song, "The Late Show."

A Large Booth Feeling So Small

When I got married in 1983, AIDS was a term unknown to the general population of the United States. Within a few years, that would change as an emerging epidemic began and caught the attention of everyone. The public knew very little, and even the medical community was mostly unaware at this point in history. My wife Jenni was a staff physical therapist at Lake Forest Hospital, beginning her career right when we were married.

In 1985, Jenni treated a patient diagnosed with AIDS who was in the hospital. However, the precautions of the medical staff were nil, and no guidance was given to any of the physical therapists regarding medical precautions to take. One day, Jenni went to the patient's room for his treatment and found a terribly sad sight. The poor man defecated in bed and over time had much of his body covered in his own feces. Jenni did not treat him as he needed cleaning, but no one had any concern about transmission from patient to caregiver.

On the flip side, the public began to be concerned as to whether this was easily transmitted or not. Mosquitoes are known to pass various deadly diseases via blood, and no one knew for sure if this was possible with HIV at the time. Even seven years later when Magic Johnson revealed that he was HIV positive, many of his NBA opponents were concerned about possible transmission on the basketball court.

The disease was 100 percent fatal at the time, and everyone was cautious about exposure.

In 1986, I made a cold call on a diner in Highwood, Illinois, trying to sell a group medical insurance policy for the owner and employees. To my delight, the owner said we could talk about it right then, rather than wait for a date in the future. I had caught them between breakfast and lunch, and so the owner could gather his small staff of seven for a quick meeting.

The AIDS epidemic had made a lot of news in the insurance world as it related to a change in claims for medical, disability, and life insurance policies. All insurance companies implemented a new system that required blood exams for every life insurance policy issued at this time.

"Let's go over to the large booth," the owner said, directing me toward a specific area of the restaurant. I slid into the booth and had six men in their midfifties climb in on either side of me.

"Gentlemen," I started, "let me ask a few questions—" when the owner interrupted me, asking that I wait for Jane. Shortly after that, a young girl in her early twenties walked up and pulled up a chair. The booth was full, and honestly, it felt a bit too crowded with me in the middle.

"OK. Now that we are all here, I'd like to start with a few questions." And I began to work into my sales presentation. I mentioned that medical insurance was very expensive, which prompted a question to me.

"Do you know why medical insurance is so expensive?" the owner asked me. I could tell the question was not one he wanted me to answer but instead one he wanted to say to me.

"No. Why?" I asked.

With a big smile on this face, he blurted out in a loud voice one word, "age." His smile seemed odd to me, especially when I thought he said AIDS.

"Well, yes, that is a problem," I agreed. "And there is nothing the medical community can do about it," I added.

"No," he said with a laugh. "They can't!"

His smile and laugh had a weird, sinister tone to my ears, and I couldn't imagine why he thought AIDS was funny.

"Well, I know the best minds are working on that problem, and until it is solved, it is going to cost a lot of money," I said, confused by his comment. And so I asked my next question: "That isn't a problem with anyone here, is it?"

"Yes, it is!" he said, smiling.

"Who?" I asked with a bit of hesitation in my voice.

"*All of us!*" he loudly said with a jovial laugh. This large booth now felt so small as six large middle-aged men were surrounding me.

"Everyone?" I asked in voice pleading for help to this now seemingly desperate situation.

"Yes," he said, "except Janey. She's only twenty-three."

My mind was in high gear, racing and replaying the conversations. *Twenty-three*, I thought to myself. *What does that have to do with anything…twenty-three…twenty-three…* And I finally figured out that he did not, in fact, say AIDS but *age*, and young Janey was too young to be the source of high cost for medical insurance.

I felt like a trauma victim but stumbled through the rest of my standard presentation and indeed sold a group policy to these nice men and young Janey too.

Bad Parenting (and Lousy Citizenship to Boot)

August 23 to 24 weekend of 2003 was a wonderful time. Kate was now a senior in high school, and Cody had started his freshman year. Jenni and I were each forty-five but felt as if we were in our thirties. We had been married for twenty years, and the future seemed bright and limitless.

"Hey, Cody, do you want to go for a swim with me?" I said, inviting Cody to join me at the Lake Bluff Beach for my daily swim in Lake Michigan.

"If we can, bring the football," Cody enthusiastically responded. We had a football that could go in the water, and it would allow for some fun father-and-son time. We hopped on our bikes and rode the one-third of a mile to the beach for some fun in the sun. It was a warm and sunny afternoon with a pleasant southerly breeze of eight to ten miles per hour.

Photo courtesy of Lucy Gray, Lake Bluff Beach

The warm waters of late August and the weekend brought out large crowds that day to the beach. The lake level was low that year, and a sandbar had developed just on the other side of the rock pile.

Cody and I wandered out on the rocks and jumped down into the waist-deep seventy-four-degree water. It was the perfect spot, and we settled into a routine of diving catches that all boys love to do in the water.

After about five minutes, I noticed something very odd. About a quarter mile or more offshore was a man swimming. He was pulling a greenish blue raft with a ten-foot line, and someone was floating on the raft. "Cody, look at that guy out there pulling that raft," I said. As Cody looked with me, I continued, "He is crazy. He is swimming in the boating lane from Great Lakes Marina. I think he will get run over if he doesn't leave."

210

"Really?" Cody asked. "Do you think he might get hit?"

I explained to Cody that he was in a blind spot. For some reason, he was swimming parallel to shore and swimming against the two-foot chop of waves. So his progress was nil. At the same time, the afternoon sun was creating a glare off the water that would make him very hard to see by a boater who was coming upon him. The raft was the same color as the water, and with the glare on the choppy lake, the raft would blend right in.

"It's as if he's playing on the highway," I added. I showed Cody how the boats like to run along the shore, and typically, they are out at the same distance that the man was because of the large breakwater just a mile north at Great Lakes Naval Base.

We kept tossing the ball back and forth and occasionally glancing out at this man. He just continued on and on to swim into the wind and parallel with the shore. It was about the dumbest thing I had seen in a long time. Some twenty-five minutes into our time of catch, a large boat was on track to go right to their vicinity. I knew enough from having grown up with boats that it is tough to see something in the water, especially with the angle of the sun and the chop on the water.

The speed at which the boat passed by them clearly indicated they could not be seen. However, as the near-miss passed, the passengers in the large boat, at last, noticed the raft. The boat captain turned around and slowly approached the raft. Even though they were a quarter of a mile or more away, I could see the people in the boat waving their arms to signal the man and the passenger to climb into their boat. Clearly, they were offering to remove them from harm's way and deliver them safely close to shore. However, the man in the water waved them off. He had no interest in the help being offered and instead continued his foolish effort.

Not five minutes later, another boat was on the same trajectory. Cody and I stopped and looked out at this pending disaster. As the boat got to the raft, suddenly the raft disappeared, being entirely run over by the boat. A few seconds later, the submerged raft shot up out of the water and into the air. It had been a direct hit.

Those in the boat saw the flying raft and turned to see who or what they had just hit. As Cody and I quickly climbed out of the water, I shouted to the crowded beach. "I need a cell phone. There is an emergency!"

A twentysomething woman held hers up, and I dialed the Lake Bluff Police Department. "My name is Tom Terrill, and I'm at the Lake Bluff North Beach. We need an ambulance here immediately. Someone has been run over by a boat." As I continued with the details, I could see the passengers in the boat carefully lifting an adolescent-looking child into the boat and the man who had been swimming climbing in as well. The boat made a beeline right for the beach. The man driving the boat shouted out for all to hear that they needed an ambulance immediately.

An ambulance arrived along with the Lake Bluff police as the girl was carefully lifted from the boat. The boat's propeller had struck her foot, and while still attached, it almost completely severed. For ten minutes or so, the emergency responders addressed the needs of the girl, driving her to a nearby park. There a waiting helicopter would fly her to Loyola Hospital.

Cody and I watched as the ambulance pulled away, and we too left the beach and headed for home. I was struck by the oddity of seeing this situation and predicting such a terrible outcome and then to have it play out exactly as I imagined. We shared our story with Jenni and Kate, and all prayed for the unnamed girl. This Sunday afternoon was one we would not soon forget.

Coming from a boating family, I knew that the man driving the boat had done nothing wrong. All fault lay with the father who put his daughter at extreme risk. But my mind imagined someone dumb enough to do this might have such a low character that he might attempt legal action against the boat driver.

So I called the Lake County sheriff's office. I had two objectives. First, to see if the police issued a citation against the boat driver. And second, to get my contact information to the boat driver in case he needed a defense witness.

As expected, the sheriff would not give me his contact information, but they agreed to take mine and to pass it on to the driver. The sheriff took down my eyewitness account, which conveyed that the fault lay entirely with the father.

A few days later, I got a call from the boat driver. Burdened by the accident and the trauma of seeing this young child so severely hurt, he felt terrible. When I told him how I was not just a random guy who glanced up and saw the collision but someone who was carefully watching for thirty minutes anticipating the accident, he was greatly relieved. Not only had I seen this but I vividly watched the man refuse help and transportation to safety just five minutes earlier.

I shared that I would go to court to be a witness if he was cited for anything by the sheriff or if the family sued him.

Two months later, to no one's surprise, I was called again as the father was trying to sue the boat driver for recklessness. It was outrageous, and I was only too glad to help. I was deposed and gave my testimony while in my dining room. The female attorney who was representing the girl and her father asked me the vilest questions and insinuated things that would disgust anyone with any character. She represented the worst of our country's legal system, and I was thrilled to see her leave my home. An awful person. Someone might say she was just doing her job, but she was not interested in the truth. Her motives did not ring true.

As I understand it, the boat driver prevailed in this frivolous lawsuit. Justice won out, and I was lucky enough to be a part of it.

Fill 'er Up

In my early forties, my insurance agency represented my cousin's business regarding their group medical insurance. Phillips Getschow Company had some one hundred nonunion employees on their group plan run out of their Oconto Falls, Wisconsin, location.

Kurt and I scheduled a business meeting at 1:00 PM to be preceded by lunch at a local diner Kurt liked. My office in Illinois was four hours away, so I started the drive at 7:30 AM. I drove straight north heading through Milwaukee along Highway 43. At 11:30 AM, I pulled into a gas station on the outskirts of Oconto Falls, and I called Kurt on my car phone.

"Hey, Kurt, I'm here getting some gasoline. I'll meet you at the restaurant in twenty minutes."

"Great. My father-in-law will join us for lunch too. See you soon," Kurt responded.

I hung up and climbed out of my Volvo. I thought to myself I'd like to by a Snapple inside the station's food mart, so I pushed "pay inside" on the pump and started to fill up my car. As the gasoline poured into my tank, it dawned on me that I shouldn't get a Snapple now because I'd be eating lunch shortly. Yes, I'd skip the Snapple and just get the gas.

The handle clicked off as my tank was full. Replacing the hose and my gas cap, I climbed back in my car and drove back out onto the two-lane highway heading east on state Highway 22. About five miles down the road, a county sheriff passed me going the other way. In my rearview mirror, I noticed the squad car go into a hard spin turning around. It was like a scene from a movie, and I thought to myself, *Boy, someone is in trouble.*

Kurt's directions told me to turn north on Highway 141, which I was approaching, but I could see the red lights coming up fast behind me too. I wanted to get out of the sheriff's way as I knew he was in hot pursuit of some dangerous criminal activity. I figured I could make the turn on the entrance ramp, and if he went straight, I'd continue uninterrupted, and if he were going on Highway 141 like me, I'd pull to the shoulder to let him pass.

Making the turn while looking in my rearview mirror, I saw him turn behind me. So I pulled way over to the side, giving him plenty of room to get by me. However, instead of flying past me in pursuit of some scofflaw, he pulled right behind me.

I was perplexed. *Why is he pulling me over? I was not speeding and had done nothing wrong.* I watched him put his hat on and exit his car walking up to mine. Rolling down my window, I began, "Hi, Officer. What's up?"

With a stern look as he sized me up, he asked, "Did you just buy some gasoline in Oconto Falls?"

"Yes, I did!" I said with a smile. I imagined something must have happened at the gas stations, and I might be a key witness. "How come?" I asked, excited about the forthcoming details.

"Did you pay for it?" he retorted.

Suddenly, I realized my terrible mistake. "Oh…no, I didn't…but…well…let me explain."

"Yes, why don't you do that," he said with an incredulous look.

"OK," I began nervously, now realizing I might be in a lot of trouble. "Well, I was going to buy a Snapple. Right? And I changed my mind…'cause I'm going to have lunch…and I didn't want to have a Snapple right before lunch, right? So I, uh, was going to go inside and pay for gas…and the Snapple…right? And then I, uh, changed my mind, so I forgot I didn't swipe my credit card at the pump…right? Um, so it was, uh…it was an accident… I'm not a thief… I never steal anything… I even pay my income taxes without cheating… Can I go back and pay now?" I finished the feeblest-sounding explanation. My heart was in my throat, and an image of me handcuffed and thrown in the squad car ran through my mind.

"Why don't you turn around, drive back to the gas station, and go inside and pay for your gas?" he recommended, but really it was more of a command.

"Yes, I will do that. Do you want me to follow you, or do you want to follow me?" I asked.

"Neither. You just go and do it," he answered.

"Yes, I will. I promise," I said with a sense of relief.

"I know you will," he explained. "Because you don't want to know what will happen if you don't."

I turned my car around and drove back to the gas station. I went in and paid for gas and left, arriving late for lunch with Kurt. We all had a good laugh when I told the story to Kurt and his father-in-law.

Vail—Here I Am to Worship

On Saturday, March 1, 2008, the sun rose over Vail Pass at 6:30 AM to begin a perfect spring skiing day. Steve was too sick to ski, so Tony and I would head out without our leader. We proceeded with our own morning rituals of dressing, stretching, and mentally preparing for a glorious day traveling across the splendor of God's creation. I love Vail. It's almost too much to take in.

We arrived at the village to meet a childhood friend of mine. I hadn't seen Bill in fifteen years, but today he joined us to explore the majesty of Vail. As the sun rose higher into the sky, the temperature climbed to a comfortable forty degrees. We went right back into Blue Sky Basin, a place where wilderness and skiing come together.

We were alone. No one else had come back this far yet, and so we tightened our boots and let our skis run. The snowcats had groomed a beautiful trail of corduroy nectar down a gentle ridge, with a ninety-degree turn into a steep pitch. We rode the ridge with the sun gleaming down upon us, ready to take the mountain head-on as we banked into the hard left turn. The cool air rushed past my face as I accelerated down the run. Leading our pack, I continued to gain speed, flying past the trees and boulders that are prevalent in Blue Sky Basin. At the bottom, we reconvened with smiles from ear to ear. What an opening run. We went right back up and did it again… And then again after that… Each run as good as the last.

We continued on with the day moving to different runs but the same experience. Wonder and amazement filled my soul… God has created such a beautiful place, and skiing provided me the means to take so much of it in.

A few runs later, we joined in with Mark, his son Brett, and seven of Mark's friends from his college days. Hard-core skiers who played hard. Still, in Blue Sky, we went to the cornice that builds over Lover's Leap. A challenging run with soft snow and a nice seven-foot drop to begin the run—each one selecting the line that looked best to them. Mine just happened to be the one that also looked the easiest to me. My legs were strong, but not like they were in my twenties. Halfway down the run, my blood was rushing, my heart pumping, and my thighs burning…but my smile was so big it hurt… the feeling of my soul filled with such joy… Skiing brings me to a place that's hard to understand, let alone explain… I guess one either knows what I feel or they don't.

As we rode up the chair for our next run, I got the chance to talk with Brett…one of my son Cody's best friends. Brett has an enthusiasm for skiing that his father passed on to him. Of greater significance is the energy Brett has for his heavenly Father. His faith has sprouted like the seeds thrown into the good soil in the Parable of the Sower. As we came off the chair, we selected the last run before lunch. A cruiser that progressively got steeper the farther along one went. I watched Brett turn for a section of the run he had scouted out, hitting a mogul and climbing five feet into the air with a beautiful back grab. He landed in a field of moguls, enough to make my back ache just thinking about it. Unfazed by the bumps, Brett rode it out without a thought. Momentarily, I was back in 1977 when I could do the same thing, but reality bit me with lactic acid flowing through my quads. I love to watch people ski who love the sport. What joy.

After lunch, we split up. My friend Bill had to head to Denver and Tony, and I went off alone. Tony is a man who took up skiing in his forties. I enjoy his company. They don't make 'em like Tony anymore…a real class act.

We went on to Game Creek bowl. A favorite spot of skiing perfect cruisers. We took several runs down Ouzo, Lost Boy, and Dealer's Choice. All high-speed runs with various grades of steepness. At this point in the day, my body was tired. The third day of hard skiing was taking its toll.

Tony and I rode over to Avanti to finish our day. As we rode up the chair, I pulled out my earbuds and decided to listen to tunes while I skied my last run. As the chairlift crested over the ridge, Mt. Holy Cross could be seen in the distance, a mountain that holds the snow in such a way to form a cross, giving countless faithful a visual reminder of our Savior's work on our behalf.

We decided to finish the day starting at Lodgepole. As my music started, I heard the beginning of a live version of "Here I Am to Worship."

> *Light of the world, You step down into darkness.*
> *Opened my eyes let me see.*
> *Beauty that made this heart adore you, hope of a life spent with you.*

I watched the range of Mt. Holy Cross to my left slowly disappear as I dipped off to my right. The evergreen trees on each side of the run still covered with snow.

> *And here I am to worship,*
> *Here I am to bow down,*
> *Here I am to say that you're my God,*
> *You're altogether lovely,*
> *Altogether worthy,*
> *Altogether wonderful to me.*

I was riding high, making big arc turns down the run, my focus completely shifted to worship. I continued with the sun gleaming down, casting a shadow of myself off to my right. Angling toward Ledges, I proceeded down praising my Lord for this moment in my life.

King of all days,
Oh so highly exalted Glorious in Heaven above.
Humbly you came to the earth you created.
All for love's sake became poor.

Yes, you are my king. "The earth you created…" How that line stuck in my mind with my surroundings.

And here I am to worship,
Here I am to bow down,
Here I am to say that you're my God,
You're altogether lovely,
Altogether worthy,
Altogether wonderful to me.

I needed to rest a little… My body was wearing out, but my soul was as strong as ever. I continued to praise God and turn toward the run Born Free for the final descent.

I'll never know how much it cost to see my sin upon that cross.

I thought about my sin…my own choices in life that had pushed me away from God. My view was of a sky so blue…deep, deep blue…

Here I am to worship,
Here I am to bow down,
Here I am to say that you're my God,
You're altogether lovely,
Altogether worthy,
Altogether wonderful to me.
I'll never know how much it costs, to see my sin upon that cross…

I skied through the maze of people and the bottom of Lion's Head past the gondola. My eyes welled up with tears, and a big smile was on my face… I'd tasted heaven on earth today… How much more would heaven itself be with my wonderful God.

Lessons in Giving a Hug

Jenni and I were invited to a party. "Dressy/Casual," the invitation read. What did that mean? We weren't sure, but we knew it would be a fun catered party hosted by a couple we know from our church. This was going to be so much fun joining fifty or so other couples for cocktails and hors d'oeuvres followed by a delicious dinner.

We drove to the neighboring town, found a parking place among the twenty plus cars already there. As we walked toward the driveway, we could see the hostess greeting people out front and sending them around back to the pool for a glass of wine. She was such an energetic person who always had something engaging to discuss. This was going to be fun!

As we walked up and said our hello, our hostess threw her arms up in the air with her hands above her head, ready to hug me. Her hands were so high that I reached my arms around her below her arms with my hands on her back, and we gave each other the stereotypical kiss on the cheek.

As we started to move back away from the hug, she dropped her arms straight down ahead of my pace. Because my arms were below hers, this forced my arms straight down. My hands moved from her middle back down to her lower back and continued straight down so that my hands made a gentle movement around her curvaceous butt.

I was stunned.

I thought I just inadvertently made a pass at our hostess. She didn't blink, and I hoped she didn't even notice. If she did, she said nothing. I walked away, kind of in a state of shock and said to Jenni, "Well, that was interesting! I just felt her butt."

Jenni gave me a peculiar look as I explained what happened. From this point forward, I always made sure at least one of my arms was on top when hugging someone.

A Long Day

March of 2010, Jenni was in Captiva. Our son Cody was flying in for his spring break during his junior year at Baylor University while I flew down from Chicago. Our planes would land essentially at the same time, with Jenni ready to pick us up at the airport. I met Cody at the baggage claim, and he asked me to help him with his suitcase. Laughing at what I thought was his joke, I took a closer look at him, and he was thin. Very thin.

"I don't feel very well," Cody told me.

He did not know what was wrong, but he had lost twenty pounds in two months. He looked weak. I grabbed his suitcase, and we headed out to meet Jenni, who was waiting in the car. No one knew what was wrong with Cody, but we did our best to take care of him this week.

A week later, he flew back to Waco, Texas, still feeling weak but a bit better from some TLC from Jenni. We knew Cody would be back in a few weeks to celebrate Easter with us. Our daughter Kate was teaching first grade at Faith Christian Academy in Arvada, Colorado, and her spring break was the week leading up to Easter. Kate flew down to Florida, and we knew Cody would join us on Good Friday.

Friday morning, Jenni and I were excited as Cody would arrive this day and our family would have four days together. As we debated who would pick Cody up at the airport in three hours, the phone rang.

"Hey, Dad," Cody said. "I'm still in Waco. I am in so much pain I can't get out of bed."

Cody had a fissure turn into a boil in his digestive tract and was in intense pain. While talking to him on the phone, I jumped on my laptop and purchased three tickets to Dallas, leaving in two hours. I hung up and told him we'd be there by midafternoon.

The immediacy of the moment barely gave us time to think. Packing our suitcases in a rush while I arranged a rental car, our family was in high gear to get to our ailing son and brother.

Jenni is a claustrophobic flyer. She had technically stopped flying fifteen years earlier and had only reluctantly been on a plane twice since then. Without time to get nervous, Jenni proceeded to move forward as we threw our suitcases in the car and drove to the Fort Myers airport. She knew without asking that I bought her a first-class ticket to help with the claustrophobia, but still, she dreaded the idea of getting on a plane.

While driving to the airport, we arranged for Cody to see a local surgeon to lance the boil. This was painful but would give him great relief. The doctor was encouraging to Cody and was sure that this was an isolated event and he'd be back to normal in a few weeks.

Around 3:00 PM, we arrived at Cody's rental home in Waco, and our family was reunited. Not as we expected on the beaches of Captiva but instead in Waco, Texas.

We went to Cody's church on Easter and had a lovely family visit before departing. Kate was flying back to Denver and Jenni and me back to Florida. Cody was much improved, and we felt that the problem was solved.

Cody did get a little better, but not much. His weight stayed low, and his pain continued. Sticking out the semester, he flew home to spend ten days in Chicago before heading to Colorado Springs for a summer program with the Focus Institute.

We arranged for Cody to see a colorectal surgeon in Chicago. Confident that we just needed a proper diagnosis and then some medication or something simple to fix it. Jenni drove Cody to Evanston to see Dr. Muldoon, a gifted and kind physician who came strongly recommended.

After the exam, the doctor came out to Jenni in the waiting room. "You have a very sick boy, Mrs. Terrill," the doctor said. "He needs to have a colonoscopy as soon as possible to get a proper diagnosis, but he needs three to four weeks to heal before that is even possible," he added.

Jenni took it in the best she could but did not really know what it meant. Cody was sick, but with what? We didn't know nor did the doctor. On the car ride back home, Jenni called me at my office to share what the doctor said. Choosing her words carefully, not wanting to reveal her fears in front of Cody. We both were so confused. This didn't fit into the plan. Cody was supposed to go to Colorado next week, and after all, our family didn't have medical issues. We were healthy.

Cody spent weeks convalescing at home, waiting for a colonoscopy from Dr. Ehrenpreis.

Dr. Eli Ehrenpreis was my gastroenterologist, which I carefully selected to do my first age fifty plus routine colonoscopy two years earlier. He devoted an extra year while in medical school to study pharmacology in addition to gastroenterology. I felt relieved to have already a relationship with such a knowledgeable physician in a specialty that we now needed more than ever.

Finally, the day came for the colonoscopy. After the surgical procedure was over, the doctor came to tell Jenni and me that all went well, but Cody had a great deal of inflammation in his digestive tract, along with one very large polyp. Dr. Ehrenpreis explained that we'd wait on the pathology report, but he was confident Cody had Crohn's disease. Tissue samples would also be sent to the University of Chicago Hospital for a confirming diagnosis.

Jenni and I did our best to be stoic and optimistic. My dear friend, Chuck Caldwell's wife, suffered from Crohn's for some twenty years. I recall when she was hospitalized for two straight months, and they tried to get her symptoms under control. I knew I could learn much from Chuck's wealth of experience in his wife's illness. Sue was doing well now, and on the top of my checklist was a call to Chuck in Los Angeles.

Two days later, the phone rang. Dr. Ehrenpreis was calling to confirm the diagnosis was Crohn's disease. Being already sure of the diagnosis, this was no surprise. He went on to say that he was concerned about this polyp, and he wanted Cody to have another colonoscopy at the University of Chicago under the guidance of Dr. Rubin. A special dye with a chromatic colonoscopy was necessary to determine if the polyp was "flat cell" or not.

"OK," I said. "We can arrange for that to be done," I said, a bit deflated, thinking about Cody needing to do the prep again for this test. He had been through so much already, and I wanted to find a way to spare him of anything that was not necessary.

The doctor explained that this could be a very high cancer risk situation, and we needed to know for sure what type of cell tissue both this polyp had and his colon in general. It might not be cancer, but if it was a flat-cell polyp, his colon would need to be removed.

"Dr. Ehrenpreis, can't we just do colonoscopies and if there are future polyps take those out then?"

"No, we need to do it now," he replied. "If it is flat cell, we need to remove his colon now."

"What? Remove his colon? Can't we just take out his colon if he gets cancer?" I pushed back.

"No. You don't understand," the doctor replied with his gentle voice.

"What am I missing?" I asked.

"If it is flat cell, then this is a very aggressive type, especially in a twenty-one-year-old. It is different because of his young age. If he has flat cells and we don't remove his colon, he will die."

I stood there silently in our kitchen with the phone raised to my ear. I was unable to speak. Trying to reply, my body just wouldn't let me produce words. A type of fear I had never known now controlled my mind and body. I never contemplated the idea that my son might die.

Eventually, I mumbled out, "OK, I understand now," and finished the conversation.

I needed to process this, but how? I went out for a bike ride to the Middlefork, Savanna. An eight-hundred-acre open lands with a bike trail running through it. I often went here, especially for times of sorting through weighty thoughts on my mind.

Riding with my MP3 player to random assortment from my music collection, my mind swirled around with Cody as the centerpiece. Thoughts of his youth. Playing baseball, fishing, skiing, ice-skating, and the many things we did together. Emotions I didn't understand welled up in my soul when Bruce Springsteen's song "Candy's Room" started to play.

This song starts out very slowly as a snare drum sets the pace with a quiet talking-style vocal. But as the song builds, more and more power develops while the tune progresses. I started to pedal harder, changing gears to gain speed. Springsteen hit certain words with an emphasis on strength, and each time he did so, I dialed up into a higher rate. Pushing as hard as I could and needing to expend a level of physical energy in a cathartic frenzy. It's my way of screaming, not with words but with my body pushed to the limits of exertion and then more. The song lasted two minutes and forty-eight seconds, which was about all I could possibly sprint in this ride. As the song ended, I stopped pedaling and begin to coast for a moment.

The next song began, and I resumed my pedaling at a robust pace but backed off considerably. Still, my body was full of adrenaline as the lyrics to Matchbox Twenty's song "Long Day" started.

I like to personalize songs to fit my own life's circumstances. Rob Thomas has a way of singing with a blend of anger and frustration wrapped up in a neediness of desperation. This song which I knew was about to touch a nerve in me that I had never seen before.

> *It's sitting by the overcoat*
> *The second shelf, the note she wrote*
> *That I can't bring myself to throw away*
> *And also*
> *Reach she said for no one else but you*
> *'Cause you won't turn away*
> *When someone else is gone.*

This made me think about God, not turning away from me, no matter what.

> *I'm sorry 'bout the attitude*
> *I need to give when I'm with you*
> *But no one else would take this s—from me.*

I knew that God accepted me, even though I was seriously flawed. I could vent my anger and frustration, and still, He would not leave me.

> *And I'm so*
> *terrified of no one else but me*
> *I'm here all the time*
> *I won't go away*
> *It's me, yeah well I can't get myself to go away*
> *Hey it's me, and I can't get myself to go away*
> *Oh God, I shouldn't feel this way now*

This was hitting me so hard. Yes, I can't get myself to go away. I'm always here. At times like this, I wish I could get out of my own head and mind, but I can't. I'm here all the time.

> *Reach down your hand in your pocket*
> *Pull out some hope for me.*

This became my prayer. My pleading. Beseeching God to reach down his hand and pull out some hope for me.

> *It's been a long day, always ain't that right*
> *And no, Lord, your hand won't stop it*
> *Just keep you trembling*
> *It's been a long day, always ain't that right.*

Yes, it had been a long day. A long day of days. I felt like I needed this to end.

> *Well, I'm surprised if you'd believe*
> *In anything that comes from me*
> *I didn't hear from you or from someone else*
> *And you're so set in life man, a pisser they're waiting*
> *Too D—bad you get so far so fast*
> *So what, so long.*

This was my confession. That I was not reliable myself. Why should God believe me? I had consistently failed in my life to live as God wanted me to live. Why should He listen to me now?

> *Reach down your hand in your pocket*
> *Pull out some hope for me*
> *It's been a long day, always ain't that right*
> *And no, Lord, your hand won't stop it*

Just keep you trembling
It's been a long day, always ain't that right
Oh, ain't that right.

I needed hope. Something to grab hold of and hang on to through the storm. An anchor to hold my boat through the waves. "It's been a long day, ain't that right." It had been long. So long.

It's me, yeah well I can't myself to go away
Hey, well it's me, yeah well I can't get myself to go away
Oh God, I shouldn't feel this way, now.

I shouldn't feel this way. In the sense that I couldn't get myself to go away. I needed to be present.

Reach down your hand in your pocket
Pull out some hope for me
It's been a long day, always ain't that right
And no, Lord, your hand won't stop it
Just keep you trembling.

The song ended, and I had a new thought of asking God to reach down and give me some hope. Emotionally spent and physically exhausted, I could only pedal the four miles home at a moderate pace. But I had a peace that I didn't have prior to the bike ride and these two songs.
Cody would have the test, and the results were good. He did not have the flat cell, and we could cross off cancer from the list of concerns. It was a huge relief. The physical struggle for my son would continue as he transitioned from being cared for by his parents to taking care of himself. Advancements in medicine gave him great relief from his Crohn's several years later. Today he is a healthy grown man.

When I hear these songs today, I am transported back to that day on my bike. The tears come, but with a knowledge of the result. I learned that God is faithful no matter what and that my will is not always His. My job is not to change His will but to trust Him. I try my best to do that today.

Great Lakes Naval Training Center

2015

In August, I went to a Cubs game. Driving to Wilmette to take the L train to Wrigley Field, I picked up grade school friends Walter Calhoun, Brett Johnson, and Brian Avery on the way. After the game, Brian and Brett stayed downtown to meet their wives while Walter and I took the L back to Wilmette to my car.

At the Howard Street transfer station, I saw five sailors dressed in the navy white uniforms on the platform waiting like Walter and me for the next train. I overheard one of them say, "We are screwed. We can't get back in time. We're dead!"

I asked this young navy man what was the problem. "We were going to transfer at Davis Street in Evanston to catch the Metra train back to the base, but the train was canceled." He began speaking with a sense of hopelessness. He continued, "But because it is Saturday, the next train is not until 10:20 PM. If we are not back at ten o'clock, we are AWOL. We are screwed."

"How many are you?" I asked.

"Five of us," he replied.

With a smile, I told them, "I have a seven-passenger car in Wilmette with only two seats taken. I live just one mile from the front gate of the naval base and could drop you off at 7:30 PM easily." They started jumping up and down in excitement. I had the solution to their problem.

On the drive home, I learned a lot about each sailor. His age, where he grew up, and what he was learning in the Navy. I stopped by our house before dropping them off, and Jenni came out bringing homemade oatmeal raisin cookies. They loved the cookies and could not stop thanking me.

I obtained their contact information and invited them to our house for an afternoon of Ping-Pong, croquette, and dinner when they had their next liberty. Four weeks later, we had them over along with my folks and my daughter and son-in-law who were in town.

We served burgers, corn on the cob, and watermelon, finishing with a dessert of homemade apple pie and ice cream. We all had a great time.

Jenni and I wanted to treat them to some good home cooking and family fun as a break from their new routine. Many mentioned how much they missed home and how nice it was to have such a fun evening. What a privilege to host and honor these young men who had volunteered to protect our nation from those who would harm us. I was grateful to have the chance to give a little back.

Baseball

"Baseball is America's pastime." I've heard that saying since I was a kid, and while it is, of course, accurate, it could also be said, baseball is Tom's pastime. Baseball is unique from every other team sport in so many ways. There is no time limit on the game; each field is different from another, and it is the only sport where the team with the ball is on defense. These are just three aspects of many that differentiate baseball from other team sports.

Since my first encounter with the game in 1966 at the age of eight, I was hooked. The Chicago Cubs played day games that were locally broadcast on WGN-TV. One summer afternoon, I came in from playing outside and turned on the TV. Channel 9 was the favorite channel of all the kids in Chicago because of the popular morning program *The Ray Rayner Show* and the lunchtime classic *Bozo's Circus*. Our TV was set was already on channel 9 when I turned it on that day.

The TV warmed up, and when the screen came on, there before my eyes was the Cubs game. I can't tell you whom they were playing or who won, but I clearly remember the first three batters I saw. Glen Beckert, the Cubs second baseman, was leading off a middle inning, and he hit a long fly ball to left field. While the left fielder easily caught it, I was amazed at how far someone could hit the ball. Billy Williams was next up. I knew nothing about this man, who would later become my hero, but he drove the ball deep into right field. At the wall, it was caught, just shy of a home run. With two outs, the Cubs third baseman Ron Santo came to the plate. He too hit a long fly ball into the outfield that was caught on the warning track for the third out.

In the box score, it was an uneventful inning, but for me, a new passion had shown its first sign of life. I was in awe at the power and strength of these batters. Every day the games were broadcast, and I was now a devoted follower of baseball and specifically my hometown favorite team, the Chicago Cubs.

I also became a participant. I didn't have a bat, but I had a straight cane that was my grandfather's. I asked my mom to purchase an air-filled ball about the size of grapefruit, and with these two, I would stand on the front walk of my parents' home and throw the ball into the air and swing the cane as if it were a bat. I hit the ball toward the street and the house across the street that conveniently belonged to my grandparents. Creating a game based on how far I hit the ball, determined whether I had an out or a hit. A far-enough hit might be a double, triple, or even home run.

Quickly, I learned the lineups of the Cubs and their rival, the St. Louis Cardinals. Playing a real game by myself, I was every batter for both teams and kept the score in my head. Hour after hour of summer days, I played this game, which had the side effect of the development of a pretty good swing. The next year, my parents bought me a hard ball and bat, and I continued my game between the two houses. After the third broken window, I was told to move my game.

My younger siblings Kathy and Jeff were more than happy to learn the game, and so the three of us played in our driveway with a rubber ball to avoid injuries and broken glass.

In the third grade, I began to play little league with my first team coached by Mr. Kenyon. I continued my baseball career into early high school, but like most young boys, eventually I was told that my services would no longer be needed, and I would be relegated to the role of fan and softball leagues.

Tom Terrill, Bill Fillion, George Haydock, and Tom Porter. My sister Kathy Terrill and my mom in hats behind us.

My parents took me to Wrigley Field to see the Cubs many times. Initially, these were just family outings, but then I had a birthday party where I was allowed to bring some friends and teammates from my little league teams.

I loved the Cubs, and it was such fun to go to Wrigley Field. My friends and I started to ride our bikes to the Wilmette Linden Avenue L station, where we could board a train that took us right to Wrigley Field. The summer after fifth grade, we no longer required parental supervision and would simply go on our own. I was ten years old, turning eleven at the end of July, with the freedom to roam down to Chicago with only the combined wisdom of my companions on any given day.

I cannot imagine in today's world any parent allowing this to happen, but back then, it was perfectly normal, and no one would think my parents were negligent. I've been to countless games, but like every fan, some stand out more than others.

A Doubleheader

On Labor Day of 1968, the Chicago Cubs would host the San Francisco Giants at the friendly confines of Wrigley Field in a doubleheader. The next day would start the school year at Joseph Sears School in Kenilworth, where good friends Tom Terrill and Ricky McIntyre would now be in the fifth grade. However, on this September 2 date, Tom and Ricky would celebrate Labor Day watching the Cubs live.

This was more than just a doubleheader, which was unique in and of itself. This day, there would be four people sitting in box seats behind the Giants' dugout. In addition to Ricky and me, of course, were my father and one of the stockbrokers whom he managed at his loop office, Billy Pierce.

Billy was an eighteen-year veteran pitcher for the Tigers, White Sox, and Giants who recorded a 3.27 lifetime earned run average. Retiring after the 1964 season with San Francisco, Billy made the career transition into the world of finance and investments as a stockbroker for McDonnell and Company where my father, Tom Terrill, Sr., was the manager.

The first game was complete with superstars, many of which were later inducted into the Hall of Fame. Juan Marichal would be on the mound for the Giants against Cubs lefty Kenny Holtzman. Bobby Bonds was in his rookie season for the Giants with a lineup including Willie Mays, Willie McCovey, and Jesus Alou who went four for five and drove in four runs for the Giants.

The Cubs lineup was packed with talent. Kessinger, Beckert, Williams, Santo, and Ernie Banks filling out the top of the card, with Smith, Hundley, and Phillips completing this impressive team. However, Game 1 was taken by the Giants, 8–4, as Juan Marichal pitched a complete game.

Game 2 had the unique history in that the game ended as a 1–1 tie, a rarity in baseball.

When the second game ended, Billy Pierce led us from our seats to a caged door where a security guard allowed us to pass. This walkway led to the Giants locker room where we'd get to meet the players.

Ricky and I were so excited. Suddenly, there we were talking with Willie Mays. The "Say Hey Kid" was a living legend widely regarded as the best center fielder in the history of the game. Billy was yaking it up with some of his former teammates and introducing them to my dad while Ricky and I each had a new official major league baseball that we were getting autographed by the entire team.

As a ten-year-old boy, these men were enormous. Larger than life, each one represented the pinnacle of sports to Ricky and me, but the moment that stood out the most was when Willie McCovey walked out from the shower to his locker right in front of us. This man really was a giant, and his naked physic was unimaginably impressive.

Unsure what to do, I handed him my baseball and asked for his autograph. There he stood without a stitch of clothing, signing his name on the ball. You don't forget seeing Willie McCovey without his clothes on. Today I still have that ball sitting in a protective plastic case on my dresser.

Billy Williams Day

Billy Williams was my favorite baseball player. Batting third in the Cubs lineup, he was affectionately known as "sweet-swinging" Billy Williams. I would study his swing while watching TV and then imitate him while looking in a mirror with a bat in my hand. I just loved this guy!

Billy played every game all the time, which was most unusual in baseball then and now. Most players needed a day off or would have some injury requiring it. But not Billy. He was the Cubs Iron Man.

At the time, Stan Musial held the National League record for consecutive games played with 895. Billy Williams had been creeping up on this milestone and would pass him on June 29, 1969, in a doubleheader against the St. Louis Cardinals. The Cubs officially announced the day as "Billy Williams Day" with festivities planned between the two games.

I had to be there, but the anticipated crowd was considerable, which meant leaving very early. Brian Avery and I agreed to go, leaving at the absurd early time of 6:00 AM. We rode our bikes the two miles in cloudy weather and got on the L train at the Linden Avenue station.

When we arrived at the Wrigley Field stop, a misty morning greeted us. Descending the steps of the elevated train platform, we walked across, ill prepared for the weather. Without an umbrella and only a London Fog coat, I was testing my luck against the weather. We walked to the end of a long line and huddled next to the outfield wall, waiting for bleacher tickets. It would be four hours before the gates would open, but this was to see my hero, so I could wait.

At about 8:00 AM, the skies opened, releasing a heavy rain upon the crowd. A month away from my eleventh birthday, Brian and I were the youngest people in this crowd of wet and getting-wetter devoted fans. We listened to the conversations around us, trying to gain an insight into the weather or odds of the games getting played. As the rain got heavier, the mood of the crowd had a sense of defeat. By 10:00 AM, we had been standing in the rain for two hours now, and there was no evidence of it letting up.

"Brian, I don't think they are going to play these games today," I said.

"Yeah, it seems impossible with this rain and how wet the field will be," Brian said, agreeing with my assessment. We knew what happened to our little league field with much less rain and figured these games would not be played.

"I think we should get out of here. What do you think?" I asked Brian. Brian was as big a fan like me, but to two ten-year-olds, the chances of one game, let alone two being played, was impossible. We bolted out of line and ran back to the L, riding home wearing our wet jeans and soaked Converse gym shoes. After arriving in Wilmette and riding our bikes back to Kenilworth, the sun came out. Blue now dominated the skies, and the warm sun dried out the wet ground very quickly.

The games were played, and Billy Williams had an incredible day. He broke the record and was honored by the Cubs and adoring fans in the friendly confines of Wrigley Field.

I watched it on TV.

Opening Day, 1971

At some point in one's life, going to an Opening Day event is a must. 39,079 people skipped work, school, or other pressing engagements to find their way to Wrigley Field on Tuesday, April 6, 1971.

It was Opening Day!

A sunny day in Chicago, but the temperature was only in the forties. The seventh grade class at Joseph Sears School was missing five boys. Tom Porter, George Haydock, Art Bergman, Brian Avery, and Tom Terrill were riding the L train from Wilmette to Chicago to get in line to buy tickets.

I'm not sure what excuse the others used for playing hooky, but my mom gladly wrote a note for me indicating that I had an excused absence. She figured it was better, to be honest, and she knew that nothing spectacular was scheduled to happen at school that day. She and I had an understanding that if I came to her openly with my desire to miss a day of school for something special, she would work with me to accomplish it.

This gift from my mom allowed me to experience a memory of a lifetime and set the tone for how I prioritized events for the rest of my life. As we got off the L train and headed to the ticket window, we saw a sea of humanity surrounding the ballpark.

"Look at all those people!" Tom Porter said with an air of excitement. The big crowd confirmed for Tom that we were where the action would be, and he couldn't wait to be in the midst of it. Brian, George, Art, and I followed Tom to the back of the crowd to wait in line. It wasn't a line with any order to it, but more like a large school of fish all bunched together trying to get to the same place.

The four of us were in the back of this crowd, but quickly, that changed as more and more people kept arriving. Soon, we were in the middle of this crowd, and being only thirteen, most of the adults towered over us. The space between the people in front of us and those behind us shrunk to nothing in a matter of moments so that we were no longer able to control where we moved. Like that school of fish that changes direction by darting left and quickly changing to right, we were flowing with the crowd, having surrendered all control of our destination.

Each of us was pushed away from one another as this gyration of the crowd developed. I could see Art the whole time as he was tall for his age, and Tom Porter was within sight too. However, George and Brian were lost to me in the chaos. At various points in time, my feet were lifted off the ground as the pack surged in one direction. This lasted five plus minutes at a time where I didn't touch the ground as my body was crushed in upon the others around me.

This was quite scary, and some of the girls in the scramble were crying out, pleading with anyone who would listen to stop the pushing. The Wrigley Field ticket windows opened up earlier, and the fans began to work through the turnstiles into park.

Once inside, we found our seats in the grandstands behind home plate. This game featured two of the best pitchers in baseball facing off against each other. Bob Gibson for the St. Louis Cardinals and Ferguson Jenkins, the Cubs ace, both future Hall of Fame players.

The Cubs team featured the same starting four of Kessinger, Beckert, Williams, and Santo; however, now at age forty, Ernie Banks was playing less often. This game, he was in the dugout while Joe Pepitone took over at first base.

The Cardinal squad had Matty Alou leading off, with a lineup that included Lou Brock, Joe Torre, and Ted Simmons. Great players each.

This pitchers' duel went into the ninth inning tied 1–1, where neither team succeeded in putting a run on the board. It was going to extra innings. Fergie Jenkins went out to pitch the tenth inning with the dangerous Lou Brock leading off. The best base stealer in the game was always a threat, but he hit a ground ball back to the mound and was an easy out. Joe Torre was next up, and he proceeded to hit a ground ball to third base where Gold Glover Ron Santo quickly threw him out at first. Jose Cardinal flew out to center field, ending the inning.

This game was moving fast, still under two hours old when the Cubs came up in the bottom of the tenth inning. Glen Beckert led off with an easy groundout to shortstop. Billy Williams walked from the on-deck circle to the batter's box to once again face Bob Gibson.

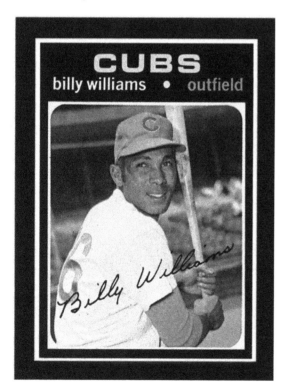

Topps® trading cards used courtesy of The Topps Company, Inc.

Billy had a walk, single, groundout, and fly out so far, and he stepped in for his fifth at-bat against the hard-throwing right-hander. Gibson had won the Cy Young Award for the best pitcher in baseball in both 1968 and 1970. No one was more intimidating on the mound.

Billy Williams was my favorite player, and I just kept repeating, "Come on, Billy. Come on, Billy."

Billy obliged the crowd and hit a walk-off home run, although that term didn't yet exist. The crowd erupted in an ovation, as did I, along with my friends. Jumping up and down, we celebrated in the stands while Billy rounded the bases to give the Cubs a thrilling victory.

This day was full of excitement and so much better than another day in the seventh grade at school.

The Day after Opening Day

The 1972 baseball season experienced a delayed start due to a player strike with opening day on Saturday, April 15. My father's office had four box-seat tickets a few rows behind the Cubs dugout, and I inquired if I might be able to take three good friends to the game.

"Tom, the opening day tickets are for the office's best clients, but you can have the second game." I accepted the free tickets, of course, but my heart was set on opening day. Having been there the year before, I wanted to relive the excitement of another opener.

No one wanted to go to the second game. Generating as much excitement as a kiss from one's grandmother, this consolation prize just didn't cut it for a true baseball fan like me. My friends were disappointed not to get the free opening day seats, but they also knew how prime these seats were.

Walter Calhoun, Chuck Caldwell, Brian Avery, and I boarded the Linden Street L train from Wilmette to Wrigley Field. This damp and cloudy day was terrible for a baseball game. We dressed as warmly as we could, but still with the wind out of the north and the temperature stuck at thirty-nine degrees, it was cold, to say the least.

"Tom, I love your dad," Walter said as we settled into our amazing seats. Looking around, we noticed so many empty seats throughout Wrigley Field. Only 9,583 came that day, and the four of us did our best to cheer on our team.

In the fourth inning, Ron Santo led off with a two-bagger. Rick Monday was then walked, leaving men on first and second. Cubs all-star shortstop came up to lay down a sacrifice bunt, but a Philly error on the play allowed Santo to score from second giving the Cubs a 1–0 lead.

I was wearing my favorite shoes, an old pair of desert boots. These tattered shoes should have long ago been thrown out, but I kept them anyway. The lady next to me saw the terrible condition of my shoes. The sole was separated from the upper part of the shoe exposing the four-inch-long opening. My socks were damp as a result, and I was shivering in the cold.

"Young man, please take this," the lady said to me, holding a ten-dollar bill.

"What for, ma'am?" I asked, a bit perplexed.

"Please buy yourself a new pair of shoes. You need them so badly," she kindly offered.

"Oh, thank you, ma'am. But I can't accept your money. My father has a good job and can afford to buy me new shoes. I'm just wearing them because I like them." She didn't seem to believe me, but then I pointed out that we did not sneak into these seats but had the tickets paid for by my dad's company. At this point, she took my word for it.

Through seven innings, Burt Hooton had still not given up a hit. And despite walking seven batters at this point, he seemed to have the game in control. In the bottom of the seventh inning, Cubs catcher, Randy Hundley, singled in two more runs, making the score 3–0.

"Guys, we are seeing a no-hitter!" Chuck said as the Cubs took the field in the top of the eighth inning. Baseball's unspoken rules were never to mention such an event for fear of jinxing the end result. Chuck had moved from Los Angeles just a year ago, and being a Dodgers' fan, he felt the freedom to talk about it. The rest of us joined in, but mostly with a developing plan to rush the field if Hooton accomplished this unlikely feat. Our seats started on an aisle that led to the top of the Cubs dugout near the on-deck circle.

"Guys, on the final out, we need to race down the last few steps, leap onto the edge of the dugout roof, and leap to the field," I said, stating the obvious.

"But we have to move fast," Brian added. "We need to time it perfectly."

As the four of us imagined ourselves celebrating on the field, Burt Hooton set down the Phillies in order in the top of the eighth inning. The Cubs scored an insurance run in the bottom of the eighth inning as Glenn Beckert singled home Jose Cardenal, who had tripled to lead off the inning.

The Cubs led 4–0 heading into the top of the ninth inning. Twenty-two-year-old Burt Hooton was pitching just his fourth major league start. Donning number 44 on his uniform, Hooton was paid $13,500 to pitch for the Cubs while Cy Young Award-winning teammate Fergie Jenkins made $125,000 that year. However, on this day, it was Burt Hooton who had Cy Young level stuff.

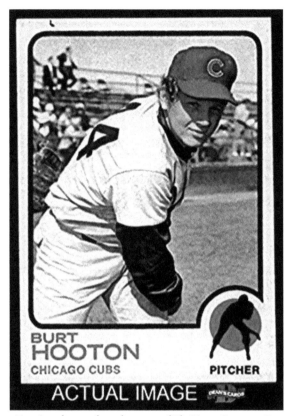

Topps® trading cards used courtesy of The Topps Company, Inc.

In the ninth inning, the Phillies quickly had two outs, and now ready to rush the field on the next out, the four of us could barely contain ourselves. As Greg Luzinski stepped up the plate, Chicago's men in blue filed down every aisle of Wrigley Field. Suddenly, our plan to run onto the field required us to get past a police officer forcibly.

On a knuckle curveball, Burt Hooton struck out Luzinski to complete his no-hitter and become a part of baseball history. We did not run onto the field but celebrated from our seats, aware of our part in witnessing this memorable event.

As it turned out, *the day after Opening Day* proved to be the game to attend. My father's clients enjoyed the festivities of Opening Day, but my friends and I can forever say we saw a No-Hitter in person and from right behind the Cubs dugout.

My Day at Wrigley Field

Summer 2008

Well, today, I had a real treat. Blue Cross hosted an outing for fifty people. Fifteen from Blue Cross Blue Shield and thirty-five top brokers. It was titled a "Field of Dreams" outing at Wrigley Field. Let me tell you about it.

We arrived and entered Wrigley Field as a group, where we were taken to the grandstands. There they divided us into two groups. My group went on a tour first and then to the field. They took us up to the press box first, and I got to sit in the seat some *Tribune* reporter I'd never heard of sat. Front row. Very high up. Then to a skybox. Very small but nice. Then out to the upper deck terrace. I'd been here many times, and it is a favorite spot of mine. It's warm, sunny, and blocked from the cold easterly winds off Lake Michigan. For some reason though, management no longer allows anyone to go to the upper deck unless they have upper-deck seats. So I haven't been able to go here in years. It was fun to see it again.

Then we move down into the locker room. We were told not to touch anything. Some guys like Zambrano get freaked out if something has moved an inch. Imagine Zambrano being touchy. Weird! It was small and rather average looking. I think I expected fancy stuff like the Ritz, but it was just ordinary. The weight room seemed very average. I guess it was nice to see things looking like the rest of the world. Then down the hall and into the dugout. This was so cool. To sit in the dugout was incredible. I moved around sitting in different seats so I could sit where some of my heroes sat. Williams, Banks, Jenkins, Sutter, and even Dave Kingman (last one not a hero ☺). I was surprised at how bad the view was. I would not want to watch a game from there versus the seats right above it, which were just as close but a higher perspective. I felt like I was in a hole. It seems kind of funny to think of managers coming out complaining about a call at first base with which they disagree. I don't think one can actually see the base if you're sitting in the dugout.

Then we went out to the field. I found a new friend and started to play catch. It was just catch, but there was ivy behind my partner, and a 368 yellow-painted sign behind me. The location was magical. The catch was ordinary. Then the guy threw one over my head, and I turned and ran. I was running on the outfield grass in Wrigley Field. This was magical.

From there, we wandered at our own pace to "The Batter's Eye" for lunch. This is the skybox in the center field bleachers. Very cool. Beautiful view with good food everywhere. I ate a hot dog. I could get good food anywhere. I was in Wrigley Field. I ate a hot dog. (I also had some artichoke and tomato and mozzarella. Yes, I had one of those pecan chocolate coconut things… OK, two of them…three, it was three, and they were delicious.)

They announced a home run derby would start soon… OK…this was tough… The last time I swung a bat hard was at a high school father-son game with Cody, and I threw my back out… My back ached every day of my life… I was not complaining, but I really didn't want to increase the pain… I wandered down… Now they were using twelve-inch softballs because the plate was in center field… Still, I watched a few guys hit. Lazy fly balls…grounders…a few guys swung and missed. Losers. I decided to at least pick up a bat and just kind of warm up after all… Some kid… maybe twenty-five…with his dad… He reached the basket, and it's the first and only one to leave the field…barely out… Maybe twenty-five guys had hit… A couple bounced off the wall… I moved in and decided my back hurts whether I would swing or not. I was in Wrigley. I walked up to the makeshift plate, and my legs were shaking… I was nervous… I couldn't believe I was nervous… The pressure was enormous… Remember this was a crowd of fifty people. The first pitch came in, and I swung hard, sending a long fly ball to the warning track… It's caught… A few comments about a nice try… The next one, I ripped a line drive to left and then repeated it again on the third hit… I had one more pitch to see. I thought to myself, *Here it comes*, and I think hard…*kept my shoulders level…don't dip…steady swing*…and there it goes…five rows up into the left-center bleachers…only the second home run and the first to leave the field and go into the stands… I felt great!…

One more guy hit one out, but that was it in the home run derby…three of them…one guy twenty-five…one guy thirty-two…and a forty-nine-year-old dude from Lake Bluff.

We then played a game of softball. It was OK but really not as much fun as one might think. Still, I played and had fun.

I went back to get some more food and just wandered around. I wanted to go to the infield, but they'd roped the grass off. I stood on the dirt next to first base. Banks, Buckner, Durham, Pepitone, Grace, and Lee, not to forget Hickman, Fanzone, Moreland, and others who stood there on this sacred ground. And those were just the Cubs.

Finally, I did something many times that serious baseball fans would understand. I spit. I spit in the infield. I spit in the outfield. I spit everywhere. Mind you, this was out of respect. I was a spitter, and it seemed liked it was my duty to spit on the field where some of the great ones had spit too.

The afternoon was over. I was standing next to my new friend, and we were looking around, trying to find what we, of course, hoped for…a goody bag. Souvenirs and keepsakes, but there was nothing. We couldn't believe it. At least give me a ball. They were treating me like I was a man. They were wrong. I was a twelve-year-old boy in an old man's body, and I wanted a goody bag. Oh well… Cubs fans would know… Maybe next year.

Playoffs 1984

I was married in September 1983, and my wife Jenni and I decided early on that for our first anniversary we'd travel to Virginia and go to Chincoteague Island. While this trip was planned well in advance, the Chicago Cubs decided to win their division and play baseball in October for the first time in thirty-nine years.

Getting tickets would be nearly impossible. Scalping was illegal and highly regulated with severe punishment. StubHub did not exist, and there were only two ways to get tickets. If you were a season ticket holder or a guest of a season ticket holder, you could attend the game. The other way was through a lottery in which one would send in a postcard with your name on it and the Cubs organization would call you up on a specific night preannounced. If you failed to answer the phone, you lost out.

The designated evening was a night Jenni and I had small group with friends from our church. There was no way I could leave the house, and so instead, Jenni went without me. Eight other couples, all very close friends, were there that evening while I desperately hoped for my phone to ring. The calls were made between 7:00 PM to 9:00 PM, and at 8:50 PM, my phone rang.

"Hello," I said.

"Can I speak to Mr. Tom Terrill please?" the voice on the other end inquired.

"This is Tom," I nervously replied.

"This is Jim Williams from the Chicago Cubs ticket office, and your name has been selected. Would you like to buy up to two tickets for the playoff series against the San Diego Padres?"

I could hardly believe my luck. I could barely talk and struggled to spit out that I would like the best two tickets available for Game 1. Jim Williams proceeded to take my order until it was time for the payment.

"Mr. Terrill, before I take your credit card, you'll need to speak to someone in our office."

The next voice I heard was my wife, Jenni. "Hi, honey. We are all playing a joke on you." It was my friend Gary Gilles on the phone, and everyone had a good laugh. Everyone but me. A dream come true was shattered with a cruel prank by trusted friends. I replied to Jenni with two words that I cannot repeat and hung up the phone. I felt a pit in my stomach and a level of anger that was new to me. I felt violated, but I also knew that Jenni would not have done this on her own. None of the other guys that night were baseball fans, let alone Cubs fans, and so it seemed like an innocent prank to them. So instead of going to the game, I went on a vacation.

We began the trip in Lynchburg, Virginia, on Sunday, September 30, and proceeded to Williamsburg on October 1. There we met up with our friend Chuck Trotter. He was with his family spending time with Chuck's brother Tom who was enrolled at William and Mary. We had a wonderful time, but my mind was elsewhere.

The Cubs, for the first time since 1945, had made the playoffs. Here I was out of town on vacation when I should have been in Wrigley Field. The Cubs won the opener by the lopsided score of 13–0, and I watched from our hotel room on Chincoteague Island. They won the second Game 4–2, taking a two-zip lead in the best of five series.

However, it was not to be our year as the Cubs dropped the next three in a row, failing to advance to the World Series. The Cubs curse was intact, and I felt partially responsible for planning a trip during the playoff season. I had missed the first chance in my lifetime to see baseball in Wrigley Field in October.

Playoffs 1989

After a thirty-nine-year hiatus, it took only five years for the Cubs to be back in the playoffs. Finishing the season with a 93–69 record, the Cubs were six games in front of the second place Mets. Vacation plans were not even considered now that our growing family had a three-year-old and six-month-old. After another failure to get tickets in the lottery, I decided to attempt a purchase at the game.

Scalping happened, but it remained illegal. I contacted both the Cubs office and the Chicago Police Department to find out what I could legally do to obtain a ticket. At the time, the rules were clear. I could only purchase it while standing on Wrigley property and only pay face value for the ticket. But the idea of paying only face value was a joke. No one would part with a coveted ticket without a profit. Both buyer and seller had to be wary of the other person in a proposed transaction to not be a victim of a sting operation.

My friend Brian Avery and I planned to drive down and hope to find tickets at a reasonable price without getting arrested in the process. Game 1, we watched on TV, and we set our sights on Game 2. Thursday, October 5, I left my home to pick Brian up. However, before leaving, I decided to make a sign. Taking a twelve-by-eighteen-inch cardboard box piece, I grabbed a thick black magic marker and printed in easy-to-read letters:

I Need

A

Ticket

"Hey, Jenni, what do you think of my sign?" I asked.

"You should add the word 'please' and put it in red," she wisely recommended.

So we got a red magic marker, and now my sign correctly said:

I Need

A

Ticket

PLEASE

Leaving Lake Bluff, I drove south to pick up Brian at his home in Chicago. From there, we drove about half a mile away from Wrigley Field and found some reasonably priced parking. As we walked the streets, people were discreetly asking the passersby, "Who needs a ticket?" After the third or fourth person who whispered this, we stopped and asked how much. "One hundred fifty dollars" came the soft-spoken reply. That was too much, and we kept going.

We got to the corner of Clark and Addison crossing onto the Wrigley Field property. I held up my sign and stood silently. Brian meanwhile was walking through the crowd, saying, "Need one," to no avail.

After five minutes, a man with his teenage son came up to me. "You need a ticket?" he asked.

"Yes, I do," I politely replied.

"Is this for you? You're not going to sell it, are you?" he inquired with a sense of importance to his question.

"No, I'm not going to sell it. I want to see the game," I answered.

"OK. You'll take my wife's ticket. She got sick, and so you'll sit with my son and me," he explained.

"Oh, OK," I said. "How much?" I nervously asked.

"Face value," he replied. "I don't want to make money. I just don't want a jerk sitting next to me," he said.

I gave him the money and told him I'd be in soon but needed to tell my friend I got a ticket. Brian came up to me as the man handed me the ticket.

"You got one!" Brian said, excited for me.

"Yes. Here take the sign. It worked great," I said, handing Brian my sign.

Within five minutes, two guys walked up to Brian and offered him a ticket. Face value. They worked for a radio station and had three tickets, and one guy couldn't make it. Brian and I were not sitting together, but we were both going in.

A stranger who saw both Brian and me get our tickets asked how we accomplished this. "It's the sign! Here, you try it," I said, now passing the sign to him. As Brian and I took a moment to see where each of us was sitting, a businessman came up to the stranger now holding Jenni's "please" sign and offered him a ticket for face value. Our new friend thanked us profusely and got his ticket also for face value.

Many times, we had gone to Cubs games over our thirty-one years of life. Most of the time with each other. Tonight was different as our feet stepped onto that hallowed ground revered by so many. This was something that other people experienced, but not Cubs fans and certainly not us. Nothing could wipe the smiles off our faces, and we soaked in the festive atmosphere.

We first went to my seat so Brian would know where I was, and we arranged to meet after the third innings. I sat down in my seat, again seeing the man and his son, who picked me to be their seatmate.

"Do you know why I came up to you?" he asked.

"No, I have no idea," I asked, looking for his explanation.

He told me, "I was going to pocket the ticket and have the seat remain open. I don't need the money and would prefer the extra room. However, when I saw your sign with the word 'please' on it, I decided then and there to offer it to you."

Jenni was right. The added word from her input had worked magic for three excited Cubs fans.

The Cubs won the Game 9–5 to even the series. But the Giants won the next two games to advance to play Oakland in the infamous BART Series marked with an earthquake just before game 3. The quake delayed the series for ten days eventually with Oakland sweeping the Giants to secure another championship for the Athletics.

The Cubs once again would wait for next year.

Playoffs 2003

Cubs vs. the Braves National League Division Series

In 2000, Eric Baker and Jeff Fluhr founded StubHub. This California start-up would soon turn the world of ticket purchases for sporting events upside down. Scalping laws began to change in various states, or at least the enforcement of it disappeared from the Wrigley neighborhood.

The Cubs had won their division and faced off against the National League's best team, the Atlanta Braves. The Braves had dominated National League baseball since 1991, winning their division every year but one. The Cubs were the underdog despite having such great players as Kerry Wood, Mark Prior, and Sammy Sosa.

The Cubs won Games 1 and 3, taking a 2–1 advantage in the best of five series into the Saturday, October 4 game at Wrigley Field. The ticket lottery was now an online window of opportunity that I failed to get through. So it would be time for a sign again à la 1989, and my fourteen-year-old son Cody and I drove down in hopes of buying a couple of tickets.

The crowd was enormous in the Wrigley neighborhood as we arrived ninety minutes before game time. We walked to the corner of Clark and Sheffield and held up the sign.

"Hey! You can't do that!" a Chicago policeman sternly told me as soon as I held up the sign.

"What? I thought we could buy a ticket legally now," I asked.

"Not on Wrigley property, you can't. You need to go across the street," he explained. How odd this was. In 1989, I had to be on Wrigley property to stay legal, and now I had to be off it. How was a person to know these changing rules? I wondered.

Cody and I walked into the street, which was closed off and full of people. I had Cody holding the sign, hoping someone might be more receptive to a kid than an adult. For fifteen minutes, we stood there getting bumped by the passing crowd without any encouragement.

"You need a ticket, man?" a skinny poorly dressed guy asked me. He didn't look like he had any tickets.

"Yes. Two," I replied. "One for my son and one for me."

"Four hundred dollars apiece," he told me.

"No, thanks," I said, shaking my head back and forth.

"Make me an offer," he answered.

"Face value," I said with a smile.

"Oh, man, you're just wasting my time," the skinny man said, giving me a dismissive hand wave as he walked away. I had split my money, so I had eighty dollars in my front right pocket and one hundred dollars in my left. I also had one hundred dollars in each of my back pockets, totaling three hundred eighty dollars. I had no plan to spend it all but was ready to do something to be sure Cody got into the game.

Cody silently watched this interaction, faithfully holding his sign the whole time. Shortly after Skinny left, a nicely dressed man in his early sixties approached Cody.

"Which is your favorite college team?" he asked Cody.

"Huh?" Cody replied, confused by the question.

"I asked you which college team is your favorite?" he nicely clarified.

"I don't know," Cody said, and the man walked away.

"Dad, what was that?" Cody asked me.

"I don't know. I guess he was just making conversation. It did seem a little weird, didn't it?" I verbally hypothesized.

Another twenty minutes or so passed without any offer within my budget when the well-dressed guy returned. "No tickets yet?" he now asked me.

"No," I said with a smile. "But we're still hoping."

He departed, and Skinny came back, saying, "OK, because I like you, I'll go three hundred dollars apiece."

"You like me!" I said with a laugh. "You don't even know me, and I just can't handle that much."

"OK, man, but you're missing out. I can sell these for three hundred dollars apiece easy, but I'm giving you a chance," he said, trying to sound persuasive. However, I was not willing yet. Game time was now fifteen minutes away, and I was hoping the prices might go down when Mr. Well-dressed returned for the third time.

"OK, I'm giving you one more chance," he began addressing Cody. "Which is your favorite college sports team?"

"Texas," Cody said.

"Texas?" he said with a tone of disappointment. "Well, I guess that is OK. Here you go," he said as he handed Cody a free "standing-room only" ticket, and he quickly disappeared into the crowd.

"Dad! What just happened?" Cody asked with an excited smile from ear to ear.

"*You are going to the game*," I said as we celebrated together.

Mr. Well-dressed had a plan of generosity to bestow upon someone, and he picked Cody out of a crowd of thousands. There could not have been a more grateful recipient.

Cody and I planned where he should stand and that if I were able to get a ticket, I'd meet him in the designated spot. As I watched Cody go through the turnstile, my spirit filled with joy. I loved baseball, and so did my son. We shared a love for the Cubs that was different from any other sports team in the United States. All Cubs fans can testify to this fact.

A few more minutes passed when I could hear the singing of "The Star-Spangled Banner" inside. I was outside still and was just not sure if I'd get a good chance at a ticket. Just then, Skinny came back.

"Hey, man, so you broke down and bought your son a ticket," Skinny said, noticing Cody's absence.

"No, a guy gave him a free ticket for standing room," I explained.

"What? No way! Well, then you have to get in there too to be with your son," he encouraged me.

"I have eighty dollars in this pocket," I said, pointing to my right front pocket.

"Turn that eighty dollars into two hundred dollars and you can have my last ticket," he offered.

"How do I know that it is not a fake ticket?" I asked. After all, Skinny did not look like a guy who would have a ticket.

"Come on, man. Get real. I'm for real. Are you?" He pushed back hard on my challenge to his authenticity.

"I can make it two hundred dollars if you'll walk up to the ticket taker and prove it is real," I said, not wanting to be taken advantage of by a scammer.

Skinny didn't say a word but motioned to me to follow him right to the ticket collector. "Sweetheart," he called out to a nice young woman accepting tickets, "will you tell my friend this ticket is legit?"

She just nodded in the affirmative. I gave Skinny two hundred dollars, and he handed me the ticket. "Man, you are one tough dude to do business with," he said laughingly. "Now go find your son," he ordered me like I was a subordinate to his command.

Dutifully, I followed his order and hustled in to find Cody. He was at the designated spot right where we planned and glad to see me. I explained that Cody would sit in this seat and I'd stand. We asked an usher to direct us to the ticket Skinny gave and walked all the way down to the thirteenth row, right behind the Cubs dugout. The seat was fantastic. Cody settled in, and I walked to the aisle behind the last row and leaned against the fence with a few hundred other holders of a standing-room ticket.

The Cubs lost that game. The series was tied at two games apiece and headed back to Atlanta. There the Cubs won by a score of 5–1 with Kerry Wood pitching a masterpiece, to advance to the National League Championship Series against the Florida Marlins.

Cubs vs. the Marlins National League Championship Series

As the Cubs advanced to the next level, once again the online lottery system was put into effect for Games 1 and 2 which would be in Chicago. To my great surprise, this time, my computer left the online waiting room and entered the ticket buying screen. Quickly, I purchased four tickets for Game 1 in the outfield.

On the evening of October 7, I took my two kids, Kate and Cody, and my good friend Syler Thomas. Syler was also the high school youth pastor, and so he knew my kids well, but of most significant importance, he was a knowledgeable and committed Cubs fan. Having grown up in Texas, he has always rooted for the Rangers, but having gone to college in Chicago and now raising his own family here, he had developed a genuine love for the Cubs.

The Cubs jumped out to a 4–0 lead in the first inning, thanks to a walk, triple, and home run by Moises Alou, followed by another triple and a run-scoring double. The 39,567 fans erupted into a continuous state of celebratory pandemonium. Not only were we high-fiving strangers but we were hugging one another too. With Carlos Zambrano on the mound, the Cubs looked invincible.

But the Marlins bounced back, taking the lead on a five spot they posted in the top of the third. The Cubs eventually tied it up, and going into the ninth inning, the game was tied. The Marlins scratched out two runs in the top of the ninth, thanks to a walk, error, and a couple of hits. It looked gloomy for Cubs fans, but we kept a never-say-die attitude in the stands.

Kenny Lofton got a one-out double, which got the crowd going, but a groundout followed Lofton's hit, leaving the Cubs down to their last out. Sammy Sosa, the Cubs' prolific home run hitter, stepped into the batter's box. If only Sammy could go long, we'd tie this game up.

With the count 1–1, Sammy crushed a line drive into the seats for a game-tying home run. Jumping up and down, it felt like the entire stadium might just collapse under the weight of the nearly forty thousand fanatics. This was our night. We just knew it.

The game went into extra innings, and the top of the eleventh, the Marlins Mike Lowell hit the first pitch for a home run, sending a shock wave into the stands. The Cubs failed to score, succumbing to a 9–8 loss in Game 1.

We went home sad and exhausted. Our emotions had been pushed to the limits, and the end result was a huge disappointment.

The Cubs went on to win the next three games in a row in this best of seven series. With a 3–1 lead, the Cubs were one victory away from going to the World Series. Cubs fever consumed the city of Chicago. Virtually nothing else was discussed at work, school, church, in restaurants and bars. It was nonstop Cubs as everyone anticipated the next victory.

The Marlins took Game 5 in Miami, but no one was worried. The Cubs would return to Wrigley Field for Game 6 and, if necessary, Game 7. Once again, the lottery was held online, and I was remarkably lucky once again. Not only did I get through on my work laptop but also my home computer, and I was able to purchase eight tickets for Game 7—four in the right field bleachers and four in the left field upper deck.

But in my heart, I did not want to have Game 7 played. In baseball history, there are some very memorable "Game sixes." In 1975, Carton Fisk belted a home run that he famously "willed it fair" as the ball cleared Boston's left field wall aptly named the Green Monster. Eleven years later, the Mets would come from behind to beat the Red Sox in an unlikely sequence of three singles, a wild pitch, and an error.

The Cubs came to Game 6 with their ace Mark Prior on the mound. The Cubs took a 1–0 lead in the first inning on a Kenny Lofton single and Sammy Sosa double. Adding a run in the sixth and seventh inning, the Cubs entered the top of the eighth with a 3–0 lead. It looked the game was a lock after the leadoff hitter flew out to left field. Only five more outs and the Cubs were World Series bound.

But the inning collapsed in a way that can only happen in baseball. The Marlins scored eight runs in an inning that would seemingly never end, going on to win 8–3. This would force a Game 7 the next night, and I had eight tickets.

I shared with Jenni that the tickets could be sold for more than one thousand dollars apiece, to which she immediately replied, "Let's sell them!"

"No, I've waited my whole life to go to this game," I said. No amount of money could take this game from me. I have a philosophy that when I do die, I will certainly still have money in the bank. So I try never to let the important things slip away because of the cost. This was one of those essential things.

In case Game 7 was necessary, I had already invited the people that would get to hand this valuable piece of paper to a man at the turnstile as they entered Wrigley Field. The four right field bleacher tickets were for my wife Jenni and my kids Kate and Cody. We'd sit as a family for this historic night. The upper deck seats went to my father, Brian Avery, my longtime friend Neal Geitner, and Syler Thomas.

Kerry Wood would be our starting pitcher for this game. The crowds were huge, with thousands of people without a ticket came to hang around and breathe in the excitement that filled the air. The game got off to a rocky start with Kerry Wood giving up a first inning three-run home run to slugger Miguel Cabrera. The mood soured with that big blow, and although the crowd tried to remain positive, it was challenging to do as the Cubs failed to score in their first at-bat.

Wrigley Field in 2019. Photo courtesy of Matt McKee.

But the bottom of the second inning changed everything with a single, a double, a run-scoring groundout, and Kerry Wood up to bat. On a 3–2 pitch, Wood crushed the ball into the stands in left field to tie the Game 3–3. My family was jumping up and down as the ball cleared the wall.

Jenni said, "What is all the sparkling in the sky?" when suddenly we were all drenched in beer. The crazy bleacher bums in unison took their expensive cups of beer and threw them into the air. The bright lights streaming down from their lofty perches created a glimmer as the droplets of beer looked like diamonds in the sky. Such an odd way to celebrate, I thought to myself. A baptism of beer made everyone sticky and damp and certainly soured the festive mood for anyone who was not drunk.

We did our best to clean ourselves, but the lingering smell, reminiscent of a fraternity party at the end of a long night, permeated the air. Jenni decided to relocate to a standing position under the center field scoreboard where she'd be safe from further episodes of impish reveling.

We were tied 3–3, but that wouldn't last long. In the bottom of the next inning, the Cubs Moises Alou hit a two-run home run to give the Cubs a 5–3 lead. Having refreshed their emptied cups of beer, the knuckleheaded fans surrounding us again tossed their beer into the air.

The Cubs' lead would only hold for a short time with the Marlins taking the lead in the top of the fifth inning, never to relinquish it the rest of the game. Jenni rejoined us for the final one-half inning as we watched the Cubs lose 9–6. It was painful to watch the Marlins celebrate on our field. The Cubs took to the dugout and locker room with their heads hanging in shame and disappointment.

The crowd, however, did not leave initially. Instead, we all called and cheered for our team to come back on the field. Yes, they lost, but the dedicated fans yearned to pay their respect and show their appreciation for a successful season. But it was not to happen. In a severe error of judgment, the players ignored their fans and hid in shame. At least that is how it felt to my family and the many fans who remained in the park.

Playoffs 2008

In 2008, the Cubs played the Los Angeles Dodgers in the first round. I went to Game 1 with Syler Thomas, who secured tickets from his sister-in-law. We sat in the right field bleachers and watched the Cubs get trounced 7–2. The Cubs also dropped the next two games, getting swept in the most forgettable of playoffs.

That is all I have to say about that.

Playoffs 2015

The new era of Cubs baseball was well underway. New ownership, off-field management, and a crop of young enthusiastic players filled out the 2015 roster. The final piece of the puzzle was the addition of Cubs manager Joe Maddon to guide this group of young studs.

The Cubs finished the season with a remarkable 97–65 record, which would have been first place in either the East or the West division, but in the very competitive Central, it was only good enough for third place. One game behind the Pirates and two games behind the Cardinals who had the best record in baseball.

The Cubs would play a one-game Wild card playoff in Pittsburgh for the right to advance to play the St. Louis Cardinals. Jake Arietta pitched a complete game shutout behind the home runs of Dexter Fowler and Kyle Schwarber to win 4–0.

The series started in St. Louis where the Cardinals won the first game and the Cubs the second. Returning to Chicago, the first game was set for the evening of October 12. I didn't have any tickets but got a last-minute offer from Matt McKee who had a single ticket for the last row in the upper deck of right field. Matt couldn't go and asked if I wanted the ticket. No charge.

I jumped at the chance and arranged for parking with my buddy Wells whose business is just one block away from the Friendly Confines. Wells reserved a spot for my car, and I arrived two hours early. I wandered around the park, enjoying the festive atmosphere. The Cubs were a better team than other playoff years, and I was excited to be there.

Tom Terrill before heading into Wrigley Field

As I prepared to go to the game, I thought of the countless games I had attended over the decades and thought of my friend Chuck Trotter who passed away less than two years earlier. Chuck and I went to many games together, and I decided to wear a favorite shirt that he gave to me years before with his restaurant logo. It was my way to honor his memory while I cheered on the Cubs this warm October night.

Behind the home run prowess, Cubs players had six dingers that night and won the Game 8–6. My time alone was not really alone as everyone was everyone's friend at Wrigley Field, especially in the playoffs. The Cubs won the next game too, advancing to the National League Championship against the New York Mets.

I set my sights on the next Internet lottery, hoping to get selected for a chance to buy tickets. I'd know in a few days.

My good friends Matt McKee and Syler Thomas have a common text thread with me. 95 percent of the content of these texts is our daily thoughts on the Cubs, but occasionally, Syler will throw in a comment on his U2 tickets for their next concert. The three of us all got selected to enter the Cubs ticket lottery for the National League Championship Series.

The Cubs would host Games 3 to 5 of the best of seven. Syler and Matt decided Game 5 was the best choice, anticipating it being the clinching game for the Cubs to advance to the World Series. I leaned toward Game 3, which would be the first one at Wrigley and assured to happen in case of a clean sweep.

I logged on to the site and watched the screen as a message told me to wait. I was not sure if I would ever get in or just stare at the screen for an hour. To my delight, after only a few minutes, my screen switched to the next level asking me which game I'd like to pick.

Quickly, I select Game 3, set for Tuesday, October 20, at 7:00 PM and got the four best seats available. I scored the coveted tickets in the upper deck on the left field side and was very excited. Almost immediately, my phone lit up with a text from Syler: "Game 5. Four tickets." Matt chimed in moments later with his success as well for Game 5.

We had agreed to take one another, and the fourth ticket would go to whoever was the holder of the tickets. The eight tickets for Game 5 would be for the three of us and one extra for Matt and one extra for Syler. This left three tickets we'd scalp to the highest bidder so we'd have seed money for

World Series tickets. This level of strategic thinking had us riding high emotionally for the eventual World Series title that no team in history deserved more than the Chicago Cubs.

I printed my tickets and came home from the office after work to share the good news with Jenni. As I walked in the door and flashed the paper tickets, I exuberantly said, "Hey, Jenni, I got playoff tickets. You're going to the game with me."

"Oh, Tom, that is great. But are you sure you want me to go? Why not bring Cody?" Jenni said.

"No, it is you. Cody can't get back in town, and I want to bring you. Matt and Syler will be there with us," I added.

"When is the game?" she inquired.

"Tuesday," I said.

"What time?" Jenni queried further.

"Seven o'clock at night," I casually said.

"Oh, you can't go," Jenni said matter-of-factly.

"What?" I said with a smile anticipating Jenni's forthcoming joke.

"That is when Kate is having her gender-reveal party," Jenni explained. Our daughter Kate was pregnant with her first child and was flying in from Denver for a party at our house. At the event, she would have prearranged pink silly string to be shot out from concealed cans by all the guests.

"What does that have to do with me? I don't go to baby showers. Why would I go to a gender-reveal party?" I asked, still a bit confused about why this conversation even needed to take place.

Jenni's next sentence was one that I will never forget. With a convincing tone of certainty, she said, "If you miss this party, you will irreparably damage your relationship with your daughter."

I could see in Jenni's face that she meant every word. This was not a practical joke but something she believed from the core of her soul. I politely asked if she was serious, and she gently said she was.

I now had to figure out an alternative plan. Reaching out to Brian Avery to see if he and his wife Janet would want to take two of the tickets and Matt and his wife Ashley could take the other two was the best idea I had, and so I contacted Brian by phone, and he was ready and willing. I then sent a text to Matt and Syler, telling them I could not go to Game 3 and would instead pass the tickets to my friend who would meet up with Matt and Ashley.

The text string went like this:

Tom: "Hey, guys. I can't go to Game 3."
Syler: "What? Why not?"
Matt: "You're not serious."
Tom: "Yes, I am serious. I can't go because Kate is flying in for her baby's gender-reveal party."
Syler: "Oh, come on. Why do you have to be there?"
Tom: "That's what I said, but Jenni has warned me not to make the mistake and go."
Matt: "Well, you'll come to Game 5 at least. But what is a gender-reveal party anyway?"
Tom: "It is where the gender of the baby is revealed to the couple by the spraying of silly string that is the color matching the baby's sex."
Syler: "Oh, sure. I get it. And you have to go."
Tom: "Yes".
Matt: "Tom, I have news for you. It is a gender-reveal party, but it is your gender that is being revealed."

Matt had just jokingly cut to the quick, and I laughed out loud. It reminded me of the *Saturday Night Live* skit with Hans and Franz and their famous "girlie man" reference.
I left the tickets on my desk in our family room and would deliver them to Brian and Matt in the coming days. Kate arrived in town on the Saturday before the game, and when she got back to her childhood home, we had an interesting exchange.

"Dad, what is this on your desk?" she asked me.

"Oh, those are Cubs playoff tickets," I answered.

"Really?" she replied. "That is great. When is the game?"

"It's Tuesday night," I said without adding any of the details. Kate knew her party was on Tuesday night. Even though I was not going to the game, I did not let on. I wanted to see her reaction.

"Oh, Dad!" she said with a deflated tone of sadness. "You're not going, are you?"

"No, Kate. I'm going to be at your party. Brian and Janet will go and meet Matt and Ashley there. I need to get the tickets to them still," I said, reassuring Kate I would be home for her.

Jenni was right. This did mean a lot to my daughter, and no game is worth more than my family and my relationship with them.

Unfortunately, the Cubs and fans like me were sorely disappointed as our team went into the tank, losing the first four games. Swept in the National League Championship Series was a huge disappointment. But most importantly, I got to shoot some pink silly string at my daughter and son-in-law and celebrate that my first grandchild would be a girl.

Playoffs 2016

The Chicago Cubs under the second year of skipper Joe Maddon continued their winning ways, finishing the season with the best record in all of baseball. A dominant season with 103 wins, a full eight games ahead of the next best team.

In the first round, the Cubs squared off against the San Francisco Giants. The Giants had accomplished an unusual feat of winning the World Series in three successive even years of 2010, 2012, and 2014. Now being the next even year, 2016 a storyline ran through baseball that the Giants were a team of "even year" destiny. Certainly, they would knock off the Cubs, which carried their own superstitious destiny of "close but no cigar."

The Cubs earned the right for home-field advantage with their unmatched record, and on October 7, Wrigley Field would be filled with 42,148 fans. I would be at home watching in the comfort of my family room as I did not succeed in obtaining any tickets. The first game was a pitchers' duel with the only run coming on the Cubs Javier Baez eighth inning home run that just barely made it out. The Cubs went on to win the series 3 games to 1, to advance to the National League Championship Series.

The Cubs had not been to the World Series since 1945. 1945! An unmatched record in futility. Even worse, they lost in 1945 to the New York Yankees. The last time the Cubs won the World Series was 1908. Now they were attempting for the fourth time in my lifetime to advance to this greatest stage sporting event. Only four victories away from advancing, but to move on, they would have to beat the red-hot Los Angeles Dodgers who had the best pitcher in baseball in Clayton Kershaw.

Once again, failing to obtain tickets in the Internet lottery, I would be watching at home, or so I thought. The game was set for Saturday night. The day before, I was sitting in my office when my phone rang.

"Hey, Tom," Matt McKee started the conversation. "What are you doing tomorrow night?"

"Well…" I started with some hesitation, trying to figure out why he was asking me this question. "I'm watching the Cubs game at home," I finished.

"No, you're not," Matt said matter-of-factly. "You're coming to the game. I have a ticket for you."

I could hardly believe it. Matt worked for a major United States bank and was hosting three extraordinarily successful and wealthy clients in the company's season tickets seats right behind the Cubs dugout. I didn't know how this was possible, and so I asked Matt to please explain.

"One of the clients had to cancel, and there is not enough time to find a client replacement. So I've been authorized to bring a suitable substitute," Matt shared.

"This is amazing, Matt," I started. "I will pay for the ticket, of course. How much is it?"

"It's three hundred twenty-five dollars. But I cannot accept the money. You'll have to be my guest," Matt said.

"Well, that is so generous. Are you sure?" I asked. "I am happy to cover my cost."

My ticket for Game 1

"No, Tom, you can't. In fact, you need to fit in with the other clients, so I need you to act and behave as if you have a net worth of fifty million dollars. If you want something to eat or drink, I will have to buy it for you. So please don't try to pull your wallet out. The other guest will expect me to pay for everything, and you need to do the same thing," Matt detailed.

I said with a sense of levity and delight in my voice, "Well, that is a tall order, but if I have to act like a rich dude to see the game from amazing seats, then I'm your guy!"

Matt would arrive separately, and I would drive down from my suburban home for a night of playoff baseball. It became my custom to arrive early for all playoff games and soak up more of the atmosphere of the excited Wrigley Field crowd. As usual, it was electric. One big pregame party where the sea of humanity lived in perfect harmony with one another. Side by side, fellow workers in the vineyard, strangers gathered to cheer together for the inevitable victory. We all knew the Cubs would win; we just didn't know precisely how.

I arrived at the seats. No superlatives can explain how good the seats were, so I took a video of it on my phone to forever have it documented. Matt introduced me to the clients who were watching the game with us, and I realized I had to hope they wouldn't ask me what my successful business was. I decided to say I inherited my wealth, figuring that it would be hard to refute if anyone doubted me. But they never asked. We were there to watch a baseball game, not talk shop.

The Cubs jumped out to an early lead in the first inning on a run-scoring double by Chris Bryant. The bottom of the second inning started great with a leadoff triple to right by Jason Heyward. Javier Baez followed with a run-scoring double. Baez advanced to third base on a wild pitch, with Cubs pitcher Jon Lester at the plate. In what was one of the most exciting plays I've ever seen live, Jon Lester squared around for a squeeze bunt, but the pitch was inside, and he pulled back the bat. Baez found himself in no man's land, too far from third base. He would be easily picked off, and the Dodgers' catcher fired the ball down to the third baseman.

However, rather than go back to third, Baez's unique instincts for the game had him take off for home plate. The throw back from third was high, and Baez slid in safely to home. He had stolen home, and from our seats, we watched it all from twenty yards away. Pandemonium broke out both on and off the field. Stealing home is such a rare event in baseball, and to accomplish this in a crucial Game 1 of the National League Championship made it all the more special.

The game continued with only one run scored by the Dodgers over the next five innings. Going into the top of the eighth inning holding a 3–1 lead had the Cubs sitting in the catbird seat. But the eighth had been a bad inning for the Cubs in baseball history, and once again, the curse of the billy goat seemed to rear its ugly head. The Dodgers scratched out two runs against three different relief pitchers, and now the game sat tied 3–3. While the events were discouraging, the faithful fans and talented athletes took it in stride as the Cubs came to bat in the bottom of the eighth inning.

Ben Zobrist led off the inning with a double, putting the lead run in scoring position without any outs. However, Addison Russell grounded out, and then Jason Heyward was intentionally walked. Javier Baez flew out for the second out, and things looked a bit less promising. Pinch hitter Chris Coughlin came to the plate with the Cubs' closer Aroldis Chapman in the on-deck circle.

The Dodgers' skipper was not going to let the Cubs have a legitimate hitter take his cuts when instead they could face the Cubs' weak-hitting pitcher. So Coughlin was intentionally walked, loading the bases. Joe Maddon responded by pulling his ace pitcher for pinch hitter Miguel Montero.

Tom Terrill and Matt McKee at Game 1 of the 2016 National League Championship Series

Quickly, the count went to 0–2, and Montero did not seem to be the guy to break the tie. In his career, Montero was out 75 percent of the time, and every five at-bats, he failed even to make contact striking out. Now with a no-ball, two-strikes count, he dug in, trying to throw out all the statistics and change the course of the game.

Dodger pitcher Joe Blanton had gotten away with a mistake on the pitch before that Montero swung on and missed. Instead of wasting a pitch out of the strike zone, Blanton came right back and challenged Montero. Miggy answered with a long drive to right field that landed deep in the stands for a pinch-hit grand slam. Matt took a video on his phone of the crowd as Montero rounded third base. I could be seen cheering and celebrating like the fanatics that we all were.

Before anyone had a chance to sit down, the next Cubs batter, Dexter Fowler, took the first pitch out to right field for back-to-back home runs. My voice was fading from all the exuberant shouting coming from the depths of my soul.

The Dodgers scored a harmless run in the top of the ninth, with the final score 8–4. We hung around after the game to continue the revelry before eventually heading home. The Cubs seemed to be a team of destiny. At least it felt that way that night.

So destiny continued as the Cubs took the series, clinching the National League title at home in Wrigley Field after Game 6. Celebrating another step closer and the furthest along in my lifetime, I once again set my hope in the lottery system for obtaining tickets.

World Series

The Cubs would face the Cleveland Indians, who even though their record was inferior, would have home-field advantage. This as a result of a silly idea to have the team that won the midseason All-Star Game gain home field for their representative team in the World Series. I didn't like this idea because it was not based upon merit. At least not the merit of your own team but instead the merit of a fake team of all stars that were not going to put their bodies on the line to win a meaningless game. The skin in the game was just not there.

So Games 1 and 2 would be in Cleveland, and I'd watch from home. The Cubs split the two games, returning to Chicago for Games 3 to 5. Once again, a failure in the Internet lottery brought me to the realization that I would not be going to a World Series game. Jenni had encouraged me to just buy a ticket from StubHub; the cost would be well over one thousand dollars, which was just not something I was willing to do.

Neither Matt nor Syler had been picked in the lottery either. However, then on Friday right before Game 3, Syler got an e-mail from the Cubs saying he could go into the Cubs virtual waiting room the next day. This did not make any sense to us as all the tickets for Games 3 to 5 had supposedly been sold. This would be only for Game 5, and apparently, some tickets had not been released yet.

Syler called to share this possibility with Matt and me. Now we could only hope that Syler's computer would take him from the "waiting room" to the option to buy tickets on Saturday morning. 10:00 AM was when it opened, and at 10:10 AM, Syler called me at my office where I was working that Saturday.

"Tom, we are going to the World Series!" Syler announced. Words that were such a delight to hear. Just maybe the Cubs were a team of destiny but also Matt, Syler, and I were fans of destiny too.

Syler and Foster Thomas at Game 5, 2016 World Series

Cleveland won Games 3 and 4 and now were within one victory of winning the World Series. Baseball is a sport where things can change so fast, and Cubs looked more than vulnerable as we prepared to drive down for our first World Series game. I was very excited to go to a World Series game in Wrigley Field, but I really did not want to see them lose this game either. I did not think I could emotionally handle watching another team celebrate as I did in 2003.

I drove down with Syler and his son Foster who would take the fourth ticket. We met Matt in Chicago at his house and drove to the ballpark together. Gone was the confidence, and an air of nervousness occupied our conversation. We tried to stay strong and convince ourselves that this was just one game, and we needed to take it one game at a time.

I've never been to a playoff game where the overall mood was more subdued. Some of that feeling was indeed what was in my own heart. My faith was weak, and I needed the Cubs to restore that for me, and I sensed most everyone felt similarly.

Our seats were in the upper deck on the first base side. Terrific seats with a great view, enhanced by my minibinoculars. In the second innings, the Indians took a one-to-nothing lead with a solo home run. That sinking feeling grew, even though it was just one run. My emotions confused me, and the facts slipped away into the recesses of my mind at times like this. Fear of failure took over, and I needed the logical input from someone who could remind me that in baseball one run is nothing. But no one was there to shake me out of this funk in the stands. It would instead require action from the players themselves.

Kris Bryant lead off the fourth inning with a solo home run, and I was immediately lifted in spirit as the crowd came alive. Rizzo followed with a double and then Zobrist with a single.

Tom Terrill, Matt McKee, Syler Thomas, and Foster Thomas

An infield single by Russell brought home the second run of the inning and finally the lead. The four of us were high-fiving one another but also everyone in our immediate vicinity.

A young boy was sitting right behind me. He was with his parents and extended family, but I was now aware that, as I stood to cheer, I blocked his view. I turned to him and said, "If you can't see because of me, just say, 'Hey, mister, please sit down.' OK?"

He looked at me, unsure of how to respond. His mom told me he was OK, but I wanted him to know that I was aware of his height disadvantage, and I would do my best to be considerate of his ability to see the game.

Everyone was standing in the entire stadium, and I was working on my squat strength so that this young man could see. I told myself that I was just working on getting my ski leg strength ready for the coming winter season. Heyward struck out, but the crowd stayed on their feet. Baez followed with a perfect bunt to load the bases, and I turned around.

"High-five me!" I shouted out to the young boy as we together celebrated the now-bases-loaded situation. He smiled and high-fived me as did his mom and dad. Next up was David Ross who hit a sacrifice fly to bring in the third run of the inning. Immediately, I turned around again and high-five my new friend. Matt too high-fived the young man. Matt has four kids, and his oldest Jack is just a little younger than this young man.

The Cubs now led 3–1 after the fourth inning, and I had a solid budding friendship. The game continued with each moment feeling critical, but in reality, it was just a game that kept moving forward. In the sixth inning, the Indians score another run, cutting the lead to a single run. In baseball, everyone is aware in a one-run game that every batter represents the tying run. So the outs come, and each one is met with a high five of everyone in your immediate vicinity.

I didn't know the name of my young new friend, and he didn't know mine. But we knew each other nevertheless. Friendships developed quickly with the common bond and heartfelt longing. His longing, which was common to a young man too inexperienced to have learned how to accept defeat, and my longing from one too experienced to accept any more defeat, we together took delight in a simple out.

We arrived at the top of the ninth inning with the Cubs closer Chapman throwing one hundred plus miles per hour strikes. Two outs came slowly with four pitches to the Indians leadoff hitter and five to the second batter. Now just one out away from a home victory and our hope for a turn in the momentum of the series.

In three pitches, Chapman struck out Ramirez for the final out, and the crowd erupted in cries of joy that could be heard a mile away. The players on the field celebrated the victory while the fans joined with one another in unison singing Steve Goodman's "Go, Cubs, Go" while the W flag is raised over the scoreboard.

Tom Terrill and his young new friend after the Cubs won Game 5.

During the singing, my young friend hugged his mom and dad and then spontaneously climbed onto my back to watch the on-field jubilation.

It seemed very natural and reminded me of my own kids climbing on Dad's back. It didn't seem that long ago, but in reality, some twenty years had passed since my kids had done this.

Matt captured a picture of the two of us and sent it to me the next day in a text that just said, "Tom with his son."

The drive home carried much emotion but an equal amount of planning regarding Game 6 and Game 7. The Cubs now trailed three games to two and had won the first game of the three required at this point to win the World Series. But it was the last game in Wrigley Field. We now moved on to Cleveland, which meant I'd be watching from my family room.

The Cubs easily won Game 6 by a score of 9–3, sending the series to a final Game 7. Game 7 would start on November 2 but not finish until the early hours of November 3. Everyone who is a Cubs fan knows where they were when Game 7 was played. I was at home, in the comfort of my family room with my big-screen TV. Cody was in town, and we watched the game with Jenni.

At the end of seven innings, the Cubs held a 6–3 lead. This would be enough to be assured victory almost every time, but once again, we had the troubling eighth inning for the Cubs to get through. The first two outs came easily, and my mind was in sync with Cubs fans around the globe who were thinking just four more outs. That was all. Only four more outs and we would win the World Series.

But an infield fluke single was all manager Joe Maddon needed to bring in Aroldis Chapman, his flame-throwing closer for a four-out Save. But Chapman was worn-out from all the recent work without rest. He had nothing left, and before my eyes, I saw the first batter double in a run, followed by a game-tying home run. Just like that, the game was tied, and the momentum had shifted to the Indians.

Somehow the Cubs stopped the damage, and the ninth inning came and went without a run scored by either team. Extra innings, but not immediately. It seemed God had other plans as the skies finally opened with a serious downpour. Rain delay.

Jenni stood up from her chair and said, "I'm going to bed. And you two better not wake me up with any shouting if something good happens."

"Mom, you can't go to bed now," Cody pleaded with her to reconsider.

"Jenni, you can go to bed, but you can forget the idea that we won't shout from the rooftops if the Cubs come back to win," I said, trying to be clear that any such thought of being considerate of others was not possible at such a time as this.

Cody and I laughed at the very idea that we could be quiet if the Cubs somehow would win this game. The rain delay lasted seventeen minutes, and play began in the top of the tenth inning.

The John Lennon memorial wall in Prague, Czech Republic, after the victory

Everyone knows the final result. The Cubs rallied in the tenth inning and took a two-run lead. The Indians fought back but came up short, only scoring a single run and capitulating the 2016 World Series to the Chicago Cubs.

Cody and I shouted and screamed. We hugged, and we cried—tears of joy. Jenni wandered downstairs with a smile on her face. We stay glued to the TV to see the postgame celebration and interviews.

Like nothing I've ever watched before on TV measures up to this moment for me.

Years and years of character development have gone into the making of me, Tom Terrill, to receive this moment. But it's not only me. It's my childhood friends Brian Avery, Walter Calhoun, Billy Castino, and Ricky McIntyre. Jeff Nielsen was watching from heaven. These were the boys who, like me, loved the Cubs and stayed true throughout our lives, to our Boys of Summer.

Epilogue

Anxiety, Panic, and God

Every Sunday evening, Jenni and I have a standing dinner with Neal and Robin Geitner. On September 24, 2017, I shared with the others how moved I was with a story our church pastor had shared a few years back. It involved a pastor and a former professional soccer player named Alan Wiley. I had saved a six-minute voice memo on my phone of the story and had recently relistened to it. The details involve events and circumstances that can only be explained by the idea of God inserting Himself directly into the lives of these men in a unique and profound way.

"When I hear this story and think of God stirring in the pastor's heart years before the remarkable culmination of events, I can scarcely take it in," I shared with everyone during dinner.

Neal, Robin, and Jenni too recalled the details and how powerful this story was to everyone who heard it. "I just can't imagine having something like that happen in my life," I added. However, then the subject changed to our planned Parcheesi game after dinner and who was the defending champion.

On Tuesday evening, I responded to Susan Neaman's e-mail invitation. Mark and Susan would host a dessert at their home on Saturday night with Luis and Pat Palau. Luis is an internationally renowned evangelist and one of the most gifted men I've ever met. I called Susan to share that Jenni would be out of town in Dallas this weekend, but I would like to come and, if OK, bring my parents. Back in the last seventies, my folks befriended Luis and Pat and would welcome the chance to reconnect. Susan confirmed this would be wonderful, but we'd all miss Jenni, of course.

Jenni was scheduled to leave Thursday with her friend Di Zavitz to visit Diane's daughter Lizzy at Texas Christian University. During the last three years, I had become increasingly anxious when home alone at night. I didn't sleep well and had a phobic notion of someone breaking into our home. This irrational fear did not exist when anyone else was at home with me but only when I was alone. Historically, I was rarely by myself, but with our kids grown and out of the house and now two granddaughters living in Denver, Jenni's out-of-town travel had increased. My level of anxiety had grown to the point of being both stressful and oppressive. It weighed me down.

"Hi, Mom," I began on the phone. "As you know, Jenni will be out of town this weekend, and I have been invited to an event with Luis and Pat Palau on Saturday night. Would you and Dad come with me?" My mom accepted immediately and was excited to see her dear old friend Pat.

The next night, my mom called me back. "Tom, our friends, the Russells just called us. It was so funny because they called to invite us to Christ Church to hear a speaker they just learned about named Luis Palau. So we accepted and will go to the 11:00 AM service. Why don't you join us?" Jenni and I had attended Christ Church since 1981, and my parents had come many times as our guests.

"I think I'll pass, Mom. I am not too fond of the eleven o'clock service. It is just too late for me, so I'll stick with the 9:00 AM service. I know that sounds rude, but I have so much work to do this time of year that I'm hoping to go to the office after church to get a jump start on the workweek. As well, I have to pick Jenni up at O'Hare at 1:30 PM on Sunday," I concluded. My mom understood, but we affirmed our plans for Saturday night.

Jenni left Thursday morning as planned, and I went to work. Coming home Thursday night to an empty house was uneventful. I had dinner, watched some TV, and went to bed. Recently, the days had been warm, but the nights were cool, so I placed a box fan in our bedroom window to draw in some fresh air. I quickly fell asleep and had a decent night's sleep this first night alone.

The next day, I went to work again and came home and at the end of the day to begin the weekend. I intended to go the office Saturday morning after a bike ride, and so falling asleep early fit right into my plans. At 9:30 PM, I woke up on the couch with the TV on still. Turning it off, I went upstairs and climbed in bed, again with the fan in the window bringing in some pleasant sleeping temperatures.

At 12:30 AM, I awoke needing to go to the bathroom—a common occurrence for me at my age. Climbing back in bed and lying down in the quiet of the night, I heard an unfamiliar sound. A noise from outside as if someone had spread out a blanket with a "whoosh" sort of noise. Lying there, I wondered what could have made the noise. I recalled that our patio table had the umbrella up, and I thought maybe the wind had picked up outside. If so, I should check in case I'd need to lower the umbrella in strong winds.

Climbing out of bed, I looked out the window from my darkened room to see a young man at the patio door. In his hand was a tool, and he was trying to jimmy the door open.

I could hardly believe my eyes. The sound I heard was the sliding of the screen door by this would-be intruder, and now he was attempting to break in. My heart was racing, and fear gripped me. My phobia of someone breaking into the house was now real and right before me. My legs were shaking, and my breathing started to get heavy as I picked up the cordless landline. Dialing the Lake Bluff police, I put the phone to my ear to hear only silence. The call failed. I redialed, but again, nothing: a third try and a third failure.

Oh my gosh, I thought. *He has cut the phone line.* I looked for my cell phone as he continued trying to pry open the door. I couldn't find it and was feeling overwhelmed. I wanted this punk caught and arrested. I was both fearful and outraged simultaneously. However, without the means to call the police, I had to do something else to end this. My window and the patio door are only some ten feet apart, and I decided to yell in my most deep, powerful, and intimidating voice. In a guttural outflow, I yelled, "Do you want to die?"

I figured this would frighten him and he'd run off into the night. Never to be captured but at least gone from a face-to-face encounter inside my domain. However, he didn't move. Instead, he stopped, turned his head to my upstairs window, and replied to me, "You scared me to death." And then he went back to working on the door.

I totally freaked out. Who would ever continue trying to break in when he knows the homeowner can see him? My imagination was running wild with only the worst thoughts. I figured he must not care that I'd seen him as he had other partners in crime working other doors and windows, and soon, they would take me out.

I thought to grab the baseball bat under my bed, my suburban security system, but instead, I found my cell phone at last. I dialed the police and this time got through.

"My name is Tom Terrill, and I live at 363 E. Washington in Lake Bluff. Someone is trying to break into my house. Please send a squad car immediately," I said, speaking as clearly and succinctly as I could.

"What makes you think someone is breaking into your house?" the dispatcher asked. Usually, such a question to me would have received a snappy answer to a stupid question, but instead, I replied, "Because I'm watching him from my bedroom window."

"Can you describe him?" she asked.

"Yes, but can you first send the police? I'd like to have them here, please," I replied. She told me they were on their way, and I went on to describe in detail the man. "He is a young man in his early twenties. Blue jeans, green sweatshirt, and backpack. His hair looks strawberry blond, but it's a little hard to tell for sure with the reflection of the light." My patio lights are bright, and they were on, clearly lighting up this young thug for me to give all the details.

"He is now leaving my patio and walking into my backyard toward the driveway," I reported, updating the dispatcher. Running into another bedroom, I could see him standing in my driveway.

"OK, he is now in my driveway and making a call on his cell phone. Where are the police?" I pleaded. I was no longer fearful for my safety but that he would get away. "I see him walking now into my front yard," I reported as I transitioned to a third bedroom to look out. "I can't see him, but he is right at my front door," I shared.

"How do you know that?" the dispatcher asked.

"Because I see his shadow across my front lawn," I explained. "Where are the police?" I asked again. The promise of their arrival seemed distant. I lived half a mile from the Lake Bluff police station. Heck, I could have jogged there by now, yet they couldn't seem to drive the short distance promptly.

"Oh no. He's leaving my yard," I explained as I watched him walk up the street on Moffett, heading north. "Tell the police to drive north on Moffett. Don't let them turn on Washington. He is north on Moffett," I urged. As the words were leaving my mouth, I saw the police coming up Moffett from the south, fortunately without their flashing lights on. However, they did precisely the wrong thing and turned left on Washington.

In frustration, I told the dispatcher that they now need to turn back and head north. Once they got back on track fairly quickly, the dispatcher reported that they had three people being questioned. I was relieved, but still, my mind was very active and my body stressed to the max.

She asked, "Could you identify the suspect?"

"Yes," I replied while another police car came to escort me the one block to these three hooligans.

When I got there, I easily identified the young man. However, when the pieces of the puzzle were put together, it revealed the following. This twenty-two-year-old was drunk. Very drunk. He had left a neighborhood brewery and was trying to find the house of a new acquaintance where others heavily indulging in alcohol consumption were hanging out. This house was exactly one block north of mine. It was a clear case of mistaken identity and not an attempted break-in. The police asked if I wanted to press charges, and I declined. What was the point? He was drunk and not a threat.

He didn't run when I yelled because he thought I was his friend messing with him. I was a confused mess of relief and anger. Also, my emotional state was still very fragile. The years of building anxiety about a break-in had culminated into a wild night, leaving me emotionally wounded.

I went home, locked the door, and sat in the dark on my living room couch. I picked up the phone and made a call. "Hi, Jenni. I'm sorry to wake you," I began. "It's one thirty in the morning, and you know I wouldn't call if I didn't need to talk." I shared with Jenni what had happened in the last sixty minutes. She could tell I was shaken up and listened patiently.

After hearing my story, Jenni shared some words of wisdom. "Tom, this is not a coincidence. God's hand is in this. He brought about this event on a night when you are, in fact, alone. Also, brought someone literally to our door who, in fact, was not a threat," Jenni shared. Her words were accurate, but I was not able to take them to heart. It was too soon as the night's events were too fresh for me to reflect on anything this deep. Jenni stayed with me on the phone for an hour, and we just talked. Finally feeling a bit better and plenty guilty for waking Jenni up, I released her to fall back asleep in Dallas. I remained on the couch in the dark, never falling asleep that night while feeling disappointed in myself and unsure how to move forward from here. I vacillated between the idea of spending the next night at my parents' home in Northfield and finding the courage to stay in my own home. After all, I did need to be able to function alone in my own home.

At daybreak, I left for the office. Being Saturday, it would be quiet there and allow me to address some lingering issues. I called my parents a bit later and let them know what happened the night before. They encouraged me to stay the night with them, and I promised to consider it. I also called my sister Kathy, who lives in Colorado, and shared the crazy night I had.

In the daylight, I felt much better. I found myself coming to God in prayer, asking for His hand upon me as I processed the event and my fear. As the day finished, I left for the Neaman's house and would meet my parents there. We arrived at the same time and walked inside with some of the other first arrivals. Seeing Luis was such a blessing, and it was delightful to be able to visit with both him and his wife. After ten minutes or so, we moved on, allowing other arriving guests to visit the guest of honor. This social event was a friendly gathering of some sixty plus people, and I knew most everyone. However, being with my parents led me to find chairs for the three of us to take a load off our feet. This meant I was not mingling with many people but instead just those in our immediate area.

About an hour into the open house, my dad was getting a bit tired. "Tom," he began, "I think Mom and I should leave soon."

"Of course, Dad. However, let me check if Luis is going to speak to the group," I suggested.

I got up to find Susan Neaman and found her in the foyer. "Susan, my folks are ready to go, but if Luis is going to speak, then they will stay. What's the plan?" I asked.

"Oh yes, he has a message he wants to share. Let me go and work on that now. I'll tell your parents too," Susan said as she left the foyer. Susan had been talking with Mark Stroh, who was a longtime friend of mine. Mark and I enjoyed each other's company and always had a great connection but found that we'd only see each other every few years. So it was a nice treat to run into him.

"How are you, brother?" Mark asked. We had met years earlier when our boys were young and played baseball together. He has a dynamic personality and is the type of person that cuts to the heart of the matter of any conversation.

"Mark, you would not believe what happened to me," I began. I started to tell him this story that had impacted me in such a powerful way. About halfway through, he interrupted me and said to me that he felt God was placing something on his heart to tell me. He wanted me to finish my story, but he needed first to let me know he felt God had something for him to say to me.

I continued my story, right up to that present moment; however, I did not tell him what Jenni had said on the phone, only that I called Jenni.

Mark began, "Tom, this is incredible. I want you to know that God brought this young man directly to your house. He wants you to be free from fear and anxiety. That fear is not from God, and he brought this about to deliver you. You have been oppressed with a weight of clay on your shoulders, and God is breaking it off." As he said this, he physically took his hands and pushed hard into my left shoulder and then my right, demonstrating a physical event to break apart the figurative block of clay weighing me down.

Continuing, Mark said, "Tom, think about this. He brought someone who was not a threat to you who has been burdened with fear. It was exactly the thing you have been afraid of. Your fear was prophetically fulfilled last night, and you need to claim this victory from God." Mark's words penetrated my being and felt accurate and true. He was articulating what I was feeling and what Jenni had shared with me in the wee hours of the morning when my mind couldn't take it in.

"Tom," he continued, "I am not supposed to be here tonight. "Did you know I was not invited? Really, I was not. I only came here at the very last minute because Ike called me to come with him. He did not want to come alone, and since being widowed, he asked me as a friend to accompany him. So here I am, and here we are."

This conversation went on for ten minutes in the middle of the foyer. People were walking past us left and right. People that I knew well and had not seen in a while. However, no one stopped to say hello. It was very odd. This party was a chitchat event where any conversation could be freely joined at any time. In fact, it would be not only unusual but bordering on rude to walk right past a friend without saying hello. Yet that was what happened. At least twenty friends of mine, whom I had not spoken with yet that evening, walked right by us without even a passing pat on the back. It was as if Mark and I were in a bubble that no one could penetrate or even see inside.

Mark finished his words for me by taking his finger and poking me in the chest while saying, "Tom, you tell your wife I told you this, and it will blow her away." So then he left. As he walked away, I found my way back to my parents and settled in to hear a message from Luis.

My heart filled from Mark's words. I did feel that God had used him to speak to me with a message specifically for me. As I processed this conversation, I heard a stirring message of God working in the ministry of Luis Palau. I could scarcely take it all in.

When Luis finished, my folks and I said our goodbyes and left. I had decided I would go to my parents' home to spend the night. On my drive down following my parents in their car, my thoughts kept focusing on the events of the last twenty hours. So much had happened. I picked up my phone to call my sister Kathy. "Hey, Kathy," I began. "I just left seeing Luis Palau with Mom and Dad, and Luis asked me specifically how you were doing and to please say hello from him." Kathy and my brother Jeff had spent a week with the Palau team back in 1979 in Scotland, and Luis's remarkable memory kept both my younger siblings fresh in his mind.

"Tom, that is so nice," Kathy began and shared some of her memories of Luis in the past. "Tom, I did want you to know I've been thinking all day about what happened to you. I feel like God wants me to tell you some things," Kathy explained. She went on to say the same message that I had heard first from Jenni and then from Mark. Kathy too encouraged me to actively claim from God the victory through Christ over my fear, and that this was what God was showing to me.

I arrived at my parents' home at 9:00 PM, and we spent thirty minutes talking in their living room. When we all decided it was time for bed, I told them, "You know what? I will go with you to the eleven o'clock church service tomorrow instead of the nine o'clock. I'll wake up early and go home first to change and then meet you there." I rarely went to this service but thought it would be a good idea to visit more with my parents, knowing they were coming up at the invitation of their friends.

I went upstairs and went to bed. While lying down in the dark, I began to pray to God. Thanking Him for everything that had happened and asking specifically for deliverance from this anxiety, claiming His gift of freedom for me. While praying, my mind went to Charlie Cardella. Charlie is a longtime friend with whom I talk regularly on the phone. He and his wife Linda live nearby in a neighboring town and attend Heritage Church some fifteen miles away. More than almost anyone else, Charlie is able to give me godly wisdom and encouragement when various trials come my way. I wanted to tell him what had transpired, and I didn't want to forget. As I fell asleep, I prayed, "God, help me to remember to contact Charlie. I need to talk to Charlie. Don't let me forget."

The next morning, I woke up early and drove home. I ate breakfast and cleaned up and changed clothes and went to my office for a few hours. I continued to do the work that was so demanding this time of year in my industry, although my thoughts continued to focus on the last thirty hours. I left my office and drove the two miles to church, arriving at 10:45 AM. I went inside and found my parents sitting in the third row with their friends. Joining them, my dad introduced me, and we spoke for a few minutes. I could tell the service was about to start and the church was very crowded when suddenly I looked to the center aisle and saw Linda and Charlie Cardella walking in. I was stunned. They did not attend our church, but there was Charlie with his infectious smile as he climbed into the same row as me but on the other side of the aisle. I had asked God not to let me forget to contact Charlie. I had forgotten, but God instead brought Charlie to me.

The service started, and I was unable to catch Charlie's attention then. The music was stirring, and Luis Palau delivered a sermon that grabbed everyone's attention. It was an incredible service.

Once the service ended, people made their way to the lobby to visit friends. I made a beeline for Charlie and said, "Charlie, my friend," as I took his hand to shake it, "you are here today by a divine appointment from God for the benefit of me." I don't usually talk like this, but it was true. It represented exactly what I felt and believed down to my core.

"Wow!" Charlie said. "Tell me about it." At this point, the sanctuary was primarily cleared out, and I began my story. As I was talking, Neal Geitner came up to join us. Neal knew Charlie but had not seen him in many years and wanted to reconnect. Neal and I had last seen each other the previous Sunday night, and so he, like Charlie, did not know of my unique last thirty-six hours. I took a full twenty minutes to share the story and how I ended my prayers beseeching God to remind me to contact Charlie, and here, God delivered Charlie in person.

The three of us prayed together, specifically for me and my anxiety. I was asking God to bless me with freedom from this fear. Moved to tears, my emotional tank was overflowing. God had injected himself into my life. When we stopped praying, Neal said, "Tom, this is just like the Alan Wiley story."

"Yes!" I exclaimed. "It really is, isn't it? That is how I feel. God has pierced my world with His presence and His will in a way I can hardly believe." We all just smiled and affirmed that God is good. Indeed, very good.

"Hey, guys, I want to see Diane Payne, and I heard she was here in the lobby. So excuse me, I'm going to run out to find her before she goes," I said, leaving the two of them to continue to talk with each other. After finding Diane and visiting with her and some other friends, I left the church to drive to O'Hare to pick up Jenni. Her flight would be landing soon, and I couldn't wait to see her. Jenni and I drove home from the airport, and I filled her in on everything that had happened. Retelling the events to Jenni painted a clear picture for me just how much God was present in these events. A case of coincidence could be made for any one of these events by themselves but, combined together, I can only explain by divine involvement.

That struck a chord for me. I've always believed that God cared for the individual person and logically then cared for me too as an individual. I believed that, and it made sense to me. However, I had not had such personal evidence in my own life of the love and care from God to bring about these things. Here and now, He had shown to me personally that I could put my faith and trust in Him and Him alone. The head knowledge is one thing, but this combined my head and heart forging a stronger bond together and solidifying for me the reality that God cared specifically for me.

That night, one week later, Neal and Robin came over for dinner at our house. Jenni and Neal knew the story, but Robin did not, and so at her request at dinner, I retold the story to Robin finishing with Charlie, Neal, and me praying together this morning in church.

Twelve years earlier, I was on an annual ski trip to Vail with Steve Holzrichter. Steve is Charlie Cardella's business partner and a strong Christian man. During this trip, I shared with Steve how my good friends Neal and Robin were struggling with their eldest daughter. She had walked away from the Christian faith that she was raised with, and it was troubling to her parents. While Steve did not know her or her parents, he committed to praying for her. That like the prodigal son, she would return. For twelve years, Steve has faithfully prayed each day for her, unbeknownst to anyone other than Charlie and me.

As I finished telling my story to Robin, Neal began, "Tom, what you don't know yet is the cherry on top." I looked at Neal with a quizzical expression as he continued. "When we were in church with Charlie, I just kept thinking that I was there that moment for you. That it was about you and your needs and that I could be supportive and help you. You then left to find Diane, and Charlie shared with me something I never knew. 'Neal,' Charlie said, 'I want you to know that my business partner, Steve Holzrichter, prays every day that your daughter will come back to the Lord.' Tom, I don't know Steve, and I never knew this. However, at that moment, I sensed God showing me that I was not there to help Tom but instead for God to be there for me."

Neal was so moved to learn of such love and care within the body of Christ. That for more than a decade, someone he didn't know had been praying for his eldest daughter, initiated from a conversation I had on a ski trip.

For me, it seemed like an endless pouring out of love from God to me. Just when I thought the story was over, something else happened.

Three weeks later, Jenni was getting ready to fly to Denver to see our grandchildren, planning to leave on an early morning flight on Friday. But in the middle of the night, Jenni awakened with the stomach flu. Disappointed, she canceled her trip, and I headed off to work.

Next door to my office is a Heinen's grocery store. I am not too fond of the store and rarely shop there myself. It's 5:00 PM, and I'm getting ready to leave my office when the phone rang.

"Tom, would you stop at Heinen's and pick me up some chicken soup?" Jenni asked. She was feeling much better but needed something healing for her empty stomach. Gladly, I stopped in on my way home. The store was crowded, which is one of the things I don't like about it. As I fill up a couple of carryout containers of soup, I thought to myself that if Jenni had left for Denver as planned that morning, I would not be here. I was thinking about how changes in life had a direct impact on other events and how different things could play out as a result.

I got in line at the checkout counter with three people in front of me, and as I moved forward, the line grew behind me—so many people. After paying for Jenni's soup, I walked the end of the checkout and stopped. Pausing for a moment, I turned around and waited.

The person in line behind me finished his transaction and walked toward me. "Excuse me," I said. "You look familiar to me."

"Oh, huh? I don't think I know you," the stranger replied. "But let's see if we can figure this out," he said as we walked out together.

"Let me ask you a question," I said. "Did you go to the wrong house at twelve thirty at night three weeks ago?"

"You're the guy!" he said to me with a shout.

I replied, "Yes, I am the guy. The guy whose house you were trying to get inside."

"I'm so sorry," he said. "I was pretty drunk."

"You were very drunk," I told him. "I thought you were a burglar." He told me his name and explained what had happened. He was quite embarrassed and quite apologetic.

God had once again stepped in. If Jenni's not sick, I would not be there, in this very crowded store with seven checkout lanes, and I happened to be right in front of the young man who started the whole thing.

As we departed, I climbed in my car and called home. "Jenni, you're not going to believe who I just ran into…"

About the Author

Tom Terrill, raconteur extraordinaire and all-around nice guy, calls the North Shore of Chicago home where he resides with his lovely wife, Jenni. He sells insurance to finance his future adventures and Glory Days.

9 781098 021641